BEYOND MY DREAMS

Mel A. Tomlinson and Karin von Aroldingen in George Balanchine's Episodes.
© *Steven Caras, all rights reserved.*

BEYOND MY DREAMS

MEL A. TOMLINSON
as told to Claudia Folts

TurningPointPress LLC

TurningPointPress 2018
PO Box 81, Teaneck, NJ 07666
turningpointpress@gmail.com
www.turningpointpressllc.com

Copyright © 2017 Mel A. Tomlinson and Claudia Folts

All rights reserved. No portion of this book may be reproduced, scanned, or distributed in any printed or electronic form without permission of the publisher and/or owners of the copyrighted material. Please do not participate in or encourage piracy of copyrighted materials in violation of the author's or creator's rights. Purchase only authorized editions.

ISBN 978-0-9973829-9-0

Photos not otherwise credited are from the author's collection or photographers unknown.

Designed by Vicky Shaw

First Edition

Cover Photos by King Douglas

Autumn Leaves
By Mel A. Tomlinson

> For dust thou art, and unto dust thou shalt return.
> Genesis 3:19

Man was created failing to realize the nature of his existence….
    finding work in maintenance-sustaining
        long enough to struggle.

Seasons change moving him to catch a glimpse of Autumn leaves….

Man struggles as morning dew and rays of hope start the new days.
    Night assumes them rest and there is harmony in nature.

He struggles, learns and forgets – faltering to that earthly reality.
    Pushing dust and webbing lies – labeling a fallen Summer with
        Autumn leaves.

Spring and Summer greenery soon melt into crunchy colors
    that beckon Man to see the light
        in the coldness of darkened Winter nights

        WHEN LIFE HAS LEFT AND
            AUTUMN LEAVES STAND TALL
        WE STRUGGLE AND THEN REALIZE
            MAN WAS CREATED TO FALL

Autumn leaves blend warm nights
    and chilly days into the harmony of a questioned haze
        that hang horizons at sunset.

Every man shall fail in time
    and every leaf will bare a different tone
        and continue to be called a leaf.

The winds will call. The rain will cry upon the earth….
    reminding others to remember – MAN WAS CREATED.

Autumn leaves return?
    Spring is coming.
        Hope is eternal!

Root yourself compassion for the tree and forget not the seed!

Dedication

To Gyula Pandi, my teacher, my mentor, my friend, I dedicate this book and all the memories held within. As a teacher, never did Gyula judge me or intimidate me, or anyone else for that matter. He was always kind, always supportive, but at the same time he made me want to work my hardest and become my best. When I grow up, I want to be like Gyula Pandi, who inspires so many others. This is one of the best things anyone could hope to aspire to. He is my favorite teacher both in and out of the ballet studio.

Throughout the ordeal I faced later in my life, Gyula was there for me, often in person, always in spirit. Without Gyula in my life, I might never have met Agnes de Mille, much less been given my first job with her Heritage Dance Theatre. I honestly believe that I would have died on a very lonely day in the mid 1990's, had Gyula not shown up, unexpected, at my house. He put in motion everything good that has happened throughout my adult life. Gyula is my guardian angel in human form, and for his love and encouragement through all my days, both the brightest ones and the darkest ones, I will forever be grateful.

The amazing Gyula Pandi, teaching class at UNCSA.

Table of Contents

Foreword by **Heather Watts** i
Chapter 1 **In the Beginning** 1
Chapter 2 **The Elephant in the Room** 15
Chapter 3 **Transitions** 25
Chapter 4 **North Carolina School of the Arts Years** 35
Chapter 5 **Touring with Agnes** 47
Chapter 6 **Graduation and Moving On** 61
Chapter 7 **Everybody Doesn't Love You** 79
Chapter 8 **My Life at the White House - Part I** 95
Chapter 9 **My Life at the White House - Part II** 109
Chapter 10 **My Life at the White House - Part III** 129
Chapter 11 **The Prodigal Son and His Ballerinas** 147
Chapter 12 **Diva Days** 167
Chapter 13 **Change is in the Air** 187
Chapter 14 **Dark Days: Down the Rabbit Hole** 199
Chapter 15 **Dark Days: Endless Agony** 219
Chapter 16 **But They Don't Check Out** 233
Chapter 17 **Thinking Ahead for the Dead** 251
Afterword 267
Index 269

Mel A. Tomlinson with the corps de ballet in Joseph Duell's Creation du Monde. New York City Ballet, 1984.

Foreword by Heather Watts
NYCB 1970-1995

Heather Watts and Mel Tomlinson, in Balanchine's Agon. © Steven Caras, all rights reserved.

The world of New York City Ballet in the early 1980's was at a peak of evolution— I know that now. George Balanchine was still omnipresent, at the helm of the company he created, and our leader in all ways. History was all around us, with the people who had made the company still present; Frank Moncion, Jacques d'Amboise, Allegra Kent... Alexandra Danilova was teaching at the School of American Ballet, and Lincoln Kirstein was everywhere. We were in every sense a tribe, Balanchine's tribe.

I had seen Mel Tomlinson dance before I knew him. On the stage with Dance Theatre of Harlem, he stood out with his tall, beautifully-etched profile and deliberate yet intuitive approach to dancing. Mr. Balanchine hired Mel to join New York City Ballet in the fall of 1981, and he cast us together in his 1957 Stravinsky masterpiece *Agon*. Our partnership in *Agon* remains a significant example of Balanchine constantly reframing his own repertory. I had already danced *Agon* pas de deux with NYCB's Peter Martins and Adam Luders, but was excited and honored to merge my understanding of the ballet with Mel's, which was built on his work at DTH under the direction of Arthur Mitchell, who danced the leading male role in the original production at NYCB. In those days, the ballets were all still new to varying degrees. The oldest among them, *Apollo, Prodigal Son*, and *Serenade*, were just over or shy of 50 years old, with premieres well within the memories of so many who were a part of our daily lives. *Agon* itself was only approaching 25 years old. It was into this vibrant world that Balanchine brought Mel.

BEYOND MY DREAMS

Our *Agon* rehearsals with Mr. Balanchine were very specific and clear and, as ever he spoke primarily about the music and his friend Igor Stravinsky's great serialist score, and tempo always tempo… but also the quality of movement to be drawn out. Balanchine brought us as a team to a new place in the *Agon* pas de deux as he pushed us to emphasize contrasts: Mel, very tall and strong, and me, smaller and sinewy; me, all raw nerves and Mel so calm and serene; Mel's skin very dark and mine quite pale—it was important to show the difference when we take hands, or when he placed his hand on my pink pointe shoe; my elongated neoclassical lines and flexibility was highlighted by Mel's ability to shine the spotlight on me as the center of attention, while still commanding the audience to see *him* move me. Balanchine made us bring attention to the very rigorous and classical side of ballet – turn way out, then way in— he insisted on clean footwork, and pointed out the allusions to *Sleeping Beauty* and *Swan Lake*, the hallmarks of classical ballet but now turned on their head. *Agon*, though "modern," demanded clean classical dancing, clean arabesques (for the time!) showing each position, and it stretched ballet to its most daring possibilities and to a danger-filled conclusion. I often felt in our performances that we kept going further and further, deeper and deeper into it all ... Balanchine's dare to Mel and me in '81 was to make what had been so challenging in 1957 still challenging in the 80's. I often felt, on our entrance, like stripped down circus performers entering the great arena for a truly dangerous high wire act. Today when I work with dancers I try to guide them forward just as Balanchine challenged Mel and me to use our own time and experiences to make the danger and risk inherent in the ballet, current, making what is a historical work alive for today. As we worked side by side adjusting our versions to merge, Mel was unfailingly kind, patient and professional, and he quickly made a home for himself at NYCB. His extraordinary dancing, charisma, and fun loving persona became central to the company. We all loved to be around him -- his was an important, strong voice in the City Ballet family of those special days.

When Balanchine and Lincoln Kirstein envisioned their original school in America in 1933, they envisioned a class of four white female, four white male, four black female and four black male students. As the 1980's dawned and Balanchine's life was ending, he was still reaching for that dream, welcoming the young Jock Soto who was half Hispanic and half Navaho, and Afshin Mofid a young Iranian dancer, among others, integrating his NYCB roster. Balanchine, who was never satisfied, hired Mel, a strong, tall, talented young African American ballet dancer to continue reaching for the great "American" New York City Ballet of which he had dreamed. Mel's presence in NYCB

FOREWORD

was a game changer in many ways. I had danced *Agon* before Mel with white partners of great distinction and was the fortunate and grateful, recipient of a wonderful personal success in the role.... However, on the night Mel and I first danced *Agon*, the reception was wild! His own brand of dance, his elegance, and personal style, and yes, I believe the statement of race relations that Mel and I, side by side brought to the performance, all contributed to a deeper conversation within the choreography.

After Mel left NYCB and continued through the great journey he has shared in these pages, he suffered and persevered in so many ways of which I only knew the half. It is a harrowing and inspiring journey over HIV, crippling losses, and adversity. Yet his faith, strength and serenity have led him to achieve remarkable things by any standard. It is humbling to know his story, and it is an important record of a remarkable man that needs to be told.

As retired dancers, Mel and I share more than memories; we share an aesthetic that will never leave either of us. We recognize each other. As rarely as Mel and I have the opportunity to see each other these days, we know where each other lives in spirit. I am so grateful for the chance to salute him in these pages, to say thank you for the dances, and for sharing these personal and poignant reflections on a remarkable life in dance and beyond. Hats off to Mel A. Tomlinson.

Heather Watts
NYCB Dancer, 1970 - 1995

© *King Douglas, all rights reserved.*

Acknowledgments

To God Be the Glory

I must say I would not have amounted to anything much without my faith and the incredible people who have been placed in my path. I do not believe that luck had anything to do with this journey I have been on. So many people, both good and bad, were purposely placed on my path because they all had something important to offer me, something that I needed to learn. I cannot begin to thank them all for their part in the madness of my life. Of course, whenever one acknowledges a group of people, someone is inevitably left out. If that happens to be you, please know that I am a flawed human just trying to do what is right and that your part in all the madness is most appreciated and honored. My dear family, teachers, and friends, you are the magic that has made my life's journey and this part of my journey that Claudia and I wrote about here, worthwhile. I love you all and have great respect and awe for who you are and what you have brought to my life.

First and foremost, I thank God for everything that has happened in my life and for all the people who so generously taught me, helped me, and loved me:

To Gyula Pandi and his wife, Gina Vidal, Bobby Lindgren and his wife, Sonja Tyven, Frank and Noel Smith, Mindi Lawrence, Mabel Robinson, Melissa Hayden, Duncan Noble, Liz Williamson, Nolen Dingman, Jane Van Hoven, Fanchon Cordell, Marcia Plevins, and Pauline Koner, Evelyn Miller, Breanetta Mason and all the ladies I worked with in the UNCSA Costume Shop – You all either taught me or taught with me. In either case (and for some of you, both cases), I learned so much from you and was so honored to have been taken into the UNCSA family. Frank and Noel Smith, Gyula Pandi, Mindi Lawrence, Mabel Robinson – there simply are no words to express how I feel about you all. Thank you, from my so very humbled heart. I feel sure that I would not still be here, but for you all.

To Betty Kovach, Agnes de Mille, Arthur Mitchell, Karel Shook, Alvin Ailey, George Balanchine, Jerome Robbins (yes….even Jerry), Lincoln Kirstein, Salvatore Aiello, Jill Eathorne-Bahr, Patti and Don Cantwell, Bruce Marks,

ACKNOWLEDGMENTS

Frank Bourman (yes….even Frank), Peter Martins, Rosemary Dunleavy, Jerri Kumery, Katherine Dunham, Alonzo King and all the directors, ballet mistresses and masters, choreographers and great teachers I had the pleasure to work with and learn from, thank you for the hours, the patience, and even the not-so-patience. Thank you for pushing me, keeping your standards high, and expecting me to give beyond what I knew my capabilities to be.

To Kevin and Michele Self, Karen Brown and family, Peter and Paul Frame, Ronald Perry, Susan Freedman, Heather Watts, Eddie Shellman, Judith Jamison, Heather Maloy, Jennifer Cavanaugh, Keith Darby, Scott Miner, Joe Duell, Dan Duell, Erika Moe Taylor, Traci Owens, Patricia Dickinson, Lydia Abarca, Dayna Fox, Robert Gosnell, Rita and Gary Taylor, LaTanya Johnson and all the dancers I had the great pleasure to work with as a dancer, teacher or choreographer in Heritage Dance Theatre, Dance Theatre of Harlem, Alvin Ailey American Dance Theatre, New York City Ballet, NC Dance Theatre (Charlotte Ballet), Charleston Ballet Theatre, Boston Ballet, UNCSA, High Point Ballet, Charlotte City Ballet, Gaston Dance Theatre, Charlotte Youth Ballet, Dance Theatre of Albuquerque, and all the other companies and schools for whom I have had the great pleasure to work, thank you for the dances. I loved every, last minute.

Thank you to all my friends who saw me through the dark days in one way or another, as well as all my dear friends throughout my life: Phil Hanes, J. E. Williams, Octavius Williams, P.U. Watson, Gregory K. Moss, Jr., Dr. Gregory K. Moss, Sr., Mr. and Mrs. Alfred Alexander, Jason Kurchner and family, Jennifer Wilder and family, Ann Heartley, Edith Diane Lockley-Williams, Branch Morgan, III, Robert Costello and family, Benjamin Schrievogel, Melvin Jones, Dana Cromartie, Mark Hinson, Nelle Fisher, Frank S. Ruark, Alfred Perry, Herbert Farrish, Haywood Ray, Tyronne Brooks, Cedric Rouse, J. E. Williams, Merle Steven Gary, Trish King, Marilyn Rowland and family, Robert Bain, Rochelle Alexander, Moses Anthony Porter, Maryhelen Mayfield, Elson Baldwin, Susan Brooks, Karen Moore, Karen Williams, Anna Kisselgolf, Maurice Gordon, Sybil Huskey, Betsy Blackmore, Eddie and Rebecca Higgs-Campbell, Pat Wall, Gay Porter, Edward Warburton, Clay Ashbie Headen, Joseph Henderson, Gregory Rowland, Leontyne Price, Norma Haywood, Mrs. Harvey Heartley, Ann Hunt Jones-Smith, Regina Reynolds, Motres Pridgeon, Raleigh Public School System.

To my families: Marjorieline (yes….even Mrs. Tomlinson) and Tommy Tomlinson, Janie, Ellen, Tommina, Dexter, Marlon, Papa and Ma Mable

ACKNOWLEDGMENTS

Tomlinson, Mama Jessie Henry, Rev. John D. Henry, Viola Perry and family, Kierron Robinson and family, Thomasina Craig, Joyce Kloninger, my favorite nurse, Shirley Stowe, Kathleen LaCamera and family, Thomas Sinabaldi, the Nuns and Chaplains at House of Mercy, all of my church families at St. Paul Baptist Church and Smith Temple Baptist Church.

Much love and gratitude to my publisher, Andrew Wentink of TurningPointPress, for giving me the opportunity to tell my story, Vicky Shaw for the beautiful job she did designing, organizing, and laying out this book. To Steven Caras and King Douglas, thank you for making our world more beautiful by recording the moments that take one's breath away. Your photographs are masterpieces. And to my co-writer, dear friend and confidant, Claudia Folts, who figured out how to untangle my jumbled story and get it down on paper. You are all artists as well as incredible people.

These are just a few of the people who were major in my life and many of my life decisions. I know I did not do this alone, and I know that there are so many more people that I may have omitted. I have been blessed to always have someone in my life on whom to lean. I love you all and want you all to know how very grateful I am for your contributions to my life. You all helped me go beyond my dreams!

Mel A. Tomlinson and Maria Calegari in Joseph Duell's Creation du Monde. New York City Ballet, 1984.

Chapter One

In the Beginning - Early Family Life

I miss my innocence and the feelings that come from being a part of something bigger than myself. To me, my childhood was normal because, in the beginning, that was all I knew. It was the first time in my life where all I knew was all that I had been taught. I was taught who my parents were and that it was their job to take care of me until I could take care of myself. I must say that I developed a sense of independence at a very early age.

I remember how hard I played and how much fun I had. I rarely asked for anything because I didn't feel the need. Later, I manufactured wants: toys, games, clothes, books, outings, and even later the need to be seen. I am from a rather large family of six children, a middle child, third born. My younger brother, Marlon, and I are about twenty months apart. I walked first and fastest, and probably furthest. Marlon was my playmate and I did everything I could to let him know that I was his big brother and his friend. We were close. We ran wild, full of ourselves and our childhood freedom and lightning-quick energy, in the fields and down the country backroads at my father's parents' farm in the country. We entertained ourselves within the vast limits of the surrounding acres of land. To my young eyes, the cotton fields, corn fields, tobacco fields and watermelon patches went on forever.

My mother named all the children except for me. She gave the girls male middle names and the boys female middle names: Ellen Henry, Dexter Gale, Marlon Dale, Tommina Jo, and Janie Robbins. My father named me, so I did not get a female middle name. I'm not sure why my father named me instead of my mother, but I think it had to do with the fact that North Carolina State University's Mel Thompson, #76, the center of the then all-white basketball team in 1954, the year I was born, led the North Carolina State University team to win the first ever Atlantic Coast Conference Tournament that year, and my father loved basketball. My middle name was in honor of my paternal grandfather, Coray Alexander Tomlinson. "Papa," we all called him. Mel is not short for Melvin. It was a simple name for me - someone who was to become a very complex person.

I was born into a completely segregated world. The societal climate in the South was that of "Separate but Equal," but whether or not life was fair and equal for "Colored" people was simply not a concern in the white southern culture of the day, nor was it ever a concern to me. I would face those battles much later, in the ballet world, from both black and white directors, despite being named for a white, star basketball player.

I was born on a bright, sunny Sunday, the third of January, 1954. This is not usually a particularly sunny time of the year, even in the South. It was the first week of a new year, a year that would bring much strength to the changes that were already under way not just in the South, but all over the United States. I was born eighty-eight years, thirty weeks and two days after the official end of the Civil War, the "War of Yankee Aggression" as it is still described in some parts of the South. Much happened during those years, two world wars, the Great Depression, inventions like the automobile and the airplane, and widespread use of indoor plumbing, electricity and the telephone. But still, in 1954, I was born at home in the projects, with the help of the local project's midwife, Miss Mitchell. I was born where my family would live for

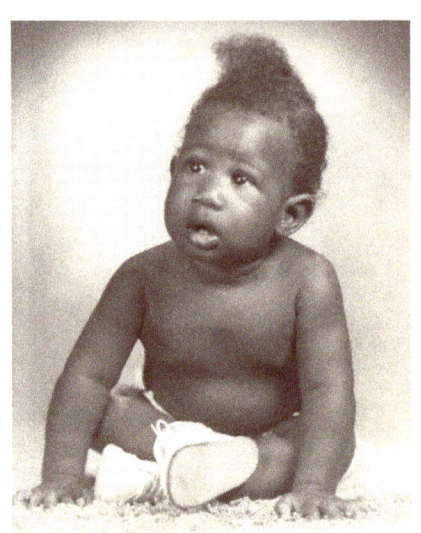

Mel Tomlinson, age one year.

the next nine years, the Chavis Heights Public Housing Development, without the benefit of a doctor or hospital equipment. It was a racially segregated community and world, where being "Colored" meant you were considered less than other humans by whites as well as by fellow "Coloreds." However, change was in the air. Little did I know, that throughout my life, I would be a part of that change.

My birth year ushered in the beginnings of desegregation in America. On May 17, 1954, when I was just four-and-a-half months old, in the now-famous Brown v. Topeka Board of Education decision, the Supreme Court of the United States unanimously overturned the 1896 Plessy v. Ferguson decision, which had allowed states to individually sponsor segregation as long as the segregation afforded each race "equal" accommodation.¹ This event was probably the single most important event in my life, though I was too young to understand the implications. The decision made it possible for me to spend much of my teen and adult life learning on an equal footing with other Americans. My battles would not be those of my parents and grandparents generations, fighting for a decent education, decent housing, the right to run a farm, open a day care center, use the local public water fountains and facilities. I would still face down the color barrier in other ways, particularly in the whitest of the white world – ballet, and even from a beloved white mentor, and a certain well-known black director.

1954 was a banner year for children born "Colored." My generation would be the first to grow up "officially" equal to white children as far as public education was concerned. The Warren court held that "Segregation of white and colored children in public schools has a detrimental effect upon the colored children. The impact is greater when it has the sanction of the law, for the policy of separating the races is usually interpreted as denoting the inferiority of the Negro group. A sense of inferiority affects the motivation of a child to learn. Segregation with the sanction of law, therefore, has a tendency to [retard] the educational and mental development of Negro children and to deprive them of some of the benefits they would receive in a racial[ly] integrated school system. We conclude that, in the field of public education, the doctrine of "separate but equal" has no place. Separate educational facilities are inherently unequal. Therefore, we hold that the plaintiffs and others similarly situated for whom the actions have been brought are, by reason of the segregation complained of, deprived of the equal protection of the laws guaranteed by the Fourteenth Amendment." ²

This was historically, one of the most important wins in the Civil Rights Movement's fight for justice for people of color.

As with all change, desegregation was a slow process. In the South, the decision was largely ignored for years. It would take the Civil Rights Movement in the 1960's, and forced busing to finally push the South into compliance, not just with the laws, but with basic human decency. I grew up in "Colored" schools. Public drinking fountains were designated "White" and "Colored" in Raleigh, North Carolina, until late 1967. At the movie theater, only whites could sit

1. "Plessy v. Ferguson." Oyez, 14 Oct. 2017, www.oyez.org/cases/1850-1900/163us537.

2. Brown v. Board of Education of Topeka (1)." Oyez, 14 Oct. 2017, www.oyez.org/cases/1940-1955/347us483.

"downstairs," as we called it, in the orchestra. "Coloreds" had to sit "upstairs," in the balcony. This was normal to me, as I had never known anything else, and throughout my childhood, I gave it little thought. I had little exposure to white people. We walked to school – a neighborhood school. Talk about "It takes a village." Our whole life as young children was that village of family, friends and neighbors. It was the South. All adults were addressed as Mister or Miss and received answers of "Yes Sir," "Yes Ma'am," "No Sir," "No Ma'am," "Thank You" and, of course, "Please". Manners were mandatory and unquestioned.

Though neighborhood schools were as important to black families as they were to white families, this was not a consideration in any of the legal decisions. For many years in North Carolina, black elementary school students living out in the country on farms, had been bussed sometimes up to 50 miles to segregated city schools. They were accustomed to long bus rides, so neither the courts nor the school boards took into consideration the effects of busing on black families. My family considered ourselves lucky to live within walking distance of neighborhood schools. The fact that the schools were not integrated was never a concern to my mother. She believed that education started at home and that it was the responsibility of the parents to ensure children had the skills they would need to succeed in the world. In school, mother expected her children to get good grades, have perfect attendance and excel at class participation. The best thing I got from mother was my love for learning and reverence for formal education. Marlon, only twenty months younger than me, did not weather the desegregated education-

Mel's mother, Marjorieline, holding Tommina, with Dexter, Marlon and Mel. (left to right)

al changes well. While I was offered a place at the North Carolina School of the Arts, and would luckily miss the traumatic changes of forced busing at the same time, Marlon would have no choice as to his immediate future. A "C" student at best, adding unfamiliar territory to the equation for Marlon's schooling was a disaster. Marlon spent two years struggling in 12th grade, only to finally give up and leave to join the Marines.

It was not until 1970, when I was in the 10th grade, and offered a place at the North Carolina Governor's School, at Salem College in Winston-Salem, that I first sat in class with white students. The NC Governor's School, the oldest statewide program for academically gifted students in the nation, was a five-week summer school program for four hundred of the State's most talented and gifted students. In most cases, students had to be rising seniors, but exceptions were made for extremely talented rising Juniors in the performing arts. All students had to be recommended by an administrator or school counselor, and were chosen according to their IQ, grade point average, and innate abilities. I was nominated by my high school counselor, Mr. Watson. My school, John W. Ligon High School, had five students attend that year: Walter Egerton, Carolyn Moore, Deborah Moore, Henry Muldrow and me. These talented students attended Governor's School in the disciplines of music, mathematics, drama, psychology and dance.

At the time, The North Carolina Governor's School, founded in 1963, was the only school in North Carolina to be fully integrated from its inception. Originally, I wanted to attend in English, but switched to dance so I would not have to wait a whole year. Drama appealed to me as much as dance, and I am not sure exactly why I chose dance, having no background in it, but I'm certainly happy I did. I really don't think I knew at the beginning of my journey into the dance world whether or not being black in the very lily-white ballet world would matter. I never thought about it. At the time, all I knew was that I loved to dance.

My siblings and I spent some of our early childhood summers with our paternal grandparents, Alex and Mable Tomlinson. "Papa" and "Ma Mable," lived "in the country," as we called it, outside of Clayton, North Carolina, which was about twenty miles south of Raleigh, or fourteen miles as the crow flies. The one-story, weathered, old-wood farmhouse was set far back off a meandering, country road, surrounded as far as one could see by fields of corn, cotton and tobacco reaching for the glorious "Carolina Blue" sky and warm sun. Papa and Ma Mable still had an outhouse, and a well from which they drew water. Pages from magazines and giftwrap were recycled for use as toilet paper. They drove to church every Sunday in a wagon pulled by two mules, Alice and Mamie, not because they did not have a car, but because the car could not hold the entire clan. The deeply-rutted roads in rural Clayton were not yet paved, so Alice and Mamie were often more dependable than the family car, especially after the rains, when the roads were muddy and slick. The simple three-bedroom house was not painted, inside or out. There were screen doors, both in the front and the back. The screens were full of holes. I vividly remember those doors because, in my mother's house at Chavis Heights, I don't remember a back door, much less a screen. In my mind, those doors represent freedom and safety. You could see the cats roaming around under the house through the plank floorboards. The wood stove heated the whole house in the winter, and there was no air conditioning, but we just didn't notice.

Some of my happiest early childhood memories came from those days spent at my grandparent's home outside of Clayton. "In the country," what we always called Papa and Ma Mable's place, we learned about the cycles of life -- birth, growth, and death. We learned early that all things nourishing came from the earth, and were sacred gifts from God. We ran free and barefoot, playing games of our own creation, in the fields and on the quiet, dirt back roads of rural North Carolina. We were poor, and that was ok. It allowed me to grow creatively, and to develop a vivid imagination.

In the 1950's, Clayton, with a population of just over 2200 people, was more a cross roads than a small town. Everyone was related, either by blood or marriage, so family was everything. Papa's house sat far back off the county road and was lined by fields of cotton, corn and tobacco. The mailbox was at the entrance – you had a long walk to get the mail. In the front of the house, which was the back, were broken-down cars, and a swing on the porch, one of my favorite places to be. The town was like TV's Mayberry. In town, the people worked in churches, factories, stores, and as teachers. Outside of town, everyone worked a farm. We always ate together as a family, sitting on benches at the picnic table in Ma Mable's kitchen.

Papa raised pigs and we ate every part of them – pig's ears, snouts, feet, chitlins, you name it. You knew when Ma Mable was cooking chitlins because you could smell them all the way at the neighbor's house, a mile away. Chitlins, or "Chitterlings," the more formal name, are the small intestines of pigs, which must be thoroughly cleaned of feces, a very smelly job, before being fried or sautéed in a sauce. During the slavery years in the American South, one of the many unpleasant jobs given to slaves was that of butchering the hogs and preparing the meat. The owners of the plantations kept the better cuts of meat, leaving the "waste cuts" for the slaves. It was said that the owners got to live "high on the hog". Slaves had to live on the less appetizing parts of the pig - ears, feet, snouts, skin, necks, and chitlins. These days, what started out back in the slave times as waste cuts have become soul food delicacies.

My paternal grandmother, Ma Mable, who was born Mable A. Jones in

1902, was one of 15 children born to James Donnie Jones and Selena Smith Jones, and most certainly the granddaughter-in-law of slaves of the prominent old-south white Tomlinson family of eastern North Carolina. Her cooking knowledge had been passed down to her the way that the most important things in life are passed down, by word-of-mouth and example.

On Saturday nights, both in the country and at home in Raleigh, the family would start getting ready for church, which was an all-day affair. As a young child, I thought of Sundays as "that long day." There was no watching TV on Saturday nights, no dancing, no games. Bible verses were read, memorized and studied on Saturday evenings, and recited at Sunday morning breakfast. The younger children were given shorter verses; the older children had more complicated ones to learn, and had to be able to explain what the verses meant. The Bible was the law of the household. There was no questioning of Christian faith, as it was as ingrained as breathing on both sides of my family.

When I was almost four, my younger brother, Marlon, and I went to live at Papa and Ma Mable Tomlinson's place because our father went to prison and mother could not handle all the children on her own. I believe she probably went on public assistance at that time. My older siblings, Ellen and Dexter, were already of school age and stayed with our mother. Daddy was apparently in the wrong place at the wrong time, and went to jail for a while, but I don't know the details. They were not important at that time in my life, as I was still too young to have a real sense of time or trauma. While in prison, daddy learned to make furniture, and alligator shoes and purses. He later made furniture for our family. I remember coming home from the country and seeing my father there. I didn't really know him before then. I don't remember him before that time. I also remember there was some new furniture, and daddy had made it.

There were so many wonderful things about living in the country. Everything about it was more relaxed than back at Chavis Heights, where my mother kept all the furniture covered in plastic, which was only removed for special visitors "important company," mother called them, and for family pictures. In the country, we got to see so much stuff for the first time – animals mating, watching seeds grow, baby animals being born. Everything was new. I really do miss my innocence. The wisdom that comes from one's journey tends to remove all the mystery and innocence that make life so special when one is young.

My grandparents were all business. Papa planted seeds and reaped that which he sowed. He worked their place hard every day. I got to see what work was and was glad that I was not old enough to do it. This was their livelihood and how they were able to feed and accommodate us while we were visiting. Papa and Ma Mable were married for seventy years before being temporarily separated by Papa's death. Ma Mable followed Papa two years later. Their beloved farm is still in the family, run now by my Uncle George Adolph Tomlinson, whom we always called Uncle Duck, and his wife, Aunt Bessie. Uncle Duck is the youngest of Ma Mable and Papa's six sons and two daughters.

I remember having my first friend, outside of family, in the country – a chicken. We became very attached to each other. I would talk "chicken talk" to him and he would follow me around. One day, I could not find him anywhere. That night, my chicken, my friend, joined us for dinner. This was one of the hardest lessons of all for a young child growing up in the country. You could be friends with the animals, but you had to remember that they were animals and part of God's food chain. Their deaths were violent. First, their necks were snapped. Then they were placed in boiling water so their feathers would come out easily. The memory of eating my friend still haunts me today. It was so hard to do. I was devastated and just couldn't swallow. I think this lesson in the reality of nature was the beginning of two very important life lessons for me: one, that we are basically here to struggle, and two, that time will go on even when we don't.

Mel, center, with his Uncle Duck and Aunt Bessie at a Family Reunion in 2016.

All in all, life was less stressful at the farm. We children only had to bathe once a week, on Saturday night, so we would be clean for church. To potty-train us, Ma Mable put us outside with nothing on but an apron. We were too little to climb up on the "john" in the outhouse, and there were no child-size training potties. At night, if we had to go after bedtime, we would use a slop pot, as the darkness was so complete that it would have been hard to find the outhouse, much less enter it. During Saturday night bath time, the bathtub was always shared with at least two others.

Ma Mable had a washing machine on the porch. It had to be cranked by hand, but that made it all the more interesting to us. Water came from the well, a fascinating place to a young boy. My "Irish twin," Marlon, and I, liked to throw rocks down the well. Papa scolded us for throwing rocks down that well, explaining that the rocks were dirty and the family had to drink that water and bathe in it. He admonished us not to get too close to the well, for if we were to fall down it, we might not get back out.

To us, every day and everything in it was new. When a child turned twelve, he could work in the cotton field. As a pre-schooler, I could not wait to turn twelve and go to work with the big boys, my youngest uncles and cousins. But that was not to be, as by the time I turned six and was ready for school, we were back in the city with my parents.

My parents' home in the city did not seem to have the same freedom as the country – more rules, more people and disagreements, no outdoor toilets or well water. Even church services were different, less free, more formal. Freedom, which was so prevalent in the country, seemed to be at a premium in the city. My mother's father, Reverend John D. Henry, a minister and elder of the Disciples of Christ Church, stayed with us in the city quite often, and became my best and oldest friend. I always felt loved and safe in his company. He would have some serious talks with us little boys from time to time and would hold our hands and walk to the corner store to buy candy and ten butter cookies for a penny. He was so rich to me. Understand, this is all from the eyes of an innocent child. I was a child full of love, hope, dreams and potential. On top of this, granddaddy became my mentor and was responsible for widening my love of learning, speaking and education. He believed that all those who found their way to the wrong side of the law had one thing in common – being raised without the benefit of strong Christian family values. Reverend Henry spent most days sitting in the Raleigh courthouse, listening to charges brought against coloreds, then offering his services free of charge to those with no hope of fair, legal representation. Although, Reverend Henry had no formal law school training, he was a very smart, educated man of God, who believed in helping those less fortunate than himself. He was, for most of his clients, the best possible representative/lawyer for whom they could hope, and made a difference in many lives.

My granddaddy, my mother's father, was the only person who could control my mother. It seems he was the only one who could keep her from beating us.

I am sad to say that granddaddy was the first loss in my young life. I guess I was around seven when he died of cancer. Mother took all of us to the funeral. I didn't understand death or dying. This was my first experience with the death of someone I loved. I knew what getting old was and celebrated that fact. I was told, "He's asleep and gone to heaven." I didn't ask any more questions.

I simply had to accept the fact that he wouldn't be able to take me to the store anymore or have long talks with me.

In Reverend John D. Henry's home, discipline had been strict and consistent. My mother, Marjorieline, the youngest of the two Henry daughters, was the disciplinarian of her own children. Having been brought up in the fishbowl life of a preacher's family, much was expected of her and her 6'5" tall older sister, Hazelline, who we called "Auntie." Marjorieline was a brilliant student, and a beautiful, young woman. If born into a later time, Marjorieline could have gone on to finish college and done anything she wanted. "Baby" was her nickname. Granddaddy called her "Baby Girl."

My mother cursed like a sailor. The preacher's daughter could literally raise holy hell. She was always model-ready from head to toe. Her beautiful, black hair was often folded away in a French Twist – nice and neat, yet not too stern. It had an air of mystery unto itself especially when she took it down. Along with this, she cultivated killer nails, which she attended to religiously. Mother was born with twelve fingers, six on each hand, and was proud of this fact. She finally had the two extra fingers removed after giving birth to her fifth child, my sister Tommina. Mother was an avid reader of "The Upper Room" a daily devotional guide, romance novels and of course, the Bible. Her children were all well-spoken, articulate and well-read. She rehearsed and corrected our speech as well as our delivery. We knew how to speak up and be heard. She indeed prepared us for school. Our clothes were always immaculate and were expected to stay that way.

As a young "Colored" woman coming of age in the mid-twentieth century in the rural South, Marjorieline did what she was expected to do. She married her high school sweetheart as soon as he returned from WWII, became a housewife and raised six children. Throughout my adult life, I have called my mother "Mrs. Tomlinson" when I speak of her. I remember her as being someone who talked out of two sides of her mouth, and very rarely praised her kids for anything. There was much good that I learned from Mrs. Tomlinson, but there was also much that created fear and distrust. I felt my mother's emotions in a different way than I felt my father's. She was the disciplinarian and he was the savior. She was an excellent housekeeper, and a deeply troubled woman. The one thing on which could be counted consistently was abusive physical discipline, with both switches and belts. Mother seldom praised us. She named the belt "Friend" and hung it in plain sight on a doorknob as a reminder. We were not allowed to scream when being beaten. I seem to remember that Mrs. Tomlinson would say, "The love is in the wood," with each merciless strike. My siblings would make fun of the welts and broken skin on my back after beatings, describing the marks as road maps and rivers. They would say I sounded like a cat meowing with every strike. Once I, as a typical six-year-old, was jumping on the couch. Mrs. Tomlinson, who was cooking breakfast at the time, was so furious that she took her frying pan, which she had been heating oil in, dumped out the oil and tried to hit me in the face with it. To ward off the blow from the sizzling frying pan, I raised my arm, and still have a huge scar on my left arm from the attack. If my father had not come running down the stairs when he heard me scream, I don't think she would have stopped battering me with that hot frying pan. That day, and for many to come, she made me wear long sleeve shirts so no one would see the blistering scar. She forbade me to talk about it to anyone, saying, "It is no one's business but ours." On that day, my mother taught me to lie.

Mrs. Tomlinson could be brutal with all of us. My oldest sister, Ellen fought back the hardest. I do believe she and I got the worst of it, but we all did get our share. Mrs. Tomlinson's favorite sayings were "Good, better, best. Never let them rest. Until your good is better and your better is best," and, "As well as I brought you into this world, I can take you out."

Years later, when I was working on both my Masters and Doctorate in Christian Counseling Psychology, from Carolina University of Theology in Stanley, NC, I wrote about my experiences with my mother: "At the time, I didn't understand. My mother often guided me to passages in the Bible, for instance, Proverbs 13:1, "A wise child loves discipline," and 12:1, "Whoever loves discipline loves knowledge." As I reflect on all this "love" I received, I can't help but recount the process. I don't know if it was love or fear. Later, I learned that the fear of the Lord was the beginning of wisdom. In Psalms 103:8, 11: "The Lord is compassionate and gracious, slow to anger, abounding in love….as high as the heavens are above the earth, so great is his love for those who fear him." It was the fear of my mother that I vividly remember, and I'm sure others can relate. If there was a problem – then disciplinary actions seemed to be the answer. Yes-the answers seemed to be found in the "rod," which showed itself in the form of a "switch." I can still hear those magic words spoken by my grandmother or my mother, 'Boy, go get me a switch…. Now!' The dreaded anticipation of a beat down created one of the longest and most dreaded walks a child can ever take: you walked slowly, to find a nearby tree that had just the right limbs and you would break one off and walk slowly back towards the executioner, hoping that by the time you got there they would have forgotten or changed their minds. You would shuck those leaves off, not realizing the poor selection you'd made in getting the smallest and skinniest limb….those are the ones that will always be remembered. The experience, which seemed endless, reminded you of the improper choices you'd made and the consequences that might follow. And of course, this was followed by an invitation to sit on the back porch in the hot sun with the Bible in tow. This time, my eyes fell upon Proverbs: chapter 7, verse 13: "My children, keep my words and store up my commandments and live, keep my teachings as the apple of your life, bind them in your fingers, write them on the tablet of your heart." Yes, this was part of my childhood development and because of it I have come to understand the power of the wood and the Word."

Mother's disciplinary lifestyle seemed relentless to me as a young boy. There was a rule for everything. No one could leave the table until they finished their entire meal because people were starving in Africa. Many families had and still have that rule. But mother always seemed to take things to the extreme. Once I dumped my breakfast in the trash when I thought mother wasn't looking. I really think she had extra eyes in the back of her head, as well as extra fingers. She caught me, handed me a fork and made me eat my entire breakfast from the trash can.

Nothing ever seemed good enough for mother. Even doing well in school was never enough. Once, she told me that I would never amount to anything because all I had was book smarts and no street smarts. I learned early how to seek revenge toward people by doing well.

Once, my mother ended up in jail, not for abusively disciplining her children, but for going after a white woman downtown at a store, who said something bad about us kids. While mother could treat us any way she wanted to, and say anything she wanted, no one else was allowed to get away with it.

To say that I was always different from my siblings would be a gross understatement. I was more than just "different." I learned early that I loved to entertain. I made it my business to get attention and not feel left out of anything. I was able to do back flips and other gymnastics naturally. There was no money for lessons of any type. I made my own skateboard, on which I learned to do many tricks, and I could Limbo lower and better than any of the other children. I taught myself how to do the popular dances of the day by tying a towel to a doorknob and dancing with it, something I had watched my sister, Ellen, do. The Twist was a dance I especially loved, and I made it my own. I used a hairbrush or a comb, whichever was readily available, as a microphone and sang all the popular songs of the day. I loved to play with paper dolls, "Dolly, Molly and Polly" and Barbies, dressing them in the latest styles. Daddy and mother let me be who I was. No one seemed to give a second thought to my interests. Nothing was ever said to me at home about doing "boy things." My older brother Dexter was a star athlete and, I believed, and still believe, he was Mother's favorite male child. As a child, I felt that I lived in Dexter's shadow so I found my own ways to get attention, learning to ride a unicycle and twirl batons. I was extremely flexible and could do many crazy contortions. One of several nicknames given to me as a child was "clown." A very talkative child, called the "snitch" and "tattletale" by my older siblings, I learned early to use silence to manipulate others into feeling guilty. This worked particularly well on my daddy, Tommy Willie Amos Tomlinson, a gentle, kind man, much loved by all his children. "Mr. Tommy" as he was known to the neighbors, worked at the local Krispy Kreme Donuts, and had a second job as a deliveryman for Janie Jolly Griffith Jewelers. Daddy was quiet, humble and humorous, and hard-working, hard-playing. He taught me to ride my sister's bike and how to swim out at Jones Lake, one of our family's favorite vacation spots.

Daddy was a "functioning alcoholic," who would spend some of his weekends out in the storage room drinking whiskey. He never drank in front of the children, but we always knew when he was drunk because he would return to the house and usually go straight to sleep, often on the floor outside on the steps. Later in life, he would lose his eyesight due to glaucoma, but was still able to find his way to the liquor store.

Ours was a traditional 1950's family in many ways. Daddy brought home the bacon and Mother cooked it up. Mother taught the girls how to cook and sew. Daddy taught the boys how to help in the yard and repair things. I remember wishing I could stay in the kitchen with the girls and learn to cook. Mother taught us all how to keep a house neat and clean, and how to properly wash clothes and dishes. Everybody had chores to do. We had to change into "play clothes" after school, neatly put our school clothes away, and then do homework before going out to play. Later that evening, the homework would have to be approved by my mother -- and you better not have gone out to play if it was not your best work. All report cards had to be seen and signed. Good grades were expected by all within our abilities and levels of learning.

Throughout my childhood, I suffered from a "Rhythmic Movement Disorder." I would go somewhere quiet, usually to a rocking chair in the living room, rock and bang my head. I would also do this at night, in my bed, to help me get to sleep. This behavior helped me to deal with stress and anxiety, most of which came from the consistently angry behavior of my mother. I continued to do this until I left for school at North Carolina School of the

Arts and started living with roommates. As I look back, the characteristics of my constant need to rock and bump my head in rhythmic patterns could be recognized as "autistic" behavior. We didn't assign fancy names to things like that when I was growing up. It was kind of like sucking your thumb. There comes a time when you realize that you have to stop….or your roommates might think you are crazy.

Each one of us children in Daddy and Mother's family had a place in the scheme of family life. First-born, Ellen, had much conflict with Mother; Tommina tended to be more neutral and diplomatic, less antagonistic than Ellen. Dexter was the athlete, and Marlon, whose nickname was "Hazard," was the "Black Sheep," constantly in trouble. I was the academically inclined entertainer, and "Robin," Janie Robbins, the youngest, was nurtured by all. I looked up to my older sister Ellen and brother Dexter. They were the most important mentors of my young life. I learned how to behave, what to do, and what not to do, from them. We were not perfect by any means – bed-wetters, closet smokers and drinkers, and over-achievers trying to find solace, approval, and love.

Chapter Two

The Elephant in the Room

It was like a Cadillac backing swiftly out of a garage, that day when I was twelve and I walked in on my parents being intimate. I had been at Vacation Bible School with my siblings and had won an award. I was so excited to share this great news with my parents that I ran all the way home, ahead of my brothers and sisters. When I burst into my parent's bedroom without knocking, my father jumped up immediately, naked. I stood frozen in my place, just staring. I do not remember exactly what I was feeling, but I would say confusion probably best describes the turmoil of feelings swirling inside of me. I remember my mother's voice, calm for once, and resigned to the reality of the situation, "Tommy, just get him, go get him." My father guided me out of the room.

We sat down on the couch, and first, he reassured me that he was not hurting my mother. He then told me that it was time for me to do some reading at the library on the subject of male/female relations. He then quietly went back to the privacy of their bedroom to finish what had been started.

For much of my life, I have been the elephant in the room in various ways, and, looking back, I believe everyone knew it but me. I was impossible to overlook, impossible not to notice, impossible to ignore, yet, until I decided not to ignore myself and my then uncomfortable reality, all the people in my world who loved me, tip-toed around it.

Until the day that I walked in on my parents, I had spent my life blissfully asexual. In many ways, I believe asexuality to be a large part of who I was then and who I have always been. But now, suddenly, I was aware of human, heterosexual sexuality. I still did not know what homosexuality was, or that being called a sissy by some of the kids had anything to do with my personal sexuality. To me, it simply had to do with the fact that some kids did not like to do the things I liked to do, like playing with paper dolls and dancing. It was not until I became aware of females as sexually attractive to males that I began to feel hindered by a confusion in my soul that I could not name or describe.

It was around this time, at twelve, that I noticed that my friends were starting to have girlfriends, so I followed suit. I even learned how to French kiss from a cousin in the back of a church bus. I did not fall in love with her – she was my cousin – but I liked it, probably because it was my first encounter. Suddenly I was seeking out more female companions. I even placed a condom, what we referred to as a "rubber" at the time, in my wallet just like my older brother, Dexter did. You never know, Dexter said at the time, you might just get lucky, whatever that was.

Three years later, at fifteen, I almost did finally get the chance to use that condom. It was at the community pool in the Chavis Heights housing project where I lived. I was in the pool with a friend who happened to be a girl and she touched me physically in such a way that I was literally moved. My mind and my emotions ran rampant. Even my dreams, from that day forward, were altered. Of course, at that time in my life, I would never have acted on my feelings because of my respect for her and my very-Christian family upbringing.

I felt that all was right with me as far as fitting in with my male friends. I listened to all their stories, but never shared mine with them. I had grown up keeping secrets and was well-versed in exactly how to do so. By this time, my male friends had, for the most part already labeled me amongst themselves. Sometimes I did catch their slings of ignorance at my expense, but it really did not click that I should be bothered by their callousness. After all, boys will be boys.

Life continued as that of a still-pretty-much-asexual teenage boy who had yet to go through puberty, until I was introduced to another experience, one that I will never fully reveal because, still, after all this time, I feel the shame of it all.

It happened at Boy Scout camp. I was sharing a tent with three other boys, who molested me. I had never seen an erection on another boy my age. It was then that I learned that all men are not created equal. I will not name them, as they have families now who do not deserve the pain and embarrassment. I worried that somehow, my school friends would find out what had happened. My discomfort was such that it felt like I was wearing clothes that were ill-fitting, like everyone could see them on me. I realize that at a certain age, boys become very curious. I was the weakest of the group and became victim to their curiosity. I was not physically hurt, but was full of confusion and shame. I kept it completely to myself. I have forgiven them and I hope that their lives have been positive and productive. At this point, I realized what it was that my older brother, Dexter would do to me sometimes when we wrestled. Up until then, I think I probably equated it to my habit of rocking and bumping my head.

I have always been late to most things in my life, except, of course, ballet classes and rehearsals. I was in my late teens before I experienced puberty. I was so happy when my voice finally changed and I began to grow hair in secret places. Looking back, my one regret is that neither my daddy nor Dexter taught me or even minimally guided me toward the facts of life. That was how it was in the late 1960's and early 1970's. I tried to learn by Dexter's example only to realize that I did not have Dexter's swagger or charming good looks. I envied so much about Dexter – his looks, his athletic ability, how easy it was for him to have girls. Even upper-class girls would jump at the chance to be in his company. He was mother's favorite and I was simply Mel – class clown, rubber man, nerd. Some of those nicknames have stayed with me throughout my life. Although I put up a good front of being friendly with everybody, inside I was so scared that I would not be able to perform in an intimate manner when the time came. Looking back now, it is a great relief that I took my time with that and did not allow pressure from my peers to force the issue.

I now suspect that all young people go through some of the same insecurities, but at that time in my life, I could not see it. Some of my peers just seemed so self-assured. I really believed that I was the only one and that I had to be vigilant and constantly try to find a way to hide that elephant in the room. I did as daddy had suggested and went to the library and read some books on human sexuality. I also spent time looking at magazines that I found under Dexter's mattress and in daddy's underwear drawer. I marveled at the pictures, but could not imagine myself doing any of those things. As I got older, I realized it just was not in me to be completely distracted by the touch of another. I married my life as an artist. That is not to say that I never got distracted. I did, but never to the point of putting my life as an artist second.

In thinking back, I remember the time when my body and mind first raged against each other. I can now imagine what Adam and Eve must have gone through. I tried very hard to hide this struggle from others. I hoped that my family would never notice the excitement of my growing body. For a long time, I controlled it even when I was alone. The nocturnal emissions that I was unable to control, mortified me. I felt so ashamed of myself. My brothers and my friends and I never talked about it, and I did not feel that I could go to daddy, and especially not to mother with my new find. The thought of being invasive enough to make a baby or get an STD was just so alien. That was not going to happen to me. I cherished and honored my space and tried to do the same with others. I just did not get it. All-in-all, I was decidedly asexual and happy to be so.

Things continued to build up and got so bad that animals would follow me when I walked past them, and even some of my friends made advances. I had no idea what was going on. This began to happen frequently until I asked a friend about it and they told me about pheromones. I tried to wrap my mind around the definition. Finally, I allowed myself personal, sexual satisfaction. It was explosive and almost addictive. I, of course, kept it private and discreet, mostly because I was sure I was going to hell. It was a couple of years before I found out that what I was doing was completely natural and normal, and that others did it, too. Once again, I was late to the party.

From the very beginnings of my sexuality, I learned that love and sex were two very different things. You could have love relationships without sex and sexual relationships without love. You could have relationships where neither were a part of the relationship, and relationships where both were part. My main concern has always been sharing my true self with anyone. Even my very first "love" was mostly mental. He would be my first roommate away from home when I was sixteen. He was heterosexual and white. I fell in love with him because he genuinely liked me and did not care what color I was or how different I was. My emotions were all over the place. I came to realize that I was in love. It was wonderfully exhilarating and painful all at the same time. I was so confused. Naturally I wanted to express my love for him, but not in words. I was in love *and* in sexual confusion at the same time.

This brings me back to that elephant in the room, the really big elephant named homosexuality. Why was I so attracted to another boy? At the time, I think I was happy that I knew how to keep a secret. I needed time to think about this. I remembered what others had seen in me, how they called me "sissy." In retrospect, I realized that I had never been sexually pushy with my girlfriends. They had been more like girls who were my friends than "girlfriends." My relationships with them had been much more intimate mentally than physically. Why was I different from the other boys? I went back to the library. Through my studies, I came to realize that for the most part sexuality is not a conscious choice. It is one's truth. My homosexuality certainly was not because of my environment. I was never taught such things. I did not choose to be gay. I just am. Throughout my life, I have always thought of God's words to Moses when Moses asked him who he was at the burning bush, and God said, "I am who I am." It was not until much later that I realized why that has always come to my mind. I am who I am, too. We are all made in God's likeness, good, bad, talented, addicted, lovable, evil, happy, sad, gay, straight, and all the rest of the possibilities. In my opinion, this likeness to God has much more to do with our souls, our thoughts, our emotions, than with our human physicality, color and sexuality. If God is all seeing and all knowing, then he must understand and relate to us all. There is a reason why no one has actually "seen" God in physical, human form. He is who he is. You are who you are. I am who I am. God does not make mistakes. People do. I therefore profess that our sexuality is part of our individual natures, something with which we are born. I believe that real love transcends sexuality, which is more about physical attraction. I have often fallen in love with heterosexuals, possibly, I suspect, because there would be no sex. Of course, I was always physically attracted to those with whom I fell in love, but what I really loved was both the act of feeling love and the glimpses into the soul and very-personal feelings of the one I loved. I could always put the physical attraction energy onto the stage.

The first person I came out to was Kevin Self. My roommate both at the University of North Carolina School of the Arts and later in New York, he is still, forty years later, my best friend. Kevin is heterosexual. When I finally decided I had to come out to him and tell him how I felt, his reaction was the kindest reaction possible. "Mel," he said, "Really? Do you think I don't know this? I love you, too, but it is platonic because I am not gay." It was as simple as that. It did not change our friendship except, probably to make it stronger.

I later discovered that one of my father's brothers was gay. He was married, had two children and fought for our country in World War II. His behavior choices were part of what was expected of him in the time in which he lived. Even in the theatre and dance world at that time, homosexuals were not free to be who they were publicly, so it certainly was not okay to be "out" in my uncle's world in Clayton, North Carolina. Then, as now, finding acceptance as gay in the black community was much more difficult than in the white community. We are expected to be "Mandingo," black men with huge libido and huge penises. Much later, my uncle was able to quietly live out the rest of his life as a gay man, at least at home, with his lover, a very quiet, kind, very effeminate man.

After I finally accepted the fact that I was homosexual, I then had other decisions to make. It is all about presentation when it comes to coming out. I chose to be conservative, the man that my father taught me to be in life, the man who could attract the opposite sex as well as the same sex, and the man that two of my ballet-world mentors, Duncan Noble and Arthur Mitchell would teach me to be as a dancer. I have loved both women and men, but feel less pressured by men when it comes time to perform intimately. The passion is different. Most of my friends and associates throughout my life have been heterosexual. For a long time, many people believed that all male dancers were homosexuals. I felt a certain amount of guilt for choosing to be a dancer because of this associated stigma. Ultimately, I am proud to be part of such an art form and happy to know that I am accepted for my talents and my convictions and that my innate sexuality and my lifestyle, like my color, do not figure into the equation. Like everybody else, I am not a "what." I am a "who." I am Dr. Mel A. Tomlinson, a man who just happens to be black, gay, intelligent, passionate, and a spiritual Christian. I only ask that people accept me just as I am.

In the words of Arthur Mitchell, founding director of the Dance Theatre of Harlem, "Be you." It was a very freeing resolve and gave me a new outlook and a realization about who I really was. People are always who they are until they realize who they really are. Then they become who they really are until the next realization comes along. This is the path of our very human lives. Through the madness, one must find a way to love oneself. This can only happen when one accepts oneself for who one really is. Once you can find this place of love for yourself, you are then free to love others. You suddenly become more positive and more productive. As Socrates said, "Be as you wish to seem."

I have never cared for those who, in their personal lives become so self-absorbed that they make a farce out of their own sexuality. The stage is one thing, but one's personal life is not necessarily, in my opinion, theatre. I remember seeing my first female impersonation show. I was in New Orleans, on tour with Ailey. It was 1977, and my tour roommate, Marilyn Banks, took me to the show. I was so innocent to what I was seeing that Marilyn had to inform me that these beautiful women performers were men. I was stunned as Marilyn went on to educate me as to what to look for: big hands, big feet, Adam's apple, Apollo's apron, the tone of the voice, the veins in their arms and legs and the size of their heads and jawlines. Although I am gay, I found myself embarrassed by the choices they had made in presenting themselves. At the time, I had a very naïve and simplistic view as to human hetero/homosexuality. I did not really understand wanting to be female, although I must admit that there were a few times in my life when I did wish that I was female, but only because, at that particular moment, I was in love with a heterosexual male, and yearned to be loved by him in every way possible. My deepest yearnings had nothing to do with being female. I was comfortable in my own skin as a homosexual male. When Marilyn explained to me that all transgender people are not necessarily gay and that all female impersonators are not necessarily transgender or gay, I became aware for the first time of just how complicated human sexuality is. There really is no "either/or" or "us vs them" situations going on here. I guess that my inability back then to wholeheartedly accept the idea of a transgender reality made me a hypocrite, prejudiced against some of my fellow human beings, in the same way that some heterosexuals were prejudiced against me. As I have said many times, I am nothing but a flawed human being, a Christian. As the years went by, I learned to accept those different from my ideas of "normal," just as many others have learned to accept me. When confronted with the argument that being gay is a choice, I have often countered with this thought: Who, on earth would choose to be gay? It is a tough life, filled with unfairness and animosity from many who do not understand or accept who you are, and seem to have the need to feel better about themselves at other's expense. I now make the same argument for those who are transgender. "Normal," as defined as fitting into the majority, carries with it a safety net, a certain amount of invisibility. The gay community has become more accepted by the majority and I believe will soon have a much better level of normalcy. There is still no safety net for transgender people. All people should be able to find their personal happiness without the fear of being ostracized or worse.

Now, if I were to comment on physical alterations, like Olympic gold medalist, Bruce Jenner's transformation into Kaitlyn, my opinions would be considered judgmental. I do not believe that God makes mistakes and so I have trouble with surgically altering what God has given. However, there are those who are born with indistinct sexuality, and doctors have been known to make mistakes. Ultimately, my opinion is this: Find yourself and find peace and happiness as long as you do not hurt anyone else in doing so. Nothing has been said in all the press given to Kaitlyn Jenner and the transgender community of late about the effects on one's children and family when one transitions. A new name? A new face? A new body? Does the complete obliteration of the former self register as the death of a loved one to one's family? To whom are you obligated and responsible to first – yourself or your children? To me, these are important questions that are not being given enough thought. I cannot help but equate it to my father staying with that woman, my mother, even though she made his and all our lives miserable. He did it because he was a man of honor, a man with great integrity. He never put himself in front of our needs. None of us could fault him for drinking a little, for he was always there when we needed him.

Since I am discussing all things sex in this chapter, perhaps I should talk about that so recently-former elephant in the room, using sex to control or manipulate others. This discussion has finally come out of hiding with the "Me, too" campaign. Women everywhere are standing up and saying, "No more," to the coercion and sexual manipulation they have put up with for time eternal. Powerful men in the business world, Hollywood and even the dance world are being outed as sexually abusive, manipulative users. Many powerful men are paying the karmic price for their behavior, losing their jobs and their families. For so many years, women without power of their own, and in certain worlds, young, powerless men, too, were the ones paying a high price for jobs, parts in productions, and promotions.

I, of course, must mention what is so far not being mentioned in the ballet world. Our world is currently reeling from the public accusations against Balanchine's successor, Peter Martins, who, as of this writing, has taken a leave of absence from NYCB while the investigation goes on. I won't go into details, but suffice it to say, where there is smoke there is fire.

However, in fairness, I think I should say this: Like all stories, there are at least two sides. Granted, we all have fallen victim at one time or another to some kind of unwanted attention or physical abuse. We have been conditioned to sweep it under the rug; to pretend it never happened. There is a dangerous duplicity here, though. As well as the many directors and administrators in the dance world of whom I have first-hand knowledge of their misbehaviors, I know just as many dancers, both female and male, who have sought out and offered sexual favors to those in power in order to get a coveted role, or to move up the ladder from corps de ballet status to soloist and principal dancer. The question I ponder is this: IF a dancer offers sexual favors in order to get something in return, like a promotion or a certain role, and that dancer gets what they want, is the exchange of sexual favors for parts and promotions alright in the eyes of both the dancer and the director/person in power? What if, as often happens, the dancer offers themselves sexually, but there has been no guarantee in advance that they will get what they want in return, and they do not get that which they wanted. Does the sexual behavior then constitute abuse on the part of the director? Or was the dancer simply naïve to think that sex would get them what they want, and the director has no culpability because he did not ask for the sex? As with everything to do with sex, this is complicated.

I am not trying to defend the bad behavior of many men in power. They deserve exactly what they are getting right now. What I am saying is simply this: In the ballet world, I know things to be more complicated than what the media is leading its' readers to believe. In fact, there is much more to the sex stories than meets the eye. Things are not as simple as male/male sexual relationships being coerced. No one is talking yet about the powerful and assumed-to-be heterosexual males who also coerce homosexual behavior when it suits their wants or even needs. Many of these men are in long-time marriages and their wives may not have a clue as to their husband's "other" interests, or if they do have a clue, they may be willing to close their eyes and allow the behavior for reasons of their own. I am speaking from personal experience here. In fact, I was once "jumped" by a heterosexual dancer at NYCB in the elevator. I am still mortified when I remember that the doors opened suddenly, and Mr. B was standing there. He simply said, "I'll take the next one," and the doors closed.

To take a complicated subject, and make it even more complicated, I must talk about sexual innuendo. The Urban Dictionary defines sexual innuendo as when something you say is meant to be totally innocent and it sounds terribly sexual. I must take this definition a bit farther than that and include the kind of subtle and often not-so-subtle repartee used when flirting with someone to which one has an attraction. Whether the attraction ends up requited or not is beside the point here. It has often been said by many friends and acquaintances that I am the king of the dry-witted one-liner as pertaining to sexual innuendo. This is something that has always come naturally to me. I have never planned, in advance to say something wittily sexual to anyone. But cleverly flirtatious one-liners have often spewed forth from my mouth without any forethought, especially when in the company of a handsome, young man. This behavior has got me in trouble a few times, and I even once lost a job back in the 1990's due to something I said to a volunteer that was absolutely meant to be harmless, but apparently made the young man uncomfortable. As an example of just how complicated this all is, if I had been a heterosexual man talking to a woman volunteer, I would never have lost my job over it. In fact, she probably would not have complained. Silence is complicity.

My homosexuality is not an excuse or a choice. It is an important part of who I am, and I am glad to be able to share myself with others. As far as companionship and friendship, gays can be a girl's best friend and even a straight man's best buddy. Like air, we are everywhere, and we are not going to disappear any time soon. We, too, are God's children. Becoming honest with oneself is the first step to living a good life, even if family and friends become disappointed in you. The rest of this step is not allowing others' disappointment to elicit negative, uncompassionate reactions or behavior from you. I remember when I came out to my family, I had been out for several years in the ballet community. Like Kevin, my family already knew. They were just waiting for me to acknowledge the elephant in the room.

Chapter Three

Transitions

It was the summer between the tenth and eleventh grades that I spent at the Governor's School that changed everything in my life. Doors started opening. People suddenly arrived in my life and brought with them such generosity of spirit that there was no way my life could take anything but a positive turn. There were people out there who appreciated me for me. They loved who and what I was, even though *I* had not figured out exactly who or what that was. One of those people was Betty Kovach, a local dance teacher in Raleigh, who first saw me on the football field, and wrote me a letter, offering me a full scholarship to her dance school.

I was in the eleventh grade, not yet seventeen, and just back from my wonderful summer at the Governor's School. I was our Ligon High School team mascot, the first male cheerleader at my high school. All the cheerleaders loved me and protected me as much as they could from some of the haters in the audience who would call out derogatory names aimed at me, and sometimes throw things. Once it got so bad that someone threw a beer bottle at me. I was able to ignore the meanness so much better than in the past, thanks to the time I spent at the Governor's School. I now knew that there were people out there who appreciated me and genuinely liked me for who I was. Even though I was still young, I had found my purpose, my reason for being. Now all I had to do was figure out how to give that purpose to my audience and all would be perfect in God's eyes,

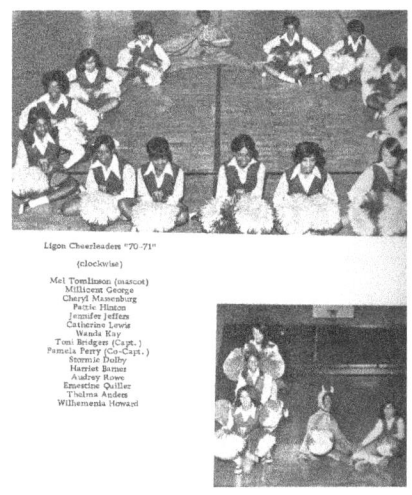

Mel, as school mascot for Ligon High School in Raleigh, NC.

and in mine.

I was different now, no longer a young boy, but a man-child, who, for so many reasons, had a much different perspective on life than the rest of my family. The most important reason was that, at the Governor's School, I had fallen in love for the first time. It wasn't sexual, not physical at all. It was completely emotional. His name was Jim, he was a dance major, and he was straight. He was my first white roommate and my first white friend. Jim genuinely liked me for who I was, and did not see the color of my skin, or my latent homosexuality. This meant so much to me. It was a huge revelation for one of my mother's children. Mother had always seen and commented on color as if color alone made you a good or a bad person, and predicted the outcome of your life. To my mother, white people were not to be trusted. In her immovable frame of mind, they were mean-spirited people who had more than we did. She believed that white people considered themselves to be better than black people simply because they had more – more money, more education, more things. It was the only thing that my mother had in common with white people. She believed just as she assumed they believed.

Publicity shot taken during rehearsal of "Biosfera" with the Dance Theatre of Harlem, mid 1970's.

My summer school experiences were the first experiences to set me apart from the rest of my family as far as beliefs about what was possible for a black person to achieve. The Governors School helped me to begin to know myself in so many ways. For the first time, it dawned on me that I was homosexual, and despite the ideas about human sexuality and skin color, that I had been raised to believe were correct, I liked who I was. By the time Betty Kovach saw me on the football field at half-time that fall, I was a performer, and I knew it.

When I got the letter from Miss Kovach inviting me to study at her dance school, I could not believe my luck. I was so excited at the thought that I would be able to take lessons. It would be like the Governor's School! It had never occurred to me that I would be able to continue to study dance once I was home again. This was huge. Of course, my mother had to be convinced.

Already that year, my mother was feeling that she had lost control over me, so I was afraid she would not let me go to Miss Kovach's school. She had made me step down as President of the eleventh-grade Honor Society because she felt that I was not spending enough time at home doing my chores. This had been my first time to try to be a leader, and I was devastated by her callous reaction. I wanted her to be proud of me for one of my accomplishments, just as she was proud of Dexter for his athletic abilities. Mother was definitely losing control and did not like it one bit. I believe that she was jealous of what she saw as the potential of my life. She had excelled in school herself and had been in many clubs but, in her day, especially for a young woman of color, these things did not lead to potential for a better life. My teachers, particularly Mrs. Allison, were trying to ingrain in us the belief that we needed to do well and get scholarships so that we could build a life on an equal footing with white people.

    For my mother, the frustration was great. That fall, the beatings accelerated, especially for me, as Ellen and Dexter were already out of the house, in college at Winston-Salem State University, leaving me to take the brunt of our mother's rage. She had taken to making my siblings and me watch each other's beatings. At this point, when it was one's turn for a beating, the instruction was even worse than, "Boy, go get me a switch." Now, it was expected that the one being beaten, strip naked and lay face down on the bed. And wait. The humiliation was complete. Even though I was bigger and physically stronger than my mother at this point, it never occurred to me to stand up to her. She would inevitably bring "friend" to the party, taking that hated belt off the dining room closet doorknob, folding it in half with the belt-buckle-side poised to teach God's lesson of consequences to one's actions. To this day, my siblings do not understand why I refuse to forget our brutal family history. As a Minister, I feel that I cannot allow myself to let it go, for I do not want to lose sight of what it feels like to be that child. I want all young people going through similar circumstances to know that I not only sympathize and empathize with their feelings, but I know exactly what they are going through. Sometimes, it seems as if my siblings' and my memories seem to be those from two different families, but I think we all do remember the same truths. The difference in our attitudes to those truths comes from the size of the worlds within which each of us have chosen to live. My broader experiences have allowed me to know that our mother's ways are not those of all mothers, and were both hateful and cruel. In fact, they were not even the actions of any of the other mothers with whom I would cross paths.

    Though I could not get there every day, and my attendance was more sporadic than the other student's, I loved going to Miss Kovach's school. Once again, everything was new and I was innocent. For the first time, I saw dancer's en pointe. Everyone was beautiful and had perfect posture. I think I grew two inches overnight from the sheer will to walk with a dancer's elegance. For the first time, I took ballet classes. Even Miss Kovach was not sure she could do anything to help my complete lack of turnout, or my feet, which looked like burned southern biscuits. I had spent years perfecting my tricks, riding a unicycle and doing gymnastics, both of which had required me to work with my legs in a parallel position. Even at Governor's School, I studied Modern Dance, Erik Hawkins technique, which grew and moved from a parallel position. Ballet training was so different, so alien. I fell in love with it immediately.

Later that year, unbeknownst to me, both the Governor's School and Betty Kovach had written letters to the University of North Carolina School of the Arts telling them about me. Miss Kovach went out of her way to convince my mother to allow me to first, audition, and second, allow me to go. Lucky for me, that my senior year, 1972-1973, was the year that the Raleigh school system was court-ordered to desegregate. That fact helped to convince my mother to let me go. She knew that desegregation was going to turn her life and her children's lives upside down. At least one of her children would have the distraction of doing something he loved. Being offered a partial scholarship, work/study in the costume shop, and a Resident Attendant job watching over the younger high schoolers, which would pay the rest of my tuition, sealed the deal. As mother said at the time, "One less mouth to feed."

The day of my audition, our car broke down. It would have been so easy for mother, in her anger and frustration with the car, to change her mind and let me down. But, to her credit, she did not. She paid our neighbor, Mrs. Farrell, a woman she despised, the huge-for-us sum of ten dollars to drive us to Winston-Salem. For that, I will always be grateful. My mother had to sit in the car for a couple of hours with this woman whom she could not stand. This, I know could not have been easy for mother. A family friend, Mrs. Jefferson, helped my parents navigate the endless paperwork associated with getting a partial scholarship and work/study at the state-run school.

Two teachers from the University of North Carolina School of the Arts, Duncan Noble and Pauline Koner, ran the audition. Many people do not know this, but Duncan Noble was the first head of the Modern Dance Department at the University of North Carolina School of the Arts, appointed by Robert (Bobby) Lindgren, the Dean of the Dance Department. Most people remember Mr. Noble for his ballet classes, amazing pas de deux classes and his wickedly dry sense of humor.

I wore red tights and a jock strap to the audition. They were the only pair of tights I owned and I think they were a hand-me-down from my sister, Ellen. At the time, I knew nothing about dance belts, those heinous pieces of dance-wear, designed to protect the male anatomy and keep it from moving around in a distracting manner, while simultaneously causing torturous chafing in the gluteal cleft area. Once again, I was an innocent, a blank slate waiting for my story to begin.

For the audition, each dancer was to have a dance made up to show to Mr. Noble and Ms. Koner. There were probably between thirty and forty hopefuls there to vie for one of very few spaces at the school, which at the time was the only arts boarding school in the country. In fact, it was the first public arts conservatory in the United States. As vain as I am, I do not remember any other dancers at the audition. As far as I was concerned, it was only about me. I do remember that it was the first time I had been in a situation with more than two boys who danced. That, in and of itself, was *huge* for me. There were others like me out there! I brought with me a single 45 rpm record of *Claire de Lune*. My "dance" consisted of some gymnastics mixed with interpretive dance steps I had learned at the Governor's School and from Miss Kovach. I remember realizing that Ms. Koner seemed to like me. She asked to see me do my dance again. I had made it up on the spot and had little idea what I had done. I danced again, keeping the new dance as similar as I could to the first dance. If they noticed, they did not let on.

Mel, center, as a Resident Assistant, with a student, right, and a mother, left. Photo courtesy of UNCSA.

At the end of the audition, the wait began. I had no idea how long it would take to hear as to whether or not I got in to the school. School would be starting in Raleigh in only a couple more weeks. It was so hard to wait; so hard not knowing in which direction my life would be heading in the next few weeks. Finally, the letter arrived and I was in! I would spend my senior year studying dance at the University of North Carolina School of the Arts. My first path as an autonomous, young adult had just opened up in front of me. I could not believe how lucky I was, but I remember sensing that something very special was happening to me. I had no idea what would be waiting for me at the School of the Arts, but I knew I had to go. My mother made it easy. She pushed us all so hard that she pushed us away. I had no regrets, and no fears about leaving home, thanks to mother. There were some things that she made so easy.

The University of North Carolina School of the Arts has always been my special sanctuary. To me, it has always been my first real home, aside from my grandparent's farm. Home, to me, is a place where one can feel safe and loved. I did not feel those things in my mother's home. Over the years, I have been lucky enough to find two other homes, which I will always hold in a special place in my heart – the Dance Theatre of Harlem and the New York City Ballet. Even though I did not know consciously that I was searching, the School of the Arts was to become the home I had been searching for, ever since returning to the projects from my grandparent's farm. Everyone there was so different, just like me, but in each his or her own original way. Rich? Poor? Mostly you could not tell. Well, except for Beverly Barwick, whose daddy would have her flown back to school in a helicopter after a weekend visit home to Atlanta. Everyone knew Beverly was rich. But none of us held it against her. She could dance, so it was ok. And no one held it against me that my family was poor and black. No one gave it a second thought, or, if they did, they didn't let on. There is a special love that is shared between students in the arts. Sure, there were petty jealousies, and full-out competition for parts, corrections, and attention, but the undercurrent was a love and support that is unmatched in any other discipline, except possibly between soldiers in the military. We all wanted success, but we wanted it collectively. None of us could imagine becoming successful without our friends.

At that time, I was one of very few black students at the School of the Arts. I had no idea what types of lives my white classmates had outside of the school. There, we were all the same in all the ways that did not matter to any of us anyway. Being poor, I had never had money to spend on anything. I had never felt that I was missing anything either, so I did not realize that I had less than my peers until years later, and by then, I had more than most in all the ways that both mattered and did not matter. As dancers, we always wore a uniform and uniforms are great equalizers. I had no appropriate dance clothes when I arrived at the school. Thank God for my work-study job in the costume shop, which was run at the time by a wonderful woman named Evelyn Miller.

Evelyn was a wiz on every type of sewing machine. One of her many specialties was working with the stretch fabrics used to make leotards and tights. She whipped up some tights for me in no time at all, on her special sewing machine called a Merrow Machine. Thanks to Evelyn, I would not have to wear the wildly inappropriate red tights I had worn to the audition. The preferred uniform of the dancers at the University of North Carolina School of the Arts consisted of well-worn tights, leotards, white t shirts, unitards, and ballet shoes. This dancer uniform helped equalize the playing field, making us all simply dancers, rather than rich dancers and poor dancers.

I loved my work-study jobs. In the costume shop, I learned many skills that I would take with me on the rest of my journey. As a Resident Assistant, I was able to help the new, younger students adjust to our crazy campus life. I always felt like I was "giving back" when I met with the new students coming to the school for the first time. I wanted them to feel as welcomed and cared about at the school as I had from my first day. One of the younger students who became a friend for life was Peter Frame. Peter was three or four years younger than me when we met, but I think we both sub-consciously recognized our kindred, introverted spirits in each other. Throughout my life, from that first meeting with Peter, we have been friends and our paths have crossed at several important junctures.

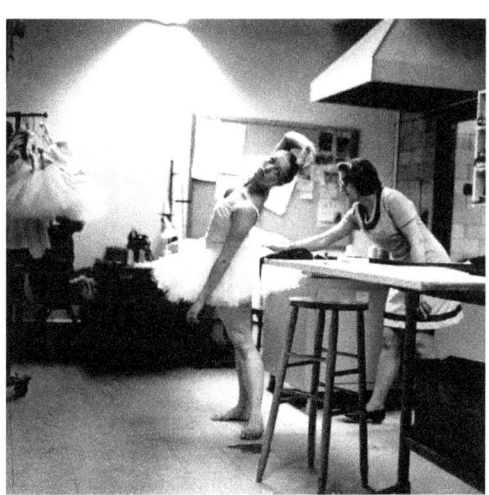

Evelyn Miller fits a tutu on a student. UNCSA costume shop, early 1970's. Photo courtesy of UNCSA.

In Peter Frame's words:

> *There are certain people you meet in your life when you least expect it that make such a lasting impression, who captivate your total attention and touch you so uniquely unlike anyone else that you have known before. It appears to be much like a serendipitous reunion of spirits that unexpectedly and out of the blue, graces your path with enthralling joy, laughter, awe and celebration.*

There I was in 1972, a joyful, shy and somewhat clueless fourteen-year-old kid from the beautiful hills of West Virginia, away from home for the first time, attending North Carolina School of the Arts as a dance scholarship recipient, wandering the campus. And there he was, Mel, like a bolt of lightning. 'Are you Peter Frame? Hi, I'm Mel Tomlinson and I will be your Resident Attendant for your dormitory and I will be looking after you,' said Mel. His words were expressed very respectfully but, his underlying unique humor and somewhat colorful delivery caught me so off guard that I just didn't know how to respond. It was a jaw-dropping moment. I had no reference point to draw upon to help me process it. I just started laughing and with every following word he uttered I continued laughing. I kept apologizing for doing so, but Mel was relentless with his quick wit and comebacks and I almost passed out from my laughing tirade and the embarrassment.

Peter Frame, with NYCB in Saratoga.

Before I could catch my breath and regain some needed dignity, Mel proceeded to demonstrate his 'One Man Cirque de Soleil Act,' with elbows twirling like helicopter blades at the speed of light, showing more flexibility than a rubber band.

He then asked me with complete sincerity, 'Would you like to see me take my foot off?'

'What?' I said, 'What do you mean take your foot off?' Before I could say no he proceeded to dislocate his foot from his ankle and let it just hang in the air with a smile on his face that completely admitted that he loved that I was in total shock. I pleaded for him to put it back in place. He said he couldn't. Before I went into utter shock, he said, 'Okay,' and without missing a beat, re-attached his foot to his leg.

A split second later, like nothing had happened at all, he then said, 'Make sure you keep your room clean. Don't make me come in there with my bucket of water.' Unfortunately for me, one day he did fulfill that promise and arrived at my door with that bucket of water.

I had never met anyone like Mel, who absolutely disarmed me so thoroughly, and who still can to this day, with his intellectual wit and contagious humor. God indeed threw out the mold when he made Mel. But at that time in my young and somewhat introverted life, I believe that God sent me a human angel to help bring me out of, no, shock me out of, my shell.

As time passed and we grew closer, Mel decided to refer to himself as my brother and then later insisted that I was his twin brother. I told him I already had a twin brother named Paul. He said, 'Okay, let's be triplets!' That's how things went between us then, and how they remain presently.

Frankly, I believe I always knew I was the lucky one, whether I was completely conscious of it or not. I was in serious need of guidance and friendship at that time, as I found myself exposed to an unfamiliar, yet exciting, artistic environment filled with such gifted dancers, musicians, actors and singers, not to mention exotic personalities, for the first time in my life. It was a world tucked into another world. Mel adopted me like a stray puppy that needed a lot of nurturing, training and attention, and helped to get me going in the right direction, a gift hard to repay.

At that time, Mel's persona was larger than life to me, like a thousand people in one magnificent body, so joyfully radiant which personally was exactly what the doctor ordered to help me feel welcomed, encouraged and with a sense of safety and security in my new surroundings. God does work in mysterious ways and I am forever grateful for that synchronistic moment that opened our hearts and souls to one another, leading us to develop and forge a most steadfast and lasting friendship.

Much of what helped to make my transition to the realities of life at the University of North Carolina School of the Arts relatively seamless was, thanks to my mother, though it does surprise me to realize that. I was already well-spoken. I was very polite. I already knew what discipline was and so could easily avoid too much social distraction. I had learned to watch and mimic my older sibling's behavior early on so that I would fit in. I continued that mission at the school by watching the most popular, self-assured students. I had already taught myself how to get the attention I needed and craved. I definitely knew how to stand out in the crowd. I fit in pretty much from the first day. I belonged. At the beginning, that was all I wanted.

Mel and Lydia Abarca in Blanchine's Agon, with the Dance Theatre of Harlem, mid-1970's. Photo courtesy of Marbeth.

Chapter Four

North Carolina School of the Arts Years

My school, the place where my life started, known these days as the University of North Carolina School of the Arts, was founded in 1963 by a very-progressive democratic governor, Terry Sanford, and opened in 1965. Still, today, those of us who went to school there before the political powers-that-be decided to change the name, call it "NCSA," not "UNCSA," and many feel very strongly about this. Many of us started our professional artistic lives there as high school students, some as junior high school students. Putting "University" in front of the name just seems to disregard most of the professional dancers of my generation and several generations beyond mine, who came out of the school, most of whom did not attend the university part.

The school was the brainchild of American Composer Vittorio Giannini who, at the time, was also a faculty member at Julliard, Manhattan School of Music and the Curtis Institute. Giannini put together his own "dream team," including North Carolina Governor Terry Sanford and Southern writer John Ehle to get the very-new idea of an American public arts conservatory off the ground. Governor Sanford appointed Ehle to be his special

Vittorio Giannini, founder of UNCSA. Photo courtesy of UNCSA.

assistant, or as Sanford referred to him as, his "one-man-think-tank" from 1963 through 1964. Ehle helped the governor to bring his very-forward-thinking, liberal educational initiatives to fruition, including the North Carolina School of Science and Mathematics, as well as the North Carolina School of the Arts. When I think about these facts, these days, during the politically conservative climate of backward attacks currently offending so many of us here in North Carolina, it makes my heart ache for those forward-thinking, great people who did so much for our state and our country in years past.

In the beginning, there was much competition between North Carolina's cities to host the arts school. Winston-Salem, a small but artistically progressive city that founded the first arts council in the country at around this same time, won out. It took Winston-Salem only two days to raise almost one million dollars through a telephone campaign, largely, I believe, due to the efforts of Phil Hanes, CEO of Hanes Dye and Finishing, and one of Winston-Salem's and North Carolina's most progressive and aggressive supporters of the arts. The money raised was ear-marked to renovate an old high school to be the first building to house the new arts school. It was the same year that Phil was appointed by President Johnson to the National Council of the Arts, where he was the only business man to sit on the board with great artists like John Steinbeck, Helen Hayes, Duke Ellington, Leonard Bernstein and Harper Lee.

Phil was an artist in his own right. He brought creative thinking to his business world, which allowed his company to grow and prosper in ways that other businesses simply did not. Phil Hanes was one of my biggest supporters and champions of my career from the very beginning. How could North Carolina School of the Arts, or I, for that matter, fail with the support of an amazing man like Phil Hanes and his equally amazing first wife, Joan?

Phil Hanes. Photo courtesy of UNCSA.

During this same time, the Ford Foundation was deciding where to place certain challenge grants nationwide in the arts. These grants, meant to help de-centralize the arts away from New York, were strategically placed around the country to help develop professional arts organizations outside of New York City. George Balanchine was part of the decision-making process as to who would receive the dance grants that year. The University of North Carolina School of the Arts received 1.5 million dollars in matching funds, a huge amount for the arts in the 1960's.

Robert Lindgren, the first Dean of the Dance Department at the University of North Carolina School of the Arts, had retired from the New York City Ballet in the early 1960's and moved to Phoenix, Arizona, where he and his wife, ballerina Sonja Tyven, had started a ballet school. Mr. Balanchine called Mr. Lindgren one day and told him that he wanted him to go to North Carolina to run the dance department for this new arts conservatory. Bobby and Sonja sold their school to retiring American Ballet Theatre dancers, Kelly Brown and Isabel Mirrow Brown, future parents of American Ballet Theatre soloist, Leslie Browne (remember the movie *The Turning Point?*). Little did I know that throughout my life, Mr. Lindgren would reappear and help me to move on to my next life-phase. For all of us in the ballet world there is only one degree of separation, and the connections tend to run deep.

Robert "Bobby" Lindgren, first Dean of Dance at UNCSA, and his wife, Sonja Tyven, who taught at the school. Photo courtesy of UNCSA.

Bobby, "Mr. Lindgren" to all of us at the time, was a great leader. He seemed to know everything and everybody. He introduced us all to so much. Mr. Lindgren was responsible for bringing Marcel Marceau, Alvin Ailey, Agnes de Mille, Liz Williamson and so many other great artists and teachers to the school. He only brought in people with generous spirits; people who were willing to give to the students and would not hold back. In those days, the early 1970's, Mr. Lindgren loved to demonstrate when he taught class, even though his hips were bad and getting worse by the year, both eventually to be replaced. He had great showmanship and style. I could see who he had been as a dancer, first, with the Ballet Theatre, then Ballet Society, the precursors to the New York City Ballet, and then with the Ballet Russe de Monte Carlo, from 1945-1952, and finally as a soloist with the New York City Ballet. Mr. Lindgren's knowledge of ballet history, the great ballets, and the dance world, in general, was surpassed by no one else. Aside from ballet, he loved football and beautiful women. I always loved his youthfulness and energy, both then and throughout his life. He would peek into all the classes, even the modern classes, and make sure everyone was working. Mr. Lindgren was good at choosing people. He never liked dancers from competition schools, "Fake smiles and bad feet," he would say, but he would take male students from any background, just as everyone else did at the time. There just were never enough of us, so being a male was a huge plus in the dance world.

The North Carolina Dance Theatre, the professional company that Mr. Lindgren founded at the North Carolina School of the Arts, was completely integrated racially, and had been from its inception. Mr. Lindgren directed the company for many years before finally leaving to take over as Executive Director from Lincoln Kirsten upon his retirement, at the New York City Ballet. North Carolina Dance Theatre, now called Charlotte Ballet, and moved to Charlotte by its second Artistic Director, Salvatore Aiello, was known from the beginning as an innovative, forward-thinking, international touring company that launched the careers of many new choreographers and dancers. Eventually, Mr. Lindgren would offer me a place in the company, but I would decline, only to come home with the intention to end my career there much later under the direction of Salvatore Aiello.

At the North Carolina School of the Arts, I often watched the most advanced ballet classes. These were the best dancers at the school. They were also the most popular group. By that time, I had figured out that it was smart to be popular. I made sure to be seen and associated with these top dancers. In my mind, guilt by association could only help me with the teachers as well as the other students. I was not wrong in this assumption.

A modern dance major at the time, I was good at it, a natural. Pauline Koner recognized this and very quickly moved me into the college classes, even though I was still a high school senior. Unfortunately, to me, it just was not enough. I found the physical control and liquid movements of the ballet dancers fascinating. After training myself to ride a unicycle, and studying modern dance, my potential for turnout was less than mediocre. Ballet is all about control, mind over body. I knew it would take enormous strength of mind to overcome my body's lack of balletic possibilities. In fact, even I did not try to fool myself as to what my body would be able to accomplish. Instead, while working for turnout and better feet, I also concentrated on enhancing what I knew I had that made me special: I re-molded my very flexible, strong legs into straighter, more elegant lines. I hoped that all that I was doing to improve my placement and lines, added to my ability to pick up choreography quickly and to remember what I had learned, would eventually make Mr. Lindgren and the ballet staff take me seriously. I was naturally musical, which I figured would be helpful, too. My long neck, height and physical strength were also assets.

I am so grateful for both the modern and the ballet training I received at the School of the Arts. From the modern teachers, I learned how to dance from the inside out. From the ballet teachers, I learned how to refine both my movements and my body. In those days, studying ballet or modern was an either/or proposition. Very few dancers did both. The current opinion was that ballet dancers should only study ballet. It was believed by many that modern training was detrimental to ballet dancers, and would take time away from the very-important repetition needed to become proficient with ballet technique. Looking back, there were definite times when my modern training gave me an edge.

The more I watched the dancers in the most advanced ballet classes, the more I wanted to be like them. They were so elegant and so graceful. They seemed smarter, too, than everyone else. It seemed as if they had a deep secret, the depths of which only the elite could fathom. By the middle of my first semester, I knew I had to be one of them, so I set about finding a way to convince Mr. Lindgren to let me switch my major to ballet.

Once again, fate stepped in to help me along the way. Gyula Pandi, then a member of the North Carolina Dance Theatre, who was to become my favorite ballet teacher, became injured and could not do the Russian variation in Mr. Lindgren's *The Nutcracker* that year. I, along with several other dancers had learned it. We all wanted to jump like Mr. Pandi. Sonja Tyven, Mr. Lindgren's wife, convinced Mr. Lindgren to give me a chance. After patiently committing to watch me do the variation, Mr. Lindgren was pleasantly surprised, and he gave me the part. In less than six months, I had gone from the team mascot at my high school to a soloist in the North Carolina School of the Arts' *Nutcracker*. And I would be going on tour with the production to Durham, North Carolina, a town, less than twenty miles from the projects where I had grown up. I knew I was on my way to something exciting. In fact, at the time, I believed I was already there.

With this opportunity, came another: Mr. Lindgren decided to allow me to double major in both Modern and Ballet beginning in my second semester at the school. I could not believe my luck once again. Now I would have to work even harder so that I could join my friends in their advanced ballet class someday. I was well-aware that Mr. Lindgren did not think I had a chance of becoming a professional ballet dancer. He was always very honest with all the students as to his opinions. I knew I had a lot to prove.

During my first semester at the school, I quickly became fast friends with several other dance majors. Many have remained life-long friends. One dance major became my best friend almost immediately and has remained my best friend for over forty-five years now. Kevin Self, from New Mexico, was one of the best ballet dancers at the School of the Arts at the time. He spent many evenings in an empty studio helping me to learn steps that he and the others had been doing repeatedly for years – *brise volé, temps de quisse, entrechat six, and the dreaded double tour en l'air*. I have never understood anyone who says they found success on their own through hard work and sheer determination. I worked hard, sure. I kept going through many failures, yes. But I also had help from some of the best, most generous people in the world. Kevin Self was and will always be at the top of that list. For the second time, I was in love with a heterosexual male.

Kevin had come to the University of North Carolina School of the Arts from New Mexico, where he had studied ballet for several years. He was my roommate and one of the top ballet students at the school. From our first meeting, Kevin and I just clicked. He shared my love of academics. We both graduated from college at the school, me, in two years; Kevin in one.

Kevin taught me so much, not just about ballet. From him I learned that we

Sonja Tyven teaching the advanced ballet class, early 1970's. Kevin Self in foreground. Photo courtesy of UNCSA.

are all just people, not black people, or white people, or male people, or female people. Just people. In fact, Kevin and I called each other "people" and still do to this day. "Hey, People," we would call out to each other in greeting each time we saw each other between classes.

Kevin helped me to realize what so many people thought would be impossible. He showed me what I needed to know and do to become a serious ballet major. Kevin loved me simply for who I was, and he believed in me. It was that simple. There was nothing physical about our relationship, though I never stopped wishing that there would be. It was fine as it was, as I have always simply loved him. Kevin would end up in American Ballet Theatre for a short career, but would decide to leave, first, to go to law school, then to work in real estate with his father, and finally to become a ballet teacher, his true destiny. Not a surprise to me, as I was probably the first student to benefit from his generous and caring guidance.

As my ballet technique improved, so did the attention I received from the ballet teachers, including Mr. Lindgren, who became more interested, more kind to me, going out of his way to help me. That Spring, Mr. Lindgren offered me another wonderful opportunity. He sent me to the Southeastern Regional Ballet Association (SERBA) Festival as a guest dancer to partner two dancers, one from Augusta Ballet and one from Atlanta Ballet. Both were black and both were named Karen. It was 1973, but it was still the South and in many places, it was seen as inappropriate for a white person to dance with a black person, socially or on stage. The term "Colored" was finally beginning to disappear, and be replaced by "Black," but the feelings and history behind the term "Colored" were still there.

I know that part of the reason Mr. Lindgren sent me was because I was black, but I believe that he also sent me because he believed I could do the job well. I was not the only black dancer at the University of North Carolina School of the Arts. Once again, I was afforded new and exciting experiences: this was my first paid job. I got to fly on an airplane for the first time. I met wealthy black people, also for the first time. Until then, I had not known that it was possible for black people to be wealthy and live the way I assumed white people lived.

First, I flew to Augusta, Georgia to dance with a girl named Karen Brown with the Augusta Ballet, under the directorship of Ron Colton. Karen's father was a doctor. Everything about her upbringing was different from mine. Her parents, Dr., and Mrs. Allen Brown, were much more practical, and more educated than my parents were. In her home, the older teenage children could drink alcohol. Karen's parents figured their children were going to do it anyway, so it would be much safer if they did it at home. My parents, particularly my mother, believed that God's word was enough to make anyone with any sense do the right thing and stay away from alcohol.

Karen took me out to dance at an after-hours club, driving her father's Cadillac. Unbeknownst to me, Karen did not have permission to take the car. We had so much fun, partying, and winning a dance contest to *Me and Mrs. Jones*, R & B singer Billy Paul's only number one hit. On the way home, Karen got the car stuck in some mud, so of course, we got caught. Being a "daddy's girl," and already a clever manipulator, Karen slyly got out of trouble by using me as her excuse.

"But Daddy, Mel wanted to go. I was just being a good hostess, Daddy," Karen said earnestly. This trip was the start of a very close friendship with Karen that has lasted throughout my life.

When I finished learning the dance with Karen Brown in Augusta, I went to Atlanta to work with Atlanta Ballet, the founding company of the Regional Dance America movement. Although San Francisco Ballet is the oldest professional ballet company in the United States, the Atlanta Ballet was founded four years earlier as a civic company, but would become a professional company much later. It is the oldest continuously performing American ballet company still in existence today. The dance I learned in Atlanta, with the other Karen – a lovely dancer named Karen Wright - was a contemporary piece, as well, called *Double Music*. The rehearsals were filmed and the film was shown behind us when we performed on stage. This piece started with me on the floor. I would rise on one leg, with the other leg extended straight up. I'm told it was spectacular-looking, but I could do it easily, as it was nothing more than one of my childhood tricks. No one had seen anything like that, and it stole the show at the 1973 SERBA Festival. We received a standing ovation and several curtain calls, even though they were not allowed then, and are still not allowed today. This is because, at regional festivals there are a large number of companies that perform, making time constraints an issue. I loved every second of the applause. I loved being loved – all children love approval. I never want to lose that quality. This very moment was what sealed it all for me. I suddenly knew exactly what I wanted to do. I wanted to have adoring fans and be loved by everyone in my audience. It would be many years before I realized that being loved by an audience of fans was not the same thing as being loved by family and true friends. But, at the time, and for many years to come, there was nothing else in my life that could compare to the feelings that came from being adored by an audience.

Karel Shook, co-founder of The Dance Theatre of Harlem, and Artistic Director, Arthur Mitchell's ballet teacher, was at the festival scouting for fresh talent for the New York-based Dance Theatre of Harlem, an all-black ballet company. He offered both Karens and me full scholarships to the company's summer program. We all accepted our scholarships and spent that summer studying in New York City. All three of us were invited to stay, join the year-round program and work with their company. At the end of the summer program, both Karens chose to stay, but I declined. I wanted to go back to North Carolina and get my college degree. It was very important to me to be the first in my family to graduate from college, as both of my older siblings, Ellen and Dexter, had recently dropped out, not finishing college. Dexter was immediately drafted into the army. To her credit, Ellen would go back much later and get her degree. I had just finished high school and already had quite a few college course credits under my belt. Being a middle child, I had always been competitive with my older siblings. The thought of getting my college degree before either of them appealed to my sense of sibling rivalry. I also knew in the back of my mind that it would matter to my mother, and her approval still mattered to me then, as it still does now.

This was a time when virtually no one in the ballet world spent time getting a college degree before starting his or her career. It was the early 1970's; thanks to George Balanchine, the Ballet Master in Chief of the New York City Ballet, the era of the "baby ballerinas" had long-since begun. Ballet dancers were expected to be ready to start their careers by sixteen at the latest. I'm not sure that I ever thought about the fact that, at eighteen, I was already at an age where I was considered "old" for a career in ballet. I just knew that, at that moment, a college degree was very important to me.

The following year brought several wonderful, new opportunities. My technique was developing at a fairly rapid pace now. I was considered a decent partner in Mr. Noble's pas de deux classes. The girls would comment that I smelled great. I figured out quickly that smelling good in pas de deux class would move me forward and give me a better chance of getting to dance with the best female dancers. They could be brutal in their opinions of the boys. If the girls thought one of the guys smelled bad, the talk behind that particular guy's back would be relentlessly tough, bordering on cruelty. I knew that if the girls wanted to dance with me, it could only help me. Our teacher, Duncan Noble taught all the boys to be like his name, Noble. He taught us how to be men on stage, strong and masculine, and how to take a backseat to the girls, presenting them to the audience and making them look beautiful no matter what. Mr. Noble's dry wit and X-ray-vision stares made one very aware that he saw right through every bit of our teenage pretense, right to our very souls. We knew that he knew everything about us, so we paid attention to everything he said with a completely single-minded focus for which not one of us even knew we had the capacity.

My hard work in the pas de deux classes paid off. Sonja Tyven decided to teach me the Snow Pas de Deux for that year's Nutcracker. Once again, she convinced Mr. Lindgren to give me a chance. I was to dance it with Julie Jordan, now an attorney, who was both strong and beautiful – I think she held us both up. Miss Tyven was beautiful. She had been with the Ballet Russe de Monte Carlo, under the name, Sonja Taanila, because her older sister, Gertrude was also in the company at the same time and did not want them confused by the audiences. This was not unusual at the time; younger siblings were often expected to change their surnames if their older sibling already had an established career. Sonja Tyven, born in New York City, had trained with the great teachers of her time, Maria Swoboda, Olga Preobrajenska, and George Balanchine. All in all, her career spanned forty-two years, and included four Broadway shows, the Ballet Russe de Monte Carlo, many TV shows, and the New York City Ballet. At that time, in her mid-forties, Miss Tyven was still so strong and elegant. She could do both the female and the male parts, full out, including *double tours en l'air*, but at the same time she had this Princess Grace-style beauty. She looked, at all times, as if she was wearing top-quality, high-karat diamonds on her fingers and around her neck. I was amazed and in awe, and very grateful to have the opportunity to learn from her and dance the Snow King.

In the fall of 1974, Mr. Lindgren brought in Agnes de Mille to look at the dancers for possible positions with her newly re-created Heritage Dance Theatre. Miss de Mille was one of the most famous American choreographers, having choreographed many signature works for Ballet Theatre, Broadway, and Hollywood. Her ballets were pure Americana, based on American folk tales and the Wild West. This new company would be touring to all fifty states over the next couple years, and would end the first year of tours in May, at the Metropolitan Opera House at Lincoln Center in New York City, as part of an all-star gala in honor of impresario, Sol Hurok's eightieth birthday. Margot Fonteyn, Rudolf Nureyev, and many other great artists would be performing on the same stage on which we would perform. These were paid positions, in a union company, for which we were auditioning. I had no idea at the time what being in a union company meant. Despite de Mille's reputation for being tough and mean, every dancer on campus wanted to be in her company.

At the audition, I quickly figured out that Miss de Mille wanted the heart, not just the steps. She wanted to see who you were and how you related to the choreography. She wanted to know your version of the story. I was sure that she liked me. I lasted through most of the audition, but finally she cut me. I was devastated. It looked as if my best friends would all get in and I would be left behind.

Once again, fate intervened in the guise of Gyula Pandi. For Mr. Pandi's belief in my abilities and willingness to push Miss de Mille to take a second look at me after cutting me at the audition, I will always be grateful. I believe that it changed the course of my life, ensuring that I would have a place in the professional ballet world.

"There simply is no place for a black male dancer in this company," said Miss de Mille to Gyula, while I stood behind the portable mirrors, listening and trembling, afraid they would discover that I was there. At the time, through my disappointment I felt that maybe she thought less of me because of my skin color. However, it was not that she was prejudiced; far from it. Miss de Mille had been a champion of black people for many years. In fact, the first ballet she ever choreographed for Ballet Theatre's Inaugural Season in 1940 was a ballet called *Black Ritual*, which featured sixteen black female dancers, known at the time as the "Ballet Theatre Negro Unit." The ballet was on the same program as *Swan Lake, Act II*, which was virtually ignored in reviews due to the scandalous black ballet getting most of the attention. *New York Times* critic John Martin called *Black Ritual* "a complete novelty for any ballet company to sponsor, and, as it turned out, an extremely interesting one." Unfortunately, it was not interesting enough to keep the Negro Unit in place. The unit was disbanded at the end of 1940 to save money for the main White company.

As I remember it, Mr. Pandi convinced Miss de Mille to give me another audition the next day. He told me to bring my whole bag of tricks – my unicycle, batons, and every trick I knew. I did. Miss de Mille decided to make a place for a black male dancer in her company, by choreographing a ballet called *Texas Fourth*, which reminded me of the western version of my days as the mascot for my high school. I got to use everything from my bag of tricks in that ballet, from riding a unicycle to twirling my batons. Miss de Mille was a master at bringing a story to life through movement. Even though I, as yet, had no idea who she was or what she had done in the theatrical world, I knew that this job would be an important stepping stone in my career. I now had my first touring company job, and it was in a union dance company. I would be touring all fifty states as a professional dancer, and I would be doing it with my new family – my ballet friends.

Chapter Five

Touring with Agnes

"The truest expression of a people is in its dance and in its music. Bodies never lie." I have always believed that this quote has so much truth in it. The great, American choreographer, and my dear mentor and friend, Agnes de Mille said it. I believe she also lived by it, as everything about her was "truth."

Miss de Mille came from an era in which the notion of a collective American history was still relatively new. When Miss de Mille was born in 1905, the United States was just 129 years old. Our history was replete with stories of cowboys and Indians, gunfights, the haves enslaving the have-nots. American ballet was even younger than American politics and religion, and had even less history on which to build. I believe that Miss de Mille saw this, whether consciously or unconsciously, and realized that by creating ballets with a uniquely American spirit, she could tell some amazing stories and, at the same time, make ballet exciting and interesting to those who lived outside the major metropolitan areas. Through small ballet touring companies, Broadway and film, Miss de Mille helped in a major way to introduce many Americans to both ballet and our country's recent history. She helped the American people to recognize and value much that was to become important and uniquely American. As I look back, I am overwhelmed and in awe that I was a part of what I now know was an important part of our uniquely American ballet history.

It was from Miss de Mille that I learned the meaning of "professionalism," that so-important link between doing something for fun and doing it for profit. I have always danced for fun, even after I became a professional and started receiving paychecks. I fell in love with dance completely, and for many years, could not imagine my life without movement. I think those of us who are lucky enough to always simply dance for the love of it are the happiest people in the world because dancing gives back so much to us. Dancing does not feel like a job; it is a passion. At the end of each day, I always felt like I had accomplished something important. That sense of accomplishment is what makes it easy to get up in the morning, even in the face of debilitating exhaustion, physical pain, and the mental anguish caused by certain choreographers. It would never have occurred to me not to show up and do my job, even if I was unhappy with casting or with any other management decision. I have always known I would be fine no matter what. I attribute this gut feeling to growing up with no money and a mother who tended to beat any sense of hope out of us. My background gave me the ability to easily live in the present, as the past was always best forgotten and the future had so many unknowns, that trying to live in it, or for it, just makes me a nervous wreck.

Becoming a professional dancer can change everything you feel about dance if you are in the wrong place with the wrong director. It can absolutely ruin your love and leave you completely empty. I think that the reason many dancers quit dancing professionally before their time is because they are not lucky enough to work with great directors who are filled with positive energy and love, so they lose heart. Whenever I think about Robert Lindgren and Agnes de Mille, my first two directors, I cannot help but marvel at my luck. From these two, extraordinary people, I learned such important lessons; lessons that would carry me through later, when faced with working in some less than perfect circumstances. If things were reversed in my life, and I had not had the experiences working under both Mr. Lindgren and Miss de Mille first, I do not think I would have been able so easily to maintain any innocence or as much enjoyment in my dance career as I did.

From Miss de Mille, I learned the simplest things, things that became so important to me that they became a part of me and I never had to think about them. I learned to be on time and prepared to go the moment rehearsal was to start. I learned to focus 100% in that moment, the moment when the choreography was being taught, and not to allow my focus to waver. I learned to grasp my part "full out," accepting and dancing the movements the way the choreographer intended for them to be danced, immediately, not tomorrow or next week. I learned to inhale and digest the choreography as well as the intent of the choreographer, and to take it and own it immediately. This was important.

Heritage Dance Theatre rehearsals were held at the School of the Arts, so during the rehearsal period, we were able to continue our academic studies. Once the actual tour started, it was harder for some of the dancers to consistently keep up with their schoolwork. I managed to keep mine up, as did my best friend and roommate, Kevin Self. Academics had always been important to both of us and that did not change although dance had taken over our lives.

Miss de Mille had a long history back then with the North Carolina School of the Arts. She, along with José Limon, was one of the original Artistic Advisors for dance at the school. Mr. Lindgren had danced in *Rodeo* when Agnes first staged it at the American Ballet Theatre. When Mr. Lindgren first secured the funding from the Ford Foundation to start his professional company, the North Carolina Dance Theater, he had invited Miss de Mille to stage two of her ballets for the opening season, an old one called *The Cherry Tree Carol*, in which Mr. Lindgren performed the lead male, and *A Rose for Miss Emily*, based on the William Faulkner short story. Back in the beginning, North Carolina Dance "Theatre" was spelled "Theater". The spelling was changed to "Theatre" when the company moved to Charlotte. Mr. Lindgren had spelled it "Theater" because, at that time, that was the accepted American version of the spelling and he reasoned that his company was an American company. Over the years, the English spelling of "Theatre" has become accepted by many arts organizations in the US as the proper spelling for an arts organization.

In the beginning, there were three directors of equal importance at the North Carolina Dance Theater – Robert Lindgren, Duncan Noble and Pauline Koner. Mr. Lindgren acted as Artistic/Administrative Director. Mr. Noble and Miss Koner were the resident choreographers.

Sonja Tyven, Bobby Lindgren, Agnes de Mille and Pauline Koner.
Photo courtesy of UNCSA.

If it had not been for the fact that one of my teachers, Gyula Pandi, had danced in the company during that first season of the North Carolina Dance Theatre, he might never have been seen by Miss de Mille, impressed her, and had her ear when needed to be able to convince her to take a second look at me.

According to Mr. Pandi's reminiscences, he performed a duet with Pauline Koner on that first North Carolina Dance Theatre opening night, in 1970, as well as dancing Limon's original part in *La Malinche*, in which, in Mr. Pandi's words:

> *She (Pauline) danced the role that she created for the Limon company some twenty-five years before. She was in her late 50's but danced superbly…...Miss de Mille complimented Pauline at the party afterwards, saying, 'This was your night, Pauline!' She wanted to know who I was. I told her that I taught in the dance department. Next day, she showed up in my class and after the class ended, she walk(ed over) to me and said: 'I want you to work with me.' She spoke in staccato, very sure of what she was saying, almost like military orders coming from her.*

Mr. Pandi went to New York to work with Miss de Mille, dancing the "Dream Pas de Deux" from *Oklahoma*, and the Champion Roper in *Rodeo*, among other ballets. Miss de Mille also sent Mr. Pandi to learn tap from Vernon Lusby, who had worked as both a dancer and assistant choreographer for Miss de Mille on several shows.

A couple of years later, in the late summer of 1972, Miss de Mille taught Mr. Pandi some of the choreography she planned to use in the Heritage Dance Theatre tour. The plan was to have Mr. Pandi go back to the school and choose 30-35 dancers to whom he would teach the movements, and then Miss de Mille would arrive and choose which dancers with whom she would work. Mr. Pandi remembered what happened at the audition a little differently than I remembered it.

In Gyula Pandi's words:

> *The audition moved slowly and Miss de Mille told me to whom she doesn't want and I had to tell the dancer 'thank you, you can leave.' I hated that. I was quietly doing my job, until she sent Mel away. I was really curious why she did that because I already knew how special Mel was. Respectfully, I asked her why she sent him away. In her typical fashion, like an order, short and sharp, she said, 'Too much teeth.' Later, I learned what that meant was that Mel was smiling too much for her liking. As the dancers were released, they left the studio, but Mel stayed behind the portable mirrors and watched what*

was going on, peering through the crack between two mirrors.

We were getting to the end and Miss de Mille asked me, 'Is there any boy who can do a big grande battements?' I told her that the black boy she sent away could do a really nice one. She just swept her hand in front of her face and repeated: 'Too much teeth.' I said: 'But Madame, he can kick his legs over his head, if that (is) what you want, he is the one who can do it.' Miss de Mille thought for a few seconds and since she really liked me and she trusted me enough to show some agreement by saying: 'Oh.... but he is already gone.' I told her, 'I can get him.' I don't remember for sure if she said something like, 'We don't have time to wait'-- so this is not a quote, but I was already moving behind the mirrors and got Mel to come out. The rest is history. Mel produced one of his patented kicks when the knee hit his chest and the foot went over the head. Miss de Mille swallowed and said to me: 'Okay, he's in,' and Mel's professional career started!

It was the next day that Mr. Pandi had me return with my arsenal of tricks, including my unicycle and batons, to show Miss de Mille what else I could do besides dance. I could see that look in her eyes – the look that said, "Oh yes. I have plans for you!" And the Acrobat in her ballet, *Texas Fourth* was born.

Really, the hardest thing about touring was not getting used to a different stage every night. It was not sleeping in a different bed in a new place either. It was those bus rides. They were long, arduous, endless rides through what could sometimes be very unfriendly territory, especially in the deep south. Unfriendly to artists in general, but sometimes to me and the four black female dancers, in particular, because of the color of our skin. Miss de Mille always did her best to shield us. She allowed me to stay youthful and happy, and would simply not have it any other way. Much as the bus tours were hard on all of us, they must have been hardest on Miss de Mille. She was almost seventy years old and rode the tour bus with us to every venue,

Agnes de Mille and Mel Tomlinson on tour with de Mille's Heritage Dance Theatre in 1973.
Photo Courtesy of Kevin Self.

when she could easily have flown, at least to some of them. I did all I could for Miss de Mille. I would have done anything for her. I knew no harm could come to me because of Miss de Mille, and that was the least of all the life gifts from her for which I will be eternally grateful.

It was during those relentless tour bus rides, that Miss de Mille noticed that I was very consistent with my studies. Often, on the tour bus, she would call me up to the front of the bus to sit with her. She would help me if I needed help, but mostly, I think she knew that it was quieter up there at the front of the bus and it would be easier for me to focus and get my schoolwork done. Sometimes, she would tell me funny stories. It was during one of those bus rides when Miss de Mille first told me to tell the reporters that I was younger than my true age. She said that I was her newest protégé and that it would be more impressive if I said I was seventeen instead of nineteen. She explained to me that even Judy Garland was older than the age she appeared to be and admitted to.

I really loved Miss de Mille's stories about all the famous people she knew. At one point, she even introduced me to Margaret Hamilton, the actress who played Almira Gulch and the Wicked Witch of the West in *The Wizard of Oz*.

I always felt that there was something oddly familiar about Miss de Mille. I think I really "got" her and she knew it. She looked to me very much like an aging, country woman, often with a large Slurpee in her hand. Do not misunderstand this. I am not saying this in a disparaging way. I am only speaking from my early, small town, rural, southern experiences. There were several very important differences between Miss de Mille and the rural country women I remember from my early childhood. First, Miss de Mille was very well-educated and well-spoken; for years I thought she had been born in England to aristocrats because of the way in which she spoke. Secondly, Miss de Mille had all her teeth, and did not use a spittoon, unlike the country women I had seen back in Clayton, North Carolina, as a child. She always made me feel safe, loved and respected, especially when we were in less-than-friendly backwoods southern towns. She never once made me aware that my skin was not the same shade as hers.

Once, in a very small town -- it was more of a truck stop than a town -- in Alabama, we stopped for lunch. As the whole company filed in and took seats at the counter of the very-Southern coffee shop, I began to feel the tension all around us. The other customers were staring at us. The waiter came out of the kitchen, and pointed at a sign which read, "We don't serve Negros here." One of the dancers, without missing a beat, said, "That's ok, I'm not that hungry. I'll just have a hotdog." We all started to laugh, but controlled it immediately, as I think we all instinctively knew that laughing would not be the wisest reaction.

The waiter, angry now at being made a fool, said, "We still don't serve their kind," nodding his head once in my direction. In an instant, just like well-rehearsed choreography, every dancer stood up and filed out the door. It was scary, but I was grateful to have so many kind, loyal friends. Suddenly, I had the realization that, not only did the white dancers consider the black dancers as equals, but we would all be there 100% for each other. For me, this was a defining moment. Never again would the thought cross my mind that not being white mattered in the least.

I think what was so magical about Agnes de Mille ballets was that one could so quickly identify with them. Miss de Mille gave you Americana in everything. She gave you small town American life that was so detailed and so full of reality that you could smell the barbeque and taste the fried chicken. It was a wonderful education that I really had no idea I was getting at the time. It was not until years later, when touring with other, larger companies, that I realized the gift that was Agnes de Mille and Heritage Dance Theatre. We did the "Charleston," the "Lazy Suzy," got to learn the "Pigeon Head Peck," and we clogged. I learned that these dances were as ingrained in America's small town, provincial culture as guns and Jesus. You could only become a true connoisseur of dance when you understood and appreciated all dance the way Agnes did.

Gyula Pandi, who had been a great character dancer in the Hungarian National Ballet before defecting and coming to the United States, and was and still is my favorite ballet teacher, danced *The Logger's Clog* in Heritage Dance Theatre. He was amazing and no one, not even a deeply southern, good-ole-boy, born and bred to clog, could have done it better than Mr. Pandi, who has more love in his soul for dance than anyone I have ever come across.

I begged Miss de Mille to put me in the ensemble in that dance with Mr. Pandi. I loved it and wanted to do it so badly. Although Miss de Mille had other plans for me, in her new ballet called *Texas Fourth*, she did put me in the back row for *The Logger's Clog*. It was my one chance to be a part of the ensemble, dancing with my peers. I was so happy.

In *Texas Fourth*, I got to do all my tricks, everything that Mr. Pandi had me show Miss de Mille at my second-chance audition. I rode my unicycle, did my gymnastics, and twirled my batons. It was fun and easy for me. We premiered it in early April 1973, at the School of the Arts, before taking it on tour.

Texas Fourth is Agnes de Mille's tribute to small town American life. It is about a parade in a small town called Baird, Texas, in 1936. The choreography is contagiously happy. It was based on the social dances of the day, including the *Lindy Hop* and the *Big Apple*. Everything about *Texas Fourth* is pure joy. At the time, I really did not realize that I was part of Agnes's inspiration for *Texas Fourth*, but when I look back now, I am honored and humbled.

Part way through that tour, Susan Carter, one of the company members, got pregnant. She was the lead majorette in *Texas Fourth*. In those days, dancers stopped dancing when they got pregnant, many for good, some for the duration of their pregnancy. Miss de Mille told me I would have to do her part since I was the only company member available at that point in the ballet. I would finish my part, leave the stage, run around to the other side, change my clothes very quickly and lead the parade back on stage, all in less than one minute. It was my first quick change and I was terrified that, unable to do it in time, I would miss my entrance. I remember that terrible, panicky feeling. Our wonderful costume designer, Christina "Stia" Giannini figured out the quick change. She soothed my worries, like all costume people I had met up to that point. She made me feel protected and loved, very much the way a mother is supposed to do. Stia approached the quick-change dilemma as a simple problem to be solved, dispassionately, and with total confidence. She made me practice it and timed it. I was amazed at just how fast it could be done. I have prided myself ever since on being able to master any quick change at lightning speed.

Everywhere we went, I got quite a bit of recognition and praise. A reviewer changed the name of the company from "Heritage Dance Theatre" to "Mel Tomlinson and the Heritage Dance Theatre". It started in Texas. Sadly, I think it was because of this that the day came in which I first lost some of my new-dancer innocence. Some of the company members, especially the professionals who had been brought in from New York by Miss de Mille, became distant to me. I had no idea why they would not be as happy about the reviews as I was. We had great reviews, and I believed that was a reflection on the whole company. If it had been one of them singled out instead of me, I would have been very happy for them. Instead, their cool reaction to my good review hurt my feelings. Unfortunately, once you lose your innocence, and the more of it you lose, the more defensiveness and distrust starts to manifest inside you. It took years, losing a little bit of innocence at a time through similar experiences, but there came a time in my dance career when I did not trust anyone and had grown to feel the need to protect myself from those who should have been closest to me.

I remember that suddenly I was very happy that I had practiced my autograph back in high school. It was one of those silly things that we all did while waiting for our stars to rise. There were people waiting for me outside the stage doors everywhere we went. I will not lie. I loved the attention. I felt like I was walking around with a spotlight on me and I reveled in it. It felt like love to me, a mistaken thought, to be sure, but something for which I had always felt so hungry. It finally clicked in my mind that I was a principal in the company, and I finally understood exactly what that meant. My contract did say that and I was paid more than most of my friends, $425 per week plus per diem, which is money for living expenses such as food and hotel. In the mid-1970's, this was a fortune to someone who had never had money before. I had no idea what to do with it, so I kept it under my mattress. Seriously, I kept it under my mattress, everywhere we went. I did not really need it, as the per diem was generous as far as I was concerned and covered all my expenses, including ice cream sundaes every day. That, was mind-boggling to me. The fact that I could eat and have the money to pay for ice cream sundaes every day! In my mind, I was more successful than I had ever dreamt would be possible. I found myself living beyond my dreams.

My roommate, Kevin had explained to me that the reason I was being paid more than the other student dancers was because I was not dancing in the ensemble. It was an odd position for someone so new to the professional dance world to be in. I was being paid as a principal along with seasoned professionals Gyula Pandi, Elaine Bauer, Charles "Honey" Coles, Jamie Jamison, Gemze De Lapp, Glory Van Scott, David Evans, and others who came and went for different legs of the tour, but I was still a kid with certainly nothing in common with them. They were grown-ups. I think it took so long to sink in because, we all knew that all my friends dancing in the ensemble were so much better at ballet than I was. They had all grown up taking ballet lessons, but there were still many ballet steps that I did not know how to do correctly. In my mind, they were doing the "real" dancing. They were the ones with beautiful training and technique. It took a while, but I started to realize that it did not matter that I did not have the technique my friends had. We all made important contributions to the company.

I danced on several legs of the tour with Agnes de Mille's Heritage Dance Theatre. Each tour was several weeks to a month or two long. Each time we returned to the school, I worried that I would be behind in my academic classes. After the first tour, I talked to Mr. Lindgren, telling him I wanted to quit the tour and focus on my academic classes. Mr. Lindgren would not hear of it. He told me that Miss de Mille would never forgive him if I left the tour. He told me not to worry. He would make sure that I got all my academic credits. As it turned out, I ended up with way too many academic credits, plus we were all given credit for the dance classes we were missing because we were working professionally. We were all very happy about this. Most of the dancers were just happy that they would receive school credit without having to sit in the academic classes.

At one point, Miss de Mille decided to send me to Chicago to learn a new ballet for the tour. It was called *Floyd's Guitar Blues*, choreographed by the legendary Katherine Dunham. It was not really a "new" ballet, as Miss Dunham had choreographed it over twenty-five years earlier, and had danced it herself with Vanoye Aikens. But it was one of Miss Dunham's "Americana" ballets, so it was a perfect fit for the Heritage Dance Theatre. The music, composed by blues guitarist Floyd Smith, was the first recording of the blues played on an electric guitar. For the first time, I had to be an independent, grown-up adult. The ballet was a mature story, far removed from *Texas Fourth*, and definitely far-removed from my everyday reality.

Mel Tomlinson and Glory Van Scott in Katherine Dunham's Floyd's Guitar Blues

Glory Van Scott was to be my partner. The ballet was for two black dancers and had a very adult theme. It was about a drug addict and a dealer, and the struggle to escape addiction. I learned the steps quickly but had to work hard on the essence of the part. I knew nothing about dealing drugs, and even less about what being an addict meant.

My partner Glory Van Scott, one of the professional dancers Miss de Mille had hired in from New York City for the tour, was older and more experienced than I was, as both a person and as a professional dancer. At nineteen, I was still unsure of myself as an adult. Glory was so patient and kind, spending hours helping me to understand the feelings I had to find, and then portray in order to live up to both Miss Dunham's and Miss de Mille's expectations.

Glory, now Dr. Van Scott, made many major contributions to the dance and theatre worlds, from being a principal dancer in both Miss Dunham's and Miss de Mille's companies, to performing in five Broadway shows, including the "Rolls Royce Lady" in *The Wiz*, and teaching Theatre at Bucknell and Fordham Universities. Thanks to Glory, I learned how to really break apart a character and find it within myself to feel things I had never experienced. She taught me how to use my body's physical reactions to certain exhilarating feelings to portray the physical reactions attributed to drug withdrawal. *Floyd's Guitar Blues* was my first experience portraying more than just great movement and the joy and exuberance that come from it.

Miss Dunham, like Miss de Mille, had already made tremendous contributions to the American dance world. She was considered "the matriarch and queen mother of black dance." The Dunham technique is still taught at The Ailey School, the school founded by Alvin Ailey. A brilliant woman, Miss Dunham like most talented people, was ahead of her time. With PhD's in Anthropology, and Philosophy, she had spent a great deal of time studying Afro-Caribbean dance. She was a well-known political activist, fighting segregation in hotels, restaurants, and even in Hollywood by refusing to sign a contract when told she would need to replace her darkest-skinned dancers with lighter-skinned-but-still-black dancers.

Miss Dunham had also studied Vodun, or Voodoo rituals, in Haiti over a period of many years and eventually became a mambo, or high priestess in the Vodun religion. At the time I worked with her, I did not know about her religious beliefs, but I remember seeing in her eyes that there was more to her than I was going to learn at that time.

Katherine Dunham was known for her beautiful legs. Jean Cocteau once said, "If we writers could say with our pens what Katherine Dunham says with her legs, our writings would be forbidden." The same year that I went to Chicago to learn *Floyd's Guitar Blues* from Miss Dunham, she was named to both the Black Filmmakers Hall of Fame and to the Entertainment Hall of Fame Foundation. Once again, I was given the opportunity to work with someone magical.

Our tours continued to be great adventures. Kevin was my tour roommate on each tour and I relied on him in so many ways. Besides helping me to improve my ballet technique, Kevin had unknowingly taken over the position once held by my older brother and sister, Dexter and Ellen. I watched Kevin constantly, so I would know how to fit in with everyone else. We stayed at many Howard Johnson's Motor Inns and often ate at their restaurants. Kevin and I always got dessert first, then our meal. The ice cream sundaes tasted wonderful; and so did the taste of freedom from my mother of which I was slowly becoming more and more aware. The first thing that Kevin and I would do when we checked into a hotel was to use the beds like trampolines. We would jump from one bed to the other if there were two beds in the room. With each jump, I found such joy and new freedom. I began to realize that there was a very different life waiting for me, one far removed from the life in which I had grown up.

Kevin was my rock. He kept me grounded at school and on tour. I was terrified that I would be lost without him. I was jealous when Kevin showed interest in one of the female dancers. This was the first moment that I realized that a part of my psyche was like that of my mother. I understood how she had felt when she knew she was losing control of us. I did not like it. I did not like feeling alone and out of control, but I also did not like understanding her side of things. I had come to the realization that I was like her in some ways, and that because of this fact, no matter how far away I traveled, I would not escape her for as long as I was alive. This revelation really shook me.

On the Heritage Dance Theatre tours, I believe that we traveled to every state, except Hawaii. My world had become much larger than that of my family. I would never be the same little boy again. Agnes de Mille had opened the world to me.

The school year flew by. Suddenly, we were preparing to leave for our final performance of the year. On May 21, we would be performing on a gala at the Metropolitan Opera House at the Lincoln Center for the Performing Arts in New York City. The gala was in honor of Sol Hurok, the great impresario who produced the performances of the cream of the crop of the ballet, opera and music worlds, not to mention helping to produce the Beatles American tours in the sixties. He had turned eighty-five that year, and it was the 60th anniversary of his work as an impresario. He was being honored by his most devoted clients: Agnes de Mille, Dame Margot Fonteyn, Marcia Haydee, Richard Cragun, Natalia Bessmertnova, Mikhail Lavrovsky, Isaac Stern, Shirley Verrett, Sir Robert Helpmann, Lynn Seymour, Alexander Grant, Jerome Hines, Mary Costa, Van Cliburn, Antonio Gades, Jan Peerce, Desmond Kelly, Roberta Peters, Robert Irving, and the dancers of the Heritage Dance Theatre. The gala raised over $150,000 which was donated to the New York Public Library for the Performing Arts. Less than a year later, Sol Hurok would be dead.

I had never heard of any of these supposedly famous people, much less the Metropolitan Opera House, or the Pickwick Arms, the hotel in which we would be staying, but the other dancers clued me in. I found it hard to believe when they said that the stage was as big as a football field. I was to find out that they were not exaggerating.

When we first got to New York, we went to the hotel to check in. Everything looked very solid, though very small. Kevin and I went to our room and immediately jumped on the beds. The Pickwick Arms was no different to us than the countless Howard Johnson's Motor Inns we had stayed in, except that the ice cream sundaes were much more expensive. I remember my hair had grown out and looked a little wild. It was the early1970's and Afro's were "in." We were in New York, so I decided to pick my hair out into a very-full Afro. Miss de Mille was not happy and told me to get it under control. A little water was all it took to shrink it down to a manageable size.

When it was time to go to the theatre, we all got on the bus and spent the whole ride with our faces pressed against the window glass. I was not the only one who had never been to New York. I remember being intrigued that the stage door to this theatre was hidden underground in a parking garage. We were barely in the stage door, when we had to check in with a security guard who had a list with all our names on it. This was nothing like the much smaller venues in which we had been used to performing. The only person whose mouth was not hanging open in awe was Miss de Mille. I do not think that any of us, least of all me, realized until that moment, that world class theaters like this were normal to Miss de Mille.

I will never forget seeing the backstage and stage area of the Metropolitan Opera House for the first time. It was not as big as a football field. It was more like two football fields. For the first time in my life I was speechless. I remember someone asking me if I was ok, but it felt like they were too far away for me to hear what they were saying. I was fine, but I was trying to calculate exactly how I would be able to dance big enough to cover that stage, not to mention how I was going to get from one side of that stage to the other and make my quick change in time for my next entrance. Many of the other dancers were nervous about dancing on the same performance as Dame Margot Fonteyn and all the other great artists of the ballet world. Since I had never heard of any of them, that did not bother me. It was that quick change that was making me hyperventilate. I kept myself calm and quiet. I knew I would need every bit of my focus to get through this performance.

There were so many differences between working at the Metropolitan Opera House and working at a small town theatre. Perhaps one of the biggest differences was that everyone allowed past the stage door here was a theatre professional. There were no "locals" hanging out. This made the atmosphere different and exciting. I loved it.

Finding our dressing rooms was an adventure unto itself. My dressing room was nowhere near my friends who were in the large-group corps dressing rooms. My name was on my dressing room door – and also a star. This was getting more and more serious by the second. It was almost as if I had been transported to a very surreal place, like a Salvadore Dali painting, or another surreal landscape. This was nothing like North Carolina School of the Arts. It was nothing like the theaters we had danced in over the past year. It was certainly nothing like my high school at home, or visiting my grandparents in the country, and it was more like being on another planet than back in Raleigh at my parent's house. Strangely enough, it felt wonderful. It took about five minutes sitting in my dressing room to start feeling comfortable. This was great! Yes, I could get used to this. And I would make that quick change, I had no doubt. The one thing that did not cross my mind until years later was that this, my first-time dancing in New York City as a professional, was in a gala at the Met for Sol Hurok, as a principal dancer in Agnes de Mille's company, in my second year as a ballet student. Wow. Just wow.

Originally, the plan for Heritage Dance Theatre was to continue to tour all fifty states, then finish in Washington, DC, for the big Bicentennial Celebration in 1976. My last performance with the Heritage Dance Theatre ended up being the Hurok Gala at the Met. The company never made it to the Bicentennial, as Miss de Mille had a terrible, massive stroke in the spring of 1975, while doing a lecture demonstration at Marymount College in New York. She fought her way back from the stroke, as only someone with her tenacity could, but it took her several years. She had become my friend for life. We kept in constant touch over the years. When I think of her, my heart feels so warm and I instantly smile. She was a tough lady, but she knew how to love and she knew how to impart strength and passion. She could make the impossible happen. Because of her, I knew that the impossible would always be a possibility.

Chapter Six

Graduation and Moving On

Throughout my life, most of my time has been spent just getting to where I was going. In some ways, I have always seemed to get there at lightning speed. I spent three-weeks at the North Carolina Governor's School in Dance in the summer of 1970, and ended up a year later, in the fall of 1971, at the North Carolina School of the Arts, majoring in both Modern Dance and Ballet. I started taking serious ballet classes and a few short months later, ended up touring with Agnes de Mille's company. I toured with Miss de Mille's company and ended up only a few months later in a dressing room with a star on the door at the Metropolitan Opera House. I graduated from college with my BFA in Dance in two, instead of four years, and, in 1974, quickly accepted an apprenticeship at the Dance Theatre of Harlem.

I remember my high school graduation, seeming more like a fun-filled school assembly than a graduation. It was short and full of humor. Nothing about the North Carolina School of the Arts was like "normal" high school. We had a Homecoming dance, but no sports teams, and our Homecoming "Queen" was two Queens, one male and one female.

Homecoming parade, UNCSA early 1970's. Photo courtesy of UNCSA.

I never had to think about what college I would attend, nor did I even have to apply. The University of North Carolina School of the Arts had taken me under its wing, and the nurturing atmosphere had me hooked. I would have been quite happy to spend the full four years of my college life at the school, however, that was not to be.

In the blink of an eye, it was time to leave the safety of my beloved School of the Arts, my wonderful home away from home. I had only spent three years at the school, one in high school and two in college, much of it on tour, but they were the most important years of my life thus far. I had learned much of great importance. I had learned that to the only people who mattered, all people were *people*, not *colors*. I had learned that there was a whole magical world of the arts out there and that lots of people thought that I had something special to share. I had figured out that I was gay and that there were plenty of people in the world who thought that was just fine. I had learned that there were black people out there who had money and education. I now knew that I could make my own way in the world, and if I so chose, I could eat ice cream sundaes before my meals.

College graduation at an arts conservatory is nothing like graduation at a regular university. We did not have the equalizing caps and gowns. Everyone wore whatever he/she wanted to wear. In fact, some chose to omit clothing entirely. It was the 1970's and "streaking" was "in". There was no mention of GPA's or class rank. No one seemed to care. The list of graduates going to professional schools on scholarship and into professional companies was announced because that was what really mattered. I managed to warn my parents in advance not to expect the expected. My mother seemed quite confused by the madness, while my father really enjoyed the whole insane process.

While I was back home in Raleigh for part of the summer before leaving for New York, my mother found all the money I was keeping under the mattress. I do not think it had ever occurred to her that I would have so much money from my dancing job with the Heritage Dance Theatre. She was flabbergasted that I had not put it in a bank. That idea had never occurred to me, as no one had ever talked to me about money or how it worked. For years, I watched my father give his paycheck to my mother every week. She decided on what the money would be spent. She was the one to help me open a bank account. I had saved more than a few thousand dollars, because it never had occurred to me to spend any of it, as I had everything I wanted and needed at that point in my life.

It was during those final few weeks that I was home before leaving for New York that my mother beat me for the last time. I do not remember much about it, but from that point on, my mother became "Mrs. Tomlinson" to me, someone akin to a stranger, with whom I had no relationship whatsoever. I had made it clear that she would never beat me again, and made it clear that there would be dire consequences if I was to hear of her beating any of my younger siblings.

By the time graduation came around, I had already decided where I was going to go. I had offers from the Dance Theatre of Harlem, the Alvin Ailey American Dance Theatre, The Joffrey, and Boston Ballet. I also received a contract offer from Mr. Lindgren to join the North Carolina Dance Theater. I was very proud that Mr. Lindgren believed in me, but he still saw me as a modern dancer and by that time, I saw myself as a ballet dancer. I chose to take the apprenticeship with the Dance Theatre of Harlem for several reasons. First, Kevin was already in New York, at the American Ballet Theatre. He had to miss graduation altogether because he had signed a contract with that company, one of the greatest companies in the world and his contract started a month before graduation. I also had my good friend Karen Brown in New York. She was already at the Dance Theatre of Harlem. Second, I had spent the previous summer there, so I felt that I knew what to expect. And lastly, I believed that I needed to see how I would fit in with other black dancers. At the North Carolina School of the Arts, I had become kind of a big deal by the end of my time there. I needed to see where I stood with other black dancers, most of whom would have had more classical training than I had. I asked myself, "Am I considered good because of the color of my skin, or can I exist in the big world of the arts WITH the color of my skin because I have *real talent*?" The Dance Theatre of Harlem just seemed to me to be the perfect place to find the answer to that question. Arthur Mitchell was the Artistic Director. At that point, very few black ballet dancers had been fortunate enough to have professional careers in the United States. Most had to go to Europe to find a place in the ballet world. There was Raven Wilkinson, who had broken the color barrier in the 1940's by dancing as a soloist for six years with the Ballet Russe de Monte Carlo touring company, where she faced some excruciatingly cruel racism on tour in small-town America, and Arthur Mitchell, who had broken through the color barrier in the 1950's, first when he joined the New York City Ballet, and again a few years later when he became the first black principal dancer in a major American ballet company, to name two. Director, George Balanchine choreographed many roles on Mr. Mitchell, from *Agon*, to "Puck" in *A Midsummer Night's Dream*.

Since Kevin had left school early to join the American Ballet Theatre in New York, he had already found a wonderful apartment on the Upper West Side. We would be roommates again. The apartment was a one-bedroom, first floor, garden apartment with a small, private backyard, on West End Avenue in the 80's. The neighborhood was a beautiful, safe, family-oriented area. Every morning, we would leave the apartment at the same time, Kevin to head down only about twenty blocks to the American Ballet Theatre's old building in the West 60's near Lincoln Center, and me, to head uptown to Harlem, in the West 150's, to the Dance Theatre of Harlem. It was the 1970's, and Harlem was still a segregated, pretty-much-Black-only neighborhood. Above 96th Street, everyone on the subway looked like me or at least had olive-toned Hispanic skin.

When I arrived at the Dance Theatre of Harlem in 1974, the company was only five years old. Arthur Mitchell and Karel Shook had already accomplished so much with this fledgling company, what I think of as the first professional all-Black ballet company in New York City. Mr. Mitchell had joined the New York City Ballet in 1955. Hand-picked by George Balanchine, Arthur Mitchell was one of the first Black ballet dancers invited to join a major professional American ballet company. Mr. Mitchell knew what it took to find success in the ballet world as a black man. I knew there was much that I could and would learn from him. It is an understatement to say that he was tough and controlling. He told us what to wear, both inside the studio and out. He told us how to behave. His expectations were higher than anyone with whom I had yet to work, even higher than Miss de Mille's. He made sure that we all knew that there was a separation between dancers and director, and that the director's opinion was really the only one that mattered.

Karel Shook, left, and Arthur Mitchell, right, co-founders of the Dance Theatre of Harlem.

Mr. Mitchell firmly believed in keeping us segregated from the white ballet world. I never really understood this, as he had spent ten very-successful years in the whitest of the white ballet world, the New York City Ballet. He had been there through much of the New York City Ballet's most important growth years. He had rehearsed at the small, wooden-floored studios on the Upper West Side and had been there for the transition to the newly-built Lincoln Center for the Performing Arts in 1965. Mr. Mitchell and the very elegant white ballerina, Diana Adams, along with ten other dancers including Todd Bolender and Melissa Hayden, were the original cast for George Balanchine's modern masterpiece, *Agon*. Balanchine had started work on *Agon* in 1953, before Mr. Mitchell joined the company, but the ballet was set aside for a few years due to several reasons, not the least of which was Balanchine's year-long sabbatical from the company to care for his last wife, Tanaquil LeClerq who had contracted polio while on tour with the company in Europe. When *Agon*, along with its Pas de Deux for Arthur Mitchell and Diana Adams premiered in 1957, it caused quite a stir. It was only three years after Brown v Board of Education, and a good six or seven years before the Civil Rights Movement was in full swing. A Black man dancing on a public stage with a White woman? The Greek word 'agon' means conflict or struggle, quite an appropriate name for this ballet in this time. Somehow, Mr. Balanchine was always able to get away with being ahead of his time, and so was Arthur Mitchell. Of course, in those days, the TV networks would not show any ballets in which a Black man danced with a White woman because Southern TV stations would refuse to air the shows. Arthur Mitchell was the first African-American to become a principal dancer in a major American ballet company. He broke the color barrier in the New York City Ballet, making it possible for first, Debra Austin, then later, me, to become soloists in the company a few years later.

According to both John Clifford and Patricia McBride, two principal dancers in the New York City Ballet at that time, Arthur Mitchell was very much loved by all the dancers as well as Mr. Balanchine. He was out-going, kind and had many friends in the company. John Clifford only remembers one racial incident within the company and that he attributed to the mother of a young female dancer from the school, who refused to allow her daughter to be one of the four girls in the Arabian variation in *The Nutcracker* if Mr. Mitchell was performing the lead in that variation. John described Mr. Balanchine as probably one of the least racist humans on the planet, and remembers the company members as feeling the same way. Patricia McBride concurred with that assessment. "Mr. B taught us all so much by his example," she remembered.

Patty remembers that there were racial discrimination incidents while the company was on tour, but never "in house." One time, when she was very young, eighteen or nineteen, she had flown to Canada with other company members to film *Agon*. Patricia had been asked by Mr. B to dance the pas de deux with Arthur, an opportunity that she considered to be quite an honor for a young dancer who had only been in the company for about three years at the time. During their down time, she and Arthur decided to catch a movie.

"It was the early 1960's," Patricia reminisced, "The other movie-goers stared at us in a hostile manner, assuming we were on a date, making us both feel a bit nervous. I think it was easier for Mel, not just because it was 1981 when he joined the company, but also because he was already a recognized dancer when he joined."

Mr. Mitchell was tough and had extreme drive and determination. He came by these traits through a difficult, young life. He had grown up in Harlem, in the same West 152 Street neighborhood where he would later start the Dance Theatre of Harlem. Nowadays Hamilton Heights, that same neighborhood, is one of the fastest growing in New York City, with gentrification in full swing. During Mr. Mitchell's childhood, however, it was a tough, hard place for a child to grow up. His own father died when he was twelve and he worked many odd jobs as a young teenager to help support his family. Much like what had happened in my youth, a school counselor first noticed his talents and suggested he audition for the High School of Performing Arts. It was there that he fell in love with ballet. Karel Shook, a retired dancer from NYCB and the Ballet Russe de Monte Carlo, and founder of Studio Dance Arts in New York City, where Arthur spent his afternoons studying, would later co-direct the Dance Theatre of Harlem with Mr. Mitchell. He was Mr. Mitchell's main teacher and mentor. A brilliant teacher, Mr. Shook returned from his tenure as Ballet Master for the Dutch National Ballet specifically to co-found the Dance Theatre of Harlem with Mr. Mitchell. A white man, Mr. Shook had been a teacher of and an advocate for black dancers for most of his career, having trained many of the best – Arthur Mitchell, Alvin Ailey, Carmen de Lavallade and Geoffrey Holder, to name only a few.

I can only imagine how tough it must have been for Mr. Mitchell. He is twenty years older than I am, and although he went through many of the same things I did, he went through them during the years before the Civil Rights Movement took off. At least he was in the North. If he had been in Raleigh, North Carolina, during those years, he would never have had a chance.

I remember my first day with the Dance Theatre of Harlem. We were taking class in a rehearsal room at New York City Center on West 55 Street, because the company was performing there at the time. I was warming up in the studio before class, trying to be unobtrusive, as I was one of the new kids. Suddenly there seemed to be quite a commotion in the hallway, and I heard, "Where is he? Where's that new boy? The one from South Carolina." It was Mr. Mitchell. He appeared in the doorway, a very neat, mass of intensely organized energy, and looked around the room. His eyes stopped when he found me. He stared. I raised my hand and politely corrected him. "My name is Mel and I am from North Carolina, which is in the South." Oops.... I realized that maybe I had spoken out of turn. The whole room heard my voice for the first time when I spoke back to Mr. Mitchell and froze. There was a sudden silence in the room that, at first, I did not understand, but soon grew to understand as I got to know how things worked with Mr. Mitchell at the Dance Theatre of Harlem.

Mr. Mitchell stared at me for what seemed to be a very long minute, then, without another word, started giving the class. First, he attacked my feet, and very quickly, without taking a breath in between thoughts, asked me where I trained and what my astrological sign was. I informed him that I was a Capricorn and had graduated from the North Carolina School of the Arts in Winston-Salem, North Carolina, to which Mr. Mitchell replied with a completely dismissive tone, "Those people don't know how to teach blacks how to dance." This was confusing to me, as both Mr. Mitchell and Mr. Lindgren had danced in the New York City Ballet and had taken company class there from Mr. Balanchine. I was still new enough to the ballet world to believe that shared history was enough to create similar teaching styles. I also could not figure out what my skin color had to do with being taught to dance ballet. Never at the School of the Arts had I felt that I was being treated or taught differently because of my skin color. Never did I understand this idea of Mr. Mitchell's.

Arthur Mitchell, stick in hand, teaching a ballet class.

Mr. Mitchell began to re-make me as a dancer. At first, he did it teaching with a stick. In those days, he always had that stick with him when he taught. In the beginning, I tried to ignore the stick and simply focused on the verbal corrections. There is a place where most ballet dancers can go to, inside their heads. It is a place of ultra-focus, and that level of concentration allows us a continuity of focus that cannot be interrupted, even by an intense ballet director with a stick.

I do not think that I realized just how much the presence of Mr. Mitchell's stick was affecting my psyche. One day, I snapped before I even consciously realized the terror that the stick had been creating in my soul. I guess he corrected me one too many times with it, and I left the class in tears. While I had grown up expecting beatings from my mother, no one else had ever hit me. For much of my three years at the University of North Carolina School of the Arts, I had trained without the added stress caused by the terror of imminent beatings. It had never occurred to me that someone else could take over my mother's place in my life and re-create the terror with which I had once lived. I had never met anyone else who came close to my mother's ability to control me. I knew Mr. Mitchell was not Mrs. Tomlinson, but I also saw that there were similarities. I was ready to pack my bags.

I had run out in the middle of the barre and found sanctuary in the dressing room. Once the barre was finished, Mr. Mitchell came to the dressing room to see about me. He found me in a puddle of my own tears. I believe that my pain deeply affected Mr. Mitchell. He promised me that he would not teach with the stick again. He honored that promise. In retrospect, I believe that, at the time, my terror, pain and honesty brought about a lot of respect from both Mr. Mitchell as well as my fellow company members. I stayed with the company, and largely because of the dancers and other staff members, I found, for the second time, a haven, a home.

Even without the stick, Mr. Mitchell could be frightening. I think I went home and complained about him to Kevin pretty much every night. If I had not grown up living in terror of, and weathering, Mrs. Tomlinson's beatings, I would have still felt the same way about Mr. Mitchell, but I do not believe that his bullying style of training dancers would have affected me quite as strongly.

Since Dance Theatre of Harlem was a small company, we toured endlessly. Having toured forty-nine states with Miss de Mille's company, I thought I knew what to expect. I was ready for the relentlessly long, boring bus rides. However, two weeks after I joined the company, I left for my first tour with the Dance Theatre of Harlem, and it was nothing like touring with Heritage Dance Theatre. It was an international tour to Mexico City. Being that Mexico City was too far away to ride on a bus, we flew. I already had a passport, as I had spent part of the previous summer studying in Italy. Mr. Lindgren had set up that wonderful opportunity. Many of the top dancers at the school, and

GRADUATION AND MOVING ON

I, had all spent several weeks that summer touring around the Italian Riviera. Every small town in Italy has a theater, and Mr. Lindgren had set up a series of performances up and down the Italian Riviera. We stayed in each town with local host families. Having done that tour in Italy, I felt that I was very much ready to go to Mexico City with The Dance Theatre of Harlem. I had always had an excellent facility for languages. In Italy, I had easily picked up the Italian language, and I already spoke a bit of Spanish. I suspected this might be helpful to the company on our many tours.

One of the highlights of my first year at the Dance Theatre of Harlem was working with Geoffrey Holder, the 6'6" tall, ultra-talented dancer, singer, actor, painter and choreographer who choreographed his ballet, *Dougla* on us.

Geoffrey Holder was another of Agnes de Mille's discoveries. She met him on the island of St. Thomas in the Caribbean and invited him to bring his company to New York where she introduced him to the impresario, Sol Hurok. Geoffrey taught with Katherine Dunham for a couple years and performed with the Metropolitan Opera Ballet Company, one of the few professional companies willing to hire black dancers in the 1950's. From there, Geoffrey moved on to Broadway and film. Twenty years later he would be director and costume designer for *The Wiz*, the black Broadway show version of the classic film, *The Wizard of Oz*.

The year before, in 1974, Geoffrey choreographed *Dougla* on us. The word "Dougla" represents the offspring created by the melding of the African and Indian cultures, in a group of people in Trinidad. Geoffrey not only choreographed the ballet, but he also designed the costumes and put together various

Mel, as an Acrobat in Geoffrey Holder's "Dougla."

African rhythms for the music.

The next season, in 1975, Mr. Mitchell created a wonderful ballet called *Manifestations* on me. It was about Adam and Eve and the Serpent. I played the Serpent. The score, by Primous Fountain III, is difficult music, but I felt that it was a perfect choice for this ballet. This role launched me into the public eye and I was both humbled and pleased. Humbled, due to the honor of having this wonderful ballet created on me, and pleased because it was both a great opportunity and honor to have a role created on me by Mr. Mitchell. By this time, my relationship with Mr. Mitchell had become one of love/hate. My terror of him made my desire to please him as my Artistic Director that much stronger. His opinion had become very important to me.

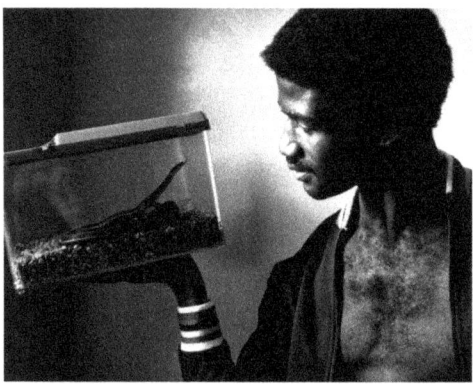

Mel with his pet snake, 1975.

Being the thespian that I am, I wanted to perfectly capture the character, nature and intent of *Manifestations*. Of course, I also wanted to please Mr. Mitchell. I bought a snake and named it Martine, after ballerina, Martine Van Hamel of ABT. No reason for this – it just felt right at the time. I watched the snake endlessly, absorbing and digesting its' every move.

Adam and Eve were portrayed brilliantly by Homer Hans Bryant and the lovely Susan Lovelle, now Dr. Lovelle, a plastic surgeon. Mr. Mitchell's choreography was creative and innovative. It caught and held the audience's attention from beginning to end. The unexpected entrance of the Serpent from above the stage, upside down on an invisible wire that supported my then 152 pounds of nervous energy, was a tour de force, which became the beginning of my celebrity with the Dance Theatre of Harlem. The music evoked another world, ahead of its time, yet it was reflective of something quite familiar. We were a great team for this ballet, dancers and choreographer working with the composer to completely understand every nuance in the music. It was a bit Stravinskyesque, but also not, at the same time. I believe we all knew that this ballet would be successful even before it premiered. For the second time in my life, I was suddenly famous in the dance world, this time thanks to Mr. Mitchell's amazing ballet.

Like so many choreographers with whom I have worked throughout my life, Mr. Mitchell instinctively gave me a certain amount of leeway to add something from my unique point of view to his choreography. In retrospect, I think that is what I most loved about the Dance Theatre of Harlem. We had strong leadership, but we were also allowed to develop as individual artists. Mr. Mitchell built *Manifestations* around my unique talents and special abilities. There were no double tours in this ballet, and that was a great relief. *Manifestations* took on wings and we performed it throughout the world – Japan, Australia, London, Germany, Ireland, Israel, and Canada. It was the mid-1970's. We were innovative movers and shakers in the dance world, sharing our unique American view on classical ballet constantly in a different part of the world.

Touring can be difficult. It is not for those who need their privacy on a regular basis, or those who need to be in control of most, if not all facets of their lives. It often means traveling in crowded, uncomfortable conditions. The wear and tear on our bodies was rough, but we were young and resilient, and built rather tough hides. We managed to not only survive the tours, but to grow into stronger dancers. We worked hard to stay healthy on tour. Between the constant traveling on planes, trains and buses, sleeping in hotels, and the close proximity to each other in which we lived, we had to be vigilant about germs and the possibility of catching various contagious diseases. The days of polio and small pox were long gone, and AIDS had not yet reared its ugly head, but we were all aware of how catching something on a tour could change one's life in a heartbeat. Tanaquil LeClerq, former principal ballerina with the New York City Ballet, was one of our teachers. She taught from a wheelchair, due to the insidious poliovirus that she had contracted while on tour with the New York City Ballet in Europe in 1956. She was only twenty-seven years old when her whole world

Mel, as the Snake in Manifestations, enters from above on a wire.

changed. None of us could even slightly imagine what that must have been like for Tanny, and we did not want the firsthand experience ourselves.

It did not take long for me to grow to deeply love Arthur Mitchell. He represented so many important pieces in my own life. I saw him and everything he had created as, not only my safe haven, but as creating almost unimaginable possibilities for a richer life, not just for me, but for so many neighborhood children. The possibilities I had dared to allow myself, a poor black kid in a very white world, to believe might be possible, came into full focus under Mr. Mitchell's mentorship. I had quickly and happily become completely dependent on him, a state of being that seemed to make Mr. Mitchell happy. My love for Arthur Mitchell grew out of my awe and respect for his talent, tenacity and commitment to both Harlem and the dance community. I believed that he had to be tough on us to help us realize our fullest potential both as dancers and as highly functioning artists.

I have never been good at hiding my feelings about anything. Of course, my roommates and fellow company members knew how I felt. In fact, my crush on Mr. Mitchell was so obvious that during a tour in my second year with the company, Mr. Mitchell finally told me that I had to get over it and just keep my mind and my thoughts on dancing. I had encountered him in a sauna at the hotel where we were staying. If I would place my complete focus on my dancing, he said, he would be pleased. Because I was so smitten, it would have been so easy for Mr. Mitchell to take advantage of me, but he did not. Instead, he reminded me that he was twenty years older than me, and that he was both my teacher and my boss. I needed to hear that because I would have done anything for him. In retrospect, I realize that I was even luckier to work for him than I realized at the time. He was a complex and passionate visionary who finished in me what Duncan Noble and Gyula Pandi had started. They taught me how to be a man on stage, and Mr. Mitchell refined and finished that process. He also showed me what great personal integrity was. His work on my technique and input into me as an artist changed my life, and I believe it changed his, too.

During this, my second year at Dance Theatre of Harlem, my roommate and best friend Kevin Self, decided to leave American Ballet Theatre, New York, and as it followed, me. Kevin was not happy in the ballet company mindset. He is one of those rare people who is good at many things. Everything he ever attempted seemed to come easy to him, or at least easier than things come to most people. Kevin was blessed not only with great ballet technique and the ability to focus and work hard, but also with an amazing mind. He always seemed to have had a great need to utilize his mind, maybe even more than his body. He decided to leave the ballet world and go to law school, back home in New Mexico. I will never forget the day Kevin left. It was one of the lowest points in my life. I watched him walk up West End Avenue. He did not even turn around and wave to me. To this day, I can feel the emptiness and loneliness I felt in that moment. Kevin and I are still best friends now, forty years later, but at the time, I was afraid that I would never see him again.

At that point in my life, living on my own was not the best option for me. Although, I have always been an introvert in my personal life, I did not like being alone. Shortly before Kevin moved out, our apartment had been broken into, making me feel even more of a sense of isolation and vulnerability. Being alone in the apartment, felt very creepy. I have always craved the feeling of "family". I had no idea how to find a roommate to share the West End Avenue apartment. In my mind, no one was Kevin, or even the least bit like Kevin. I was not a partier, despite the times in which I was living. I went to church every Sunday. Finding a roommate with whom I would be happy and comfortable was not going to be easy. In many very important ways, I was still so innocent.

I ended up losing the apartment, and moving a few blocks away to the Beacon Hotel on Broadway in the West 70's. I was depressed and lonely, and was having a difficult time living alone. I was completely distracted by my predicament, and had become a distraction to others. Looking back, my dependency on Kevin had been complete and I was now totally lost. On one occasion, I was followed home to the Beacon by a stranger who wanted to do me harm just for being me. I thought I was safe once I got inside the building, made my way to my room and locked the door. A few minutes later, he started pounding on my door. I was completely terrified and refused to open the door. He said that I would have to come out eventually, and he would be waiting for me. The next day, I brought my troubles into Dance Theatre of Harlem. As has been the story of my life repeatedly, another friend stepped in to help me.

Ronald Perry, a soloist at the Dance Theatre of Harlem, was a brilliant, classically trained ballet dancer. His technique, feet and legs were flawless. As is often the case with such technical perfection, Ronald's focus on the technical aspects of his training had been so complete that he had not developed the charismatic performance qualities that were also such an important part of the total success equation. I believe our weaknesses grew stronger, largely due to each other's influence. Many of the dancers in the company called Ronald "Mr. Perry" because he was so serious and focused when it came to his work. I simply called him Perry, and he always called me Tomlinson. We developed a healthy competition in class and even on stage. I loved dancing with Perry and watching him perform. He had what I lacked, perfect technique, and I had more of what he lacked, a charismatic personality. In many ways, Perry became my new Kevin. I always felt free and safe when I was in his company. I came to understand that Perry loved being somewhat of a mystery, but I figured him out and even knew what buttons to push to get a reaction out of him. Every now and then, I would push a button just to aggravate his peace of mind. He was one of the few people in my life with whom I would let down my guard. I saw a lot of my Daddy's character and strengths in Perry.

Perry saw that I was in trouble and invited me to come live at his mother's home in Great Neck, out on Long Island. It was a long, hour or more commute each way, daily between Harlem and Great Neck, but that was fine. I had a new home. I loved Ronald's mother and sister, Edith, and they made me feel like I was part of the family. The Perry's was the home I wished I had had when I was growing up. Having the experience of family that I got with the Perry's is what sealed in me the knowledge that what Mrs. Tomlinson had done to us was undeniably wrong. My brothers and sisters and I were all such broken human beings. Mrs. Perry was like a splint, setting my brokenness and healing my psyche through her kindness and unwavering emotional support. If my brothers and sisters had had a Mrs. Perry in their lives, things would have been so much easier for them, and they would have understood my unwillingness to forget Mrs. Tomlinson's cruelty.

Ronald's mother, Mrs. Viola Perry was from the South. She and I had much to talk about from that first day. She was the mother that Mrs. Tomlinson should have been. A gentle, patient, kind woman who only saw the good in people, Mrs. Perry gave me solace from the cold, hard ballet world. She never judged Ronald or me, even when we stayed out all night at Studio 54 and came home in less than decent shape. We came home to wonderful, family-style dinners and great conversations most nights. Years later, when my parents came to visit me while I was with the New York City Ballet, I took them out to Long Island to meet Mrs. Perry. I had an ulterior motive. I wanted Mrs. Tomlinson to see who my mother should have been.

I had started out as an apprentice making $75 a week at the Dance Theatre of Harlem, but was quickly moved up to full corps de ballet member status. During my second year, about the time I first performed *Manifestations*, I became a soloist with the company. We were still touring constantly. When in rehearsal, Mr. Mitchell did not allow us to sit down, even when it was not our turn to dance. He expected us to learn everyone's parts, constantly shadowing in the background. The company was not officially in the American Guild of Musical Artists back then, the union for dancers, singers and musicians, so there was little that could be done to make Mr. Mitchell allow the dancers to rest when it was not their turn to dance.

"You cannot learn by osmosis of the behind," he would say.

This could be physically exhausting, but in the early days, since the company was not part of a union, we dancers had no recourse to complain and remedy the situation. We were a small company, and, in retrospect, I do see that it was necessary for us all to know each other's parts, as otherwise two or three injuries would have shut down an entire performance.

On tour, the dancers were expected to help our very small stage crew to lay the flooring and put the barres together, and then later, after the performance, we were expected to help with the strike and load out. This would never have been allowed in a union company, however, the crew really appreciated our help. In those days, the Dance Theatre of Harlem was like a family. Everyone helped each other out. We all became very close. We laughed together, cried together, danced together, traveled together, and were housed in the same hotels together. We even called one another by family names: Father, Mother, Son, Daughter. I think almost everybody had a nickname which made everything so personable in terms of caring for each other. My nickname was "Betamax" because I picked up choreography very quickly. The nickname came from the name of the videocassette recording format developed by Sony and first introduced in 1975. Beta was a Japanese word that described how the tapes recorded images and sounds, and "max" was short for "maximum," meaning large or great.

Mr. Mitchell had a brilliant costumer named Zelda Wynn Valdes. We all knew her simply as Zelda Wynn. I remember that she seemed to me to be ancient, and to have as much, if not more knowledge as the wonderful women I had worked with in the North Carolina School of the Arts costume shop, Christina "Stia" Giannini, Evelyn Miller, Brenetta Mason, and the other talented women. When I first joined Dance Theatre of Harlem, Mr. Mitchell was not happy with my classroom and rehearsal attire. I was wearing unitards that I had designed while at school, and Evelyn and Brenetta had helped me sew up. I loved them. They were comfortable and quite flattering. Over the years, many of the dancers would ask me to have my unitard designs made for them by Evelyn Miller. I even showed Zelda how to make unitards and she designed my *Manifestations* costume around my unitards. My costume was airbrushed to make me look even more serpent-like.

Being unhappy with my attire, as well as with my explanation that I did not make enough money to go out and buy other dancewear, Mr. Mitchell sent me down to Miss Wynn, whose costume shop resided in the basement of the Dance Theatre of Harlem building, to see if she could help me out. Miss Wynn and I became fast friends. She saw immediately that I was quite comfortable with sewing machines and sergers. Miss Wynn's life was fascinating. She had been a fashion and costume designer, who dressed some of the top black stars – Josephine Baker, Ella Fitzgerald, and Dorothy Dandridge, just to name a few. She even had a few white clients as far back as the 1930's, 1940's and 1950's, including Mae West and Marlene Dietrich. Miss Wynn was all about dressing the figure to flatter and bring out the personal beauty and sexiness of her clients. At a time in our history before various stretch fabrics came into being, Zelda Wynn understood a woman's body and knew how to accent it in just the right way to show it off to its very best. She knew sexy and she knew how to create it. Like Barbara Karinska at the New York City Ballet,

Geoffrey Holder discusses the costume designs for Dougla with Dance Theatre of Harlem costumer, Zelda Wynn.

Zelda came to design for ballet during her retirement years. Like Karinska, she was not a stranger to costume design, having designed both costumes as well as personal gowns for her famous clients. In fact, at one point, Miss Wynn used to use space at the Playboy Club to hold her fashion shows. This relationship led to Miss Wynn designing the original, iconic Playboy Bunny outfit. Now, in 1974, Miss Wynn was Dance Theatre of Harlem's main costume designer and technician, a job she would keep for thirty-one more years, until her death at the age of ninety-six. In many ways, she was the company's mother figure. We all loved her.

On this particular day, Miss Wynn was able to make me a few pairs of tights, which helped keep Mr. Mitchell a bit happier. She designed many of our ballets, and built many designed by other wonderful designers. I was always fascinated by the special little tricks she had to make our costumes fit perfectly and feel comfortable.

My third year at the Dance Theatre of Harlem started out like the other two, traveling the world. We danced in front of European kings and queens. Mr. Mitchell would constantly remind us that we were American ambassadors to the world. We were not only representing the Black community, but the American dance scene, as well.

At this point, I was becoming bored with the repetitiveness of my roles and all the travel, and at the same time, I was hearing about some of the great teachers downtown, Robert Denvers, Maggie Black, David Howard, and others. Under no circumstances, according to Mr. Mitchell, were we allowed to venture out of the confines of Harlem. We were all so sure that Mr. Mitchell would know if we were to take a class elsewhere. We were afraid of the repercussions. Ronald Perry had left the company that year for greener (and whiter) pastures, having joined the American Ballet Theatre. He was now dancing as a soloist with arguably one of the greatest companies in the world. I was still living at his mother's house and got to hear about all his adventures working at American Ballet Theatre, under Mikhail Baryshnikov. I started thinking that maybe it was time to venture out of my comfort zone. I had heard that the Bejart company in Brussels, Belgium, was full of male dancers, all of whom were special in one way or another, and that Mr. Bejart honored their differences and special talents through his choreography. The idea of being respected for my uniqueness appealed to me. I was at a point where I was starting to feel that Mr. Mitchell had become bored with me and had no interest in creating more roles for me. Artistically, I was in a rut and needed a challenge.

To prepare to audition for Bejart, I decided that I would need to go back to my dance roots and take a few modern classes, something that was not taught at the Dance Theatre of Harlem. I decided to venture downtown to the eastside to take a few modern classes at the Alvin Ailey School. Once I had made up my mind to leave the Dance Theatre of Harlem, it no longer mattered to me if Mr. Mitchell found out that I had gone downtown to take some classes. In my heart, I had already left.

Chapter Seven

Everybody Doesn't Love You

Funny, but throughout my life I have found myself to be loved one minute and the next minute, not so much. This dichotomy of emotions seems to have followed me no matter where I go. Sometimes, it felt like love had simply left, or at least taken a break for a while. In the past, when punished by my mother, it felt like she had stopped loving me. For a while, I felt loved at the Dance Theatre of Harlem, then suddenly, not so much. When I was "that new boy with the amazing facility and incredible extensions," there was an excitement virtually swirling around me. After a while, rather than excitement, something had changed. It had become, "What are we going to do with Mel?" It was the same question I saw on Miss de Mille's face when she was telling Gyula Pandi that there was no place for me in the Heritage Dance Theatre, before she found a place for me. Suddenly, now, at the Dance Theatre of Harlem, my special talents and facility had seemed to cease to be a positive. I felt that I had become an albatross. Now, somehow, I had become more trouble than I appeared to be worth. In rehearsal, I had learned so many ballets, but only got to

Mel, wearing one of his unitards, in a rehearsal.

do some of them. Often, when I did not get to do something I had worked hard to learn, and do well, it felt like punishment to me. "What did I do wrong?" I would ask myself. It was that same old question from my childhood; the one I had so often spent time in my head asking my mother.

After Ronald Perry left the Dance Theatre of Harlem for American Ballet Theatre during my third year there, I started to get impatient. Impatient for parts. Impatient for attention. Finally, impatient to leave. I was still living with Ronald and his mother and sister, so luckily, I had not lost touch with him. Almost from the beginning, he had been my rock in the company. Ronald was my protector. He also was better able than anyone else to keep my insecurities in check, but he was gone from the company now and had his own new life with which to deal. Dance Theatre of Harlem was having its own growing pains, having added more dancers to the roster. Although not an official member of the American Guild of Musical Artists (AGMA) back then, Mr. Mitchell still tended to follow many of the official union rules, and tried to keep our pay in line with the union.

One of the newer dancers to arrive during the middle of my second year was a young man who encompassed the best qualities of both Ronald Perry and me. His name was Eddie Shellman. Looking back, I can see now that Eddie represented the beginning of major changes for me, for Ronald, and for the Dance Theatre of Harlem.

To me, Eddie was beautiful, physically and mentally. From the first time that I met him, Eddie took my breath away. Neither Ronald or Karen Brown thought about Eddie in the same way I did. In fact, neither one of them cared much at all for Eddie. Eddie was heterosexual, very heterosexual. In fact, Eddie loved young women, all of them. Karen found his behavior disgusting and would have nothing to do with him. I saw it, too, of course, but I did not care. I just loved being around Eddie and my feelings for him blinded me to the realities of Eddie's character weaknesses. His weakness for young women that had already started in those early years, would grow, but none of us really noticed it to be as serious a problem as it was until it was much too late to help.

Eddie had one personal, physical weakness as a dancer. It was his feet. They were worse than mine. I had been so lucky to have good friends to help me figure out how to work properly so that I could make my feet better, so I decided I would pay that kindness forward and help Eddie. I admit I had an ulterior motive. By coaching him privately, I would have a good reason to be around him more. I found out very quickly that Eddie also seemed to have a slight learning disability. He did not pick up choreography quickly. However, when he did get it, he not only had it forever, he could make it look so good that you might believe he had invented it. Eddie became the latest object of my love and devotion. Once again, I was in love with a straight male. My feelings for Eddie put a great deal of stress on my relationship with Ronald.

Eddie and I became friends, and roommates on the company tours. Ronald liked to room alone on tour only seeing me when he felt like it. He was a private person who needed his space. Eddie was like me in many ways, but like Ronald Perry in other ways. He seemed to embody the best of both of us. He did not stay out late and party. He was not a big drinker or drug user. He did not smoke cigarettes. Eddie was a hard-worker who took his passion for dance very seriously and was consistent in his work ethic. He was also, as I've said, committed to his heterosexuality -- much to my disappointment. I admit that I tried to seduce Eddie, but to no avail. Because he loved beautiful young women and had no interest in beautiful young men, I found myself feeling jealous of many of the young girls in the company, leading to bad behavior and rudeness on my part.

It was 1977. I was 23. It was time for me to venture forth into the world, as I had become impatient for so many different reasons. Ronald had left for American Ballet Theatre. I was in love with Eddie Shellman, a potential relationship with virtually no potential. Mr. Mitchell was not using me to what I believed was my fullest potential. As a dancer, I was no longer young, and I needed to dance just as I needed to eat. It was sustenance for my soul. I decided that to cure my complacency, I needed to take a leap of faith and leave the Dance Theatre of Harlem, even though I had nowhere in particular to go. My thought was to go to Europe, Brussels, to be exact, and audition for Maurice Bejart's company. I had heard that his innovative choreography featured dancers like me, with my peculiar talents and passions. The idea of dancing in a company like Maurice Bejart's where the men were honored really appealed to me. I did not talk about my feelings or my final decision with anyone at the Dance Theatre of Harlem, not Karen or Eddie, and not even Ronald Perry. My Bejart intentions were to lead me to Alvin Ailey's American Dance Theater instead.

In my mind, the first step in getting into the Bejart Company, was to get back to my modern dance roots, so I arrived at Alvin Ailey's Eastside studios to take a class. Having been so sheltered by Arthur Mitchell, I had no idea how fast news traveled in the dance world. It never even occurred to me that I had a following in the dance community outside of Harlem, and my leaving the Dance Theatre of Harlem would be news. About halfway through the class, I realized that all the people vying for a place in the door were there to watch me. I was flattered and quite happy about it. Immediately, I started what I always did when people were watching. I performed, pulling out all my most interesting movements and extensions. I was in my zone, my happiest place.

The next time I stole a glance at the doorway, Alvin Ailey was standing there.

After class, Mr. Ailey walked right up to me, introduced himself, and invited me to take a walk up to his office with him. While we climbed the stairs in the old, dilapidated, but somewhat renovated church building which housed the school and the company on East 59 Street, Mr. Ailey told me that he had heard that I had left the Dance Theatre of Harlem and asked me what my plans were. I told him that my plan was to go to Brussels to audition for Mr. Bejart. In the office now, Mr. Ailey offered me a seat, sat down himself behind his desk, leaned back and, tilting his head, considered me. After a minute or two, he spoke. "Now why would you want to travel so far away from your friends and family, from all you know, when you can dance right here?"

He went on to say he was sure that my mother would be very unhappy at the prospect of me living in a foreign country. "How does he know her so well?" I thought.

"Why don't you stay here and dance with us? I'm looking for a new partner for Judy," he said. Dance with Judith Jamison? Really? For one of the few times in my life, I was speechless for about ten seconds. I desperately needed a change. I wanted to go back to my modern roots, at least somewhat. I would not have to move, but I could continue to travel the world, but in higher style than I had done at the Dance Theatre of Harlem. The Alvin Ailey American Dance Theater was an established company, one that had been around since 1958. Judith Jamison was a huge star, probably one of the five most well-known female dancers in the world at the time. Suddenly, my world had shifted. I walked into that old building a little over two hours before, simply to take a modern dance class. Now, two hours later, I was negotiating my principal dancer contract with Alvin Ailey. How, and why, on earth did these miraculous things keep happening to me?

Mr. Ailey wrote a number on a piece of paper and slid it across the desk to me, knowing full well what kind of affect that number would have on me. It was much more than I had been making as a soloist at the Dance Theatre of Harlem. As has often been the case throughout my life, but not always with the best of consequences, my mouth started talking before my brain started thinking. "Is this what Judy makes? If I'm being hired to dance with her, I want to be paid what she is making." Once I had said it, I could not take it back, so, terrified as I was, I simply held his gaze. He stared at me, not blinking for a few seconds, then, lowering his gaze, he wrote another number on a piece of paper and slid it across the table to me, saying, "I'm not going to pay you what Judy makes. She has earned every penny. But.... I will offer you this. It is my final offer."

Even though he did not give me the same salary as Judy, it was still more than his first offer. And I knew better than to push things any further. It was done. I was now a principal dancer with the Alvin Ailey American Dance Theater. I insisted on only signing a six-month contract, as I still could not wrap my mind around the fact that I was not going to Europe to dance. At the end of that six months, I signed one more six-month contract with Ailey. By that time, I knew that this was not the company for me for many reasons.

I would have to say that, of all the companies I have worked with, including Agnes de Mille's Heritage Dance Theatre, the Alvin Ailey American Dance Theater was the company that toured the most. Our tours were both national and international. We performed in all kinds of situations and circumstances. We traveled by bus and by plane, and somehow, by the grace of God, we always managed to get to our destinations. There were a few times when we only just arrived in time to get off the bus and put on our costumes and make up. Once, in South America, our already very-late plane was stuck on the tarmac for three hours after landing. By the time we got to the theater, it was almost ten o'clock. Our sold-out audience had patiently waited.

The company structure was different than the Dance Theatre of Harlem had been. Although class was usually offered, it was never mandatory there as it had been at the Dance Theatre of Harlem. I usually did my own warm-up, as I was now to that career stage where I believed I knew what I needed and what worked best for my body. Looking back, I believe that one of the things that made the Dance Theatre of Harlem company such a great team was the fact that we had no choice but to take class together as a group. There seemed to me to be many more factions at the Ailey company, and much less of the feeling of being a part of something bigger and more important than the individual. It may be that that feeling came with the territory afforded to a principal dancer. I was reveling in my new-found status and the freedom to make my own training and warm-up decisions. For the first time, I felt like a very successful, autonomous adult, in charge of my present and future.

A lot goes into being an Ailey dancer. It is definitely not for the faint of heart. We had to be proficient in many types of dance - jazz, modern, tap, ballet, and even hip hop. The company had long been a member of AGMA. Since I had joined the union back when I first toured with Agnes de Mille's Heritage Dance Theatre, and had kept up my dues, I did not have to apply for membership. Generally, the Ailey company adhered to the union rules, but when they did not, it affected me greatly and is probably one of the reasons I left the company after only a year. I tend to be a rule-follower and do not much care for constant changes to my routine without proper warning.

Alvin kept his word and soon I was rehearsing with the incredible Judith Jamison. I was in awe of her every move. Judy was a top professional and set a great example of both leadership and class. I admired her for that. She was humble and very giving and patient. Judy knew her roles and was one with the music and its history. She was also quite aware of her surroundings, her audiences and the strengths and weaknesses of her various partners. Her true artistry and beauty were magnetic, and it was indeed an honor to be in her presence. However, dancing with her could be a challenge. Judy rehearsed one way, but when on stage in front of a live audience she would completely change into another form of energy that made you have to work even harder to keep up with her just to try to equal her glorious statuesque beauty and high level of confidence. She had mastered the art of doing much by doing little, something that I had only begun to notice all dancers with star status seemed to have in common.

The two ballets I immediately learned and danced with Judy were the company's showstopper, Ailey's *Revelations*, and Lucas Hoving's *Icarus*, the mythological tale of an imprisoned young lad who asks that his father make him wings so that he can escape. His father obliges him with the instructions not to fly too close to the sun or the wings, which were made of wax, would melt. In *Icarus*, Judy played the Sun and I played the Son. Judy was dressed in a bright yellow dress. It was no ordinary dress, but was so full that it literally covered most of the stage. Judy would revolve and so would this magnificent dress. As in the story, I met my demise when I got too close to her on stage.

Mr. Ailey was quite deep in his thoughts and creative processes. He had a knack for giving everything purpose. He was the real deal and sought truth in every aspect of his creations. I could sense his beautiful intelligence. Mr. Ailey sought out the same artistry and respect from his dancers that he generously gave. I really liked that about him. I felt that I was getting that for which I had been yearning. Thanks to Mr. Ailey, I was increasing my knowledge of myself and developing my craft and delivery. I only had two regrets while dancing for Alvin Ailey. I wished I could have had the chance to do the lead in *Blues Suite*, an incredible ballet based in the far reaches of Mr. Ailey's southern roots, and set to blues music, which he once called, "hymns to the secular regions of the soul." I would also have loved dancing Donald McKayle's *Rainbow 'Round My Shoulder*, the individual stories of the men on a chain gang. Mr. Ailey always seemed to put me in the classical stuff with my shoes on. This was very frustrating for me. It made me think of something Arthur Mitchell used to say to me. "You have no rhythm," he would say. "But I hide it with musicality," I would answer back. I believe that Mr. Ailey probably saw that I really did not have the proper depth of "blackness" simmering in my soul.

During my short time with the Ailey troupe, I got to work with Lar Lubovitch, another brilliant modern dance choreographer. Mr. Lubovitch created a pas de deux for me and the beautiful Sara Yarborough, who had also originally danced with the Dance Theatre of Harlem. Sara had a wonderful technique and was quite stable in her delivery. She was a lovely island woman who did things her own way. Sara was tough, yet direct. I loved dancing with her.

It probably goes without saying, but I will say it anyway: My favorite work will always be *Revelations*. I did the role of "Pole Boy" and later graduated to "Sinner Man." I performed the second variations, duets and trios. The signature piece of the company, *Revelations*, was and still is such an amazing ballet. It was inevitably performed last on our programs, and paved the way for standing ovations, at least at every performance that I can remember. Mr. Ailey staged a short curtain-call-reprise of *Revelations* for the audiences since, by the end of that ballet, they were so spirit-filled that they did not want to go home. I always thought it unfortunate that so many of the company members did not feel what that ballet so generously gave its audiences. It was often danced with some of the company members high on various drugs rather than on the Holy Spirit. Back in the early years, when Alvin had first choreographed *Revelations*, he did set it on one other company, Ballet Folklorico de Mexico, to be performed during the opening ceremonies of the 1968 summer Olympic Games in Mexico City. Since that time, no other company in the world has been granted the rights to perform *Revelations*. I have always thought that the Dance Theatre of Harlem could really do that amazing work of art and spirit justice, and probably en pointe.

At first, the thunderous applause and devotion wherever we went was so exciting to me. Each audience was different, but they were always open and ready to receive us. We had many devout fans in each city, some whom had seen the company many times. These were the people who waited for us at the stage door, calling out our names, asking us about our families as if they knew us personally.

Probably my other favorite ballet that I danced with Judy would have to be *Pas de Duke*. Originally choreographed on Judy and Mikhail Baryshnikov, to the glorious music of Duke Ellington, this ballet was supposed to represent the two worlds of dance in the form of ballet versus modern. Very tongue-in-cheek, it was full of treats for both the audience and the performers. Mr. Ailey knew exactly what would appeal to our audiences, and he knew what little inside jokes would be most inspiring to the performers. *Pas de Duke* was a friendly, campy competition of sorts between Judy and me. This was where I really learned about this great artist, Judith Jamison. I found out that she had also been discovered by Agnes de Mille, and was one of the original "*Four Mary's*" at American Ballet Theatre for Miss de Mille during the 1964 season. Soon after, she joined Mr. Ailey's company and danced there for fifteen years, with a short, one-year stint with the famed Harkness Ballet in 1966 when the Ailey company had a financial layoff. Judy also danced on Broadway in *Sophisticated Ladies*, but I believe her heart was always with the Alvin Ailey American Dance Theater, where she became Artistic Director when Mr. Ailey passed in late 1989, and held that title for twenty-one years.

    I like to think that I got along well with everyone in the company for the short time that I was there. I especially clicked with the newer dancers, those who joined the company around the same time that I did: Keith McDaniels, Marilyn "Bunky Lee" Banks, who was my tour roommate, Milton Myers, Steve Mones and Maxine Sherman. My secret mentor and hero was Melvin Jones. I loved his swagger and his energy on stage. He was also quite handsome and reminded me a lot of my father. His warm smile and patience were enough to make you want to spend time around him. I knew only one person in that company before I joined, and that was the powerhouse, Sarita Allen. I danced with Sarita in Miss de Mille's company. She was one of the guest artists that Miss de Mille had brought down from New York. At that time, she seemed much more experienced than the rest of us, even though we were very close in age. She was savvy and upfront; a very strong, opinionated woman. Sarita and I had remained friends over the years. Because of this friendship, I allowed myself to party heavily with Sarita during one of my first tours with the company, a trip to Brazil. I must be honest and say that I had the time of my life, skipping my normal bedtime and staying out all night with Sarita. We partied into the morning and went straight to class and rehearsal. I am glad that I did that, if only for the memories. At the time, I knew that I would probably never do it again.

    I fell in love, at least for a little while, during the time I spent working with the Ailey company. His name was Duane Talley and he was the company costumer. For only the second time, I thought I was in love with a gay man, Ronald Perry having been the first gay man I had loved. Like Ronald, and my other good friends, Kevin and Eddie, Duane protected me and made me feel safe. He made me some extraordinary clothes, too, which I wore with great pride. Duane was quiet, smart and interesting. We lasted together for about four months, but I had to end it. He was much more sexual than I was, wanting intimacy much more than I did. I needed to keep my edge, as I used it on stage. I needed this, I discovered, more than I needed a steady boyfriend.

It was right after one of our South American tours that I left the company. I had never felt that I fit in completely. Unfortunately, Alvin was dealing with his own demons, which in the long run would lead to his death twelve years later. He had lost a lot of weight and only went on a few of our tours. When he wasn't there, he left our ballet mistress, Mary Barnett, in charge. I tried my best to get along with Mary, but to no avail. I believe that Mary did not like me because I was asked by Alvin to join the company as a Principal, rather than having to work my way up. Asked why I left the company, I would have to say that Mary was the main reason. Although the company belonged to the union, Mary repeatedly ignored the rules. Those rules are in place to protect and serve the dancers. I was constantly asked, or rather expected by Mary, to perform on my days off. This was totally against union rules, unless the dancer who was asked to fill in was given a twelve-hour notice. This happened many times without any notice at all. I resented the fact that I was constantly expected to fill in for other company members who could not meet their obligations, most often due to their partying and over-indulging in drugs and drink. I felt used and abused by Mary. My body needed recovery time, too, even if I was not a heavy partier. Looking back, it was at a time in our human history when cocaine and marijuana were cheap and readily available, and, of course, alcohol was always there, too. We were all young and in many ways felt that we were invincible. The difference was that I believed that to stay invincible, I needed to take care of my body. I had come to a time in my life where I was not going to allow anyone to push me around again. I'm sure I was perceived as a bit of a "diva" in those days, because of what some might have perceived as my self-righteous attitude, but I did not care.

In the end, I must say that Mr. Ailey and I also butted heads once, but we both managed to survive the confrontation unscathed. It was during a performance on one of the tours. I had just come off-stage and Alvin waived a lit joint in front of my face, asking me if I would like a hit. I pushed his hand away, glared at him, and prepared to make my next entrance. Before going back out on-stage, I looked at him and said, "We need to talk as soon as this performance is over."

Afterwards, Alvin and I walked back to the hotel together. I told him not to ever pull a stunt like that again. "Like what?" he asked, confused. I could not believe that he had no clue what I was talking about. I told him that I did not smoke pot and did not appreciate him trying to hand me a joint in the middle of a performance. I went on to tell him that I was concerned about his, and much of the company's over-indulgence and felt that what he had just pulled backstage proved that he was in over his head. Anyone who did not have the common sense to realize that encouraging someone to get high in the middle of a performance was irresponsible and wrong, needed to re-think what they were doing. Alvin apologized to me immediately. He did not resent me for expressing my opinion. He was a wonderful man, despite his demons.

    By this point, I was homesick for the camaraderie of my friends and my "home," the Dance Theatre of Harlem. I literally fired myself from the Ailey company by finally refusing Mary when she expected me to jump in and perform at the last minute once again for Carl Paris.

    I called Mr. Mitchell, hoping to resume my place in the company and "family" I had left behind, but it was not to be that simple. Mr. Mitchell accepted me back, but he was only willing to give me a corps de ballet contract, along with an "I told you people – the grass is not always greener on the other side." It was alright. I was returning a better dancer, having conquered the dreaded *double assemblé en tournant en l'air*. My confidence overcame my shame in returning. I was the prodigal son, returning from a stint as a principal dancer in a company which, at the time, had more status than the Dance Theatre of Harlem. I knew it was only a matter of time before Mr. Mitchell would forgive me. I would like to think that Mr. Mitchell was proud of me and all that I had accomplished, and happy that I returned. He just never said so directly.

    Everything seemed to fall back into place. Eddie immediately became my tour roommate again. It was as if he had been waiting for me to come back. Even though I had a corps contract and was making much less money than I had been making in the Ailey company, nothing else had really changed. I was still doing my soloist and principal roles. Although there were still some of the same old frustrations, most of which were related to Mr. Mitchell's need to control us all so thoroughly, the company had grown stronger during my absence, both artistically and financially. The tours were getting more and more exciting. We were treated like royalty all over Europe. We were exotic and sought after. I was returning not as the young wannabe dancer that I had started out as at the Dance Theatre of Harlem, but as a fully professional ballet dancer with an international following. Life was pretty wonderful.

During all the touring, the dancers would love to take souvenirs, mostly hotel towels and bathrobes. Most of us were not from families who had been well-traveled, and were not sophisticated, cosmopolitan travelers. Going to so many exotic places kept us all in awe. Once, in Japan, I took four bathrobes from one hotel and Karen Brown took even more. Our plan was to dye them different colors and give them away for Christmas presents. We were young and living quite the adventure.

I stayed with the Dance Theatre of Harlem for almost three more years. During that time, I was afforded many great opportunities to learn wonderful ballets. Unfortunately, there were many ballets of which I learned that I was never given the opportunity to perform: Balanchine's *Bugaku*, and *Divertimento #15*, and the Prince in John Taras's *Firebird*, to name a few. I had a rather large repertoire, and was proud of my quick-change abilities, which I had perfected over the years. Surely, I thought, I can do ballets back-to-back without a problem. Mr. Mitchell had other ideas.

I was very happy that I got to do the leads in most of the Balanchine ballets in the company's repertoire. My favorite ballet, at the time, was *Concerto Barocco*, in which I got to dance with my female idol, the unconquerable and classically-trained M. Elena Carter. Elena, elegant and exotic, hailed from Mexico. She was passionate and saucy and so much fun when we danced together. We developed a solid bond. Elena was such a joy just to be around. She was a great partner and knew how to compliment us as a duo. There will never be another M. Elena Carter, God rest her soul. She passed away much too early, in 2006 from ovarian cancer. I remember when Mr. Mitchell brought in *Paquita* for her. She danced it with her husband, company member, Joseph Wyatt. She was right at home. I learned so much watching her create the character and dazzle everyone with that steady and dependable, but completely exhilarating technique. I felt so lucky to have been afforded the chance to dance with such a quiet beauty and thoughtful soul.

It was during this time that I learned "Phlegmatic" in *The Four Temperaments*. It was a difficult role to relate to. One day, Mr. Mitchell's friend, the dancer and Broadway star, Ben Vereen, came to watch rehearsal. Mr. Mitchell had him coach me, even though he had never done the role. He was a Broadway star, not a ballet dancer. I was pleasantly surprised at how much his coaching helped me. He told me to immerse myself completely into the role so that I would be able to become more comfortable. I started approaching my rehearsals in a completely different manner, immersing myself in the music and the choreography. I stopped trying to consciously make sense of it, and allowed myself to explore the role unconsciously.

All the ballerinas I danced with at the Dance Theatre of Harlem were outstanding, but beyond words was Lydia Abarca. This completely gorgeous, magical beauty was the ballerina I got to do *Agon* with for the first time. Lydia turned this young boy into a man on stage and I will always be indebted to her. Everything about her, from how she moved her little finger to how she moved the souls of everyone who ever saw her, created an awe in me that I have never felt for any other ballerina. I think she affected Mr. Mitchell that way, too, but even more profoundly, as I once heard that he proposed marriage to Lydia.

Arthur Mitchell working with Ronald Perry and Lydia Abarca.

During my second year back, with DTH, I suddenly seemed to be in demand for appearances away from the company. This did not make Mr. Mitchell happy. Looking back now, I realize that changes to the rehearsal schedule affected the whole company and gave Mr. Mitchell more work, between re-scheduling and catching me up on missed rehearsals. At the time, his annoyance came across to me that he did not care about my future as an artist. In my naiveté, I felt that he simply wanted to own me and use me for his own gain. I was only seeing what I felt was in my best interests, and not the interests of the whole company.

Agnes de Mille's 1980 Kennedy Center Honor was the catalyst that opened the door for many opportunities for me. At first, when I was asked to participate, Mr. Mitchell refused to allow it. It was not until Miss de Mille called Mr. Mitchell personally, and assured him that I would not be gone long and that the Kennedy Center would bill me as appearing courtesy of the Dance Theatre of Harlem, that Mr. Mitchell relented. He was not happy about it, especially since I would be performing *Texas Fourth*. Mr. Mitchell felt, and at that point, I agreed, that I was no longer an acrobat/juggler/gymnast, and to perform in that way would demean me as a ballet artist. I felt that I had no choice but to do what Miss de Mille wanted, as I owed her everything. I did call her and express my concerns with doing *Texas Fourth*, but she countered my argument with one of her own, stating the fact that a great performing artist should be able to be great in any role. A true artist must be completely versatile. There was no arguing with Miss de Mille. I had not ridden a unicycle or twirled a baton in years. I had some work to do.

The Kennedy Center was much like the Metropolitan Opera House in that it was a huge and completely professional union house. The Honors were a big deal. It was only the third year that the Honors were held. Aside from Miss de Mille, 1980 Honorees included Leonard Bernstein, Leontyne Price, James Cagney and Lynn Fontanne.

Meeting Leontyne Price was an extra added bonus as far as I was concerned. She was brilliant, beautiful and wise, not to mention the fact that she had one of the most amazing voices I have ever heard. Listening to her in person was almost a religious experience; one could feel her voice reverberating in one's very soul. I was still feeling torn about going out on that stage and performing my acrobat role in *Texas Fourth*, and I shared my concerns with Miss Price. She encouraged me by telling me to go out on that stage and continue to be fabulous. She also told me that talent has no color, it just is. A wise woman, that Leontyne Price. I remember thinking at the time that it was too bad that Mr. Mitchell, in my opinion, did not seem to believe that, as often his casting decisions seemed to have more to do with the lightness of a dancer's skin than with the dancer's talent and abilities. This was most apparent in his female casting decisions, probably because most of the males in the Dance Theatre of Harlem were very dark-skinned so he did not have as much choice where we were concerned. It was hard watching some brilliantly talented ballerinas be passed over repeatedly for roles because they were too dark in Mr. Mitchell's eyes. My friend, Karen Brown was passed over for years, as was Susan Lovelle, Yvonne Hall, Cassandra Phiffer, Gayle McKinley, and Shanequa Nowlin, to name a few. Racism can be just as rampant within the black community as it is in the larger world community.

In the end, I was so happy and honored that Miss de Mille had asked me to be a part of this, her greatest honor. I was able to give some love back to that incredible lady, who had believed in me and given me my first job. I was also so happy to be able to reconnect and catch up with most of the other dancers from the Heritage Dance Theatre. For me, it was like we had never left each other.

Back at the Dance Theatre of Harlem, I was suddenly in demand, but mostly everywhere else. After being seen on the televised Kennedy Center Honors,

Hollywood was calling. Agents, film producers and directors were offering me work. It was overwhelming. It did not endear me to Mr. Mitchell.

In years to come, I was to have a wonderful friendship with Maya Angelou during her tenure at Wake Forest University in Winston-Salem, North Carolina. When asked how long she planned to stay there, Maya simply stated, "As long as I am pleased." I loved that response and understand it whole-heartedly. One must be content, or one must leave to find peace of mind. Being an artist had never been about money for me, and by this time, I had begun to learn that fame was fleeting. Being an artist has much more to do with being in touch with, and completely in sync with one's soul.

My last year at the Dance Theatre of Harlem seemed to be filled with one disappointment after another. The company was to be featured on Dance In America on PBS. The prospect of Mr. Mitchell choosing *Manifestations* to be one of the ballets filmed had my hopes of reaching a larger audience, very high, only to be dashed. When Mr. Mitchell not only did not choose *Manifestations*, but also did not choose to feature me at all, I was supremely disappointed. At one point, while on an airplane heading off on tour, Mr. Mitchell told me that I would be getting the cover on a Dance Magazine story about the company. I was thrilled. After the tour, we were off for a week or two, so I headed home to North Carolina to rest and visit with family. During my absence, the Dance Magazine shoot was scheduled, and Mr. Mitchell gave it to Eddie

Dance Theatre of Harlem. Mel is second from the top right.

Shellman since he lived in New York and was readily available. If he had called, I would have been on the next plane, but he did not. My disappointment was so great that it colored everything I felt for the company from that moment on. I became very quiet. I am sure my silence must have caused some concern because it was very out of character. I have never been one to keep my thoughts about myself and my future under wraps. Things had gotten a bit too political for me. I am not one to be comfortable with confrontation, so I held all my feelings in check. Inside, I was feeling rejected and dejected. I was now absolutely sure that there was something more for me on the outside of the company, but as yet, I had no inkling of what was waiting for me. I would never have imagined that it would be Mr. Mitchell who would be the one to put my future in motion.

Salvatore Aiello's, "Journey."
North Carolina Dance Theatre, early 1990's.
© King Douglas, all rights reserved.

Chapter Eight

My Life at the White House - Part One, Spellbound

I never realized how much of my life was taken up with color issues, many based in reality, but some born within my own mind, until my co-author and I started on this project. All my early dance training took place at predominantly white ballet schools. Once I got to the Dance Theatre of Harlem, Mr. Mitchell repeatedly made a huge point of telling me that white people did not know how to properly ballet-train black dancers. When I was asked to join the New York City Ballet, the whitest and certainly one of the greatest of the world's ballet companies, it felt like my whole life's journey had been made complete. I realized that I could compete in the whitest of the white worlds, the mainstream professional ballet world. This was huge because back in Mr. Mitchell's dancing days, there was no Dance Theatre of Harlem yet. The professional ballet world was not thought of as having a separate professional ballet company just for black people. It was no small fete for Mr. Mitchell to have been accepted in the mainstream ballet world in the 1950's and 1960's. Mr. Mitchell started the Dance Theatre of Harlem to give talented black dancers like himself a home where they would be taken seriously as ballet dancers and could train and become great artists. He built that company in record time, turning it into a world-renowned touring company. He also unwittingly managed to expand upon segregation in a time when many white people were still more than happy to keep "the blacks" in their place. For me, joining the New York City Ballet was a huge statement. I had lived and worked most of my life in the black community. I was now going to get the chance to prove myself in the white world. The New York City Ballet is, to me, my "White House." In fact, I almost used the title of this chapter as the title for the book. Even though it is a bit contrived, it does fit my personal reality.

I have often wondered why Mr. Mitchell recommended me for the guest artist job that was to become the beginning of this next chapter of my life. It could be that he was trying to play fair after the recent disappointments I had suffered at his hands. Whatever the reason, I will always be grateful to Mr. Mitchell for taking me downtown to meet with Mr. Balanchine, so that I could be approved to dance as a guest artist in his upcoming *Dance in America* project, *L'Enfant et les Sortileges*, better-known in the United States as *The Spellbound Child*. Masterfully directed by Emile Ardolino, who was to earn a Directors Guild of America award for his direction of this wonderful project, for me, *The Spellbound Child* was to be a new beginning. With the likes of Edward Villella, Rosemary Dunleavy and Susan Freedman from the New York City Ballet and Jim Henson and his Muppets on board, I could smell success all over this project from the first moment that I walked in the door. Mr. Balanchine had already seen me dance back during my first year with the Dance Theatre of Harlem. We were in Chicago, and I was in the back row, performing in *Dougla*. As always was the case when I was relegated to the back row, I was pulling out all the stops, performing to be seen. Mr. Balanchine apparently noticed and asked who I was, that very-happy boy in the back row.

Mr. Mitchell had received a call from Mr. Balanchine asking if he was in shape and could perform the part of the dancing teapot in this production of *The Spellbound Child*. I believe he was in a production of it in the past. Mr. Mitchell, being out of dancer-shape by that time, and having a bad knee, declined, but said he had a young dancer whom he believed would please Mr. Balanchine. That young dancer was me.

Mr. Mitchell instructed me not to do two things when I met his mentor, "Mr. B." The first thing was not to talk. The second thing was not to take my shirt off. I often took my shirt off in class and rehearsal because I tend to sweat profusely, and it just felt better not to have a soaking-wet shirt sticking to me. This habit of mine had always annoyed Mr. Mitchell who was always pristinely-clean, immaculately-dressed, and never seemed to sweat. When we arrived at the rehearsal studio on the fifth floor of the New York State Theater at Lincoln Center for my audition, I learned a foxtrot and danced with the magically beautiful, Susan Freedman, "Susie," of the New York City Ballet, who would play my delicate tea cup. Mr. Balanchine, his assistant, Rosemary Dunleavy, and Edward Villella would run the rehearsals. The filming would take place in Nashville, Tennessee. Susie and I would become fast friends on the set, a friendship which has lasted through the years, though it is sustained these days on Facebook.

Giving me the once-over, Mr. Balanchine seemed doubtful at first. Looking at me with a quizzical expression, he said to Mr. Mitchell, "He looks very thin." Mr. Mitchell then asked me to take my shirt off. I looked at Mr. Mitchell, completely confused, and said, in the very-quick repartee that I often used when surprised, "But Mr. Mitchell, you told me not to take my shirt off…." Mr. Mitchell immediately interrupted me and told me, "Don't be ridiculous. Do as I asked and take your shirt off." I was confused, and said, "But Mr. Mitchell, you told me not to…." The look he gave me said it all. He was not happy with me for not doing as he had instructed, and talking, but he was also not happy with me for doing what he had originally instructed me to do and not taking my shirt off. Apparently, the rules had changed. Now he wanted me to take my shirt off, but he also still wanted me not to talk. In my confusion, I had managed to do exactly what Mr. Mitchell did not want me to do, even though one of those things was the opposite of what he had told me he did not want me to do. Keeping my mouth shut, I took my shirt off.

Mr. Balanchine was happy enough with my muscles and I got the job. He did comment that he wished I would gain a little weight, which I did manage to do in time for the taping, by immediately joining a gym. I kept the vision of a thoroughbred prize fighter in my mind while I trained. Unfortunately, this extra weight would cause my costumes to be too tight, and last-minute adjustments had to be made.

A few weeks later when I went to the White House with the Dance Theatre of Harlem to perform the lead with Virginia Johnson in Balanchine's *Allegro Brilliante*, that costume was tight, as well. I felt that I danced better, remembering some of the corrections and thoughts that Mr. B had given me. In fact, I danced so hard in our rehearsal in the East Wing at the White House, that I managed to *sauté* right into a crystal chandelier, knocking off some of the crystals. When I tried to pocket one of the crystals as a souvenir, I was stopped by one of the Secret Service agents, and informed that the crystal was government property. Needless to say, Mr. Mitchell was more than a little annoyed.

From our very first meeting, Mr. Balanchine seemed to have a keen sense of who I was and who I could be. As I reflect on how I felt when I first worked with Mr. Balanchine, I remember the sense of security that his wisdom and gentleness gave me. I was completely comfortable with him, and felt that we were two souls who had known each other well in another time. He took the time to consider each direction he gave me, and good student that I was, I always did the best that I could to please him. Working with him was magical. He was calm, always, and musical to the point of perfection.

The set for *The Spellbound Child* looked like something out of a children's coloring book. It was designed to look two-dimensional even though it was not. All the magic was being made right there in front of me, and I was a part of it. The working space was much smaller than what we had in our rehearsals, and felt a bit confined, but we made it work. I simply let myself trust Mr. Balanchine. He had Edward Villella assisting him on the set. I was beside myself when I met Eddie. I was very much in awe of his presence because I knew of his accomplishments and his rightful place in the Balanchine legacy. The only slight bit of conflict between Mr. B and me, came during the taping in Nashville. He looked through the camera and remarked that the hair on my chest looked dirty. He suggested I shave it. I did not want to do that. Edward Villella, a natural interpreter and peacemaker, stepped in and quietly told me to use Vaseline to flatten my chest hairs and no one would be the wiser. I was grateful for his wisdom. He was right, and the performance went off without a hitch.

The filming was a great success. In between takes, I found myself in conversation with Mr. B. We, or rather I, talked about a lot of things. I told Mr. B that, in two weeks, I would be going to the White House to dance the lead in his *Allegro Brilliante* with the elegant Virginia Johnson. In fact, I told him that I did all the leads in his ballets with the Dance Theatre of Harlem. Instinctively, I wanted to impress him. I wanted him to like me. I was not thinking about trying to join the New York City Ballet. At that point, I still thought of his company as the whitest "White House" in the country, and would not have allowed myself to even think that I would have a chance to be in that company.

Mel, as the Dancing Tea Pot in L'Enfant et les Sortileges.

Our conversations became more thoughtful as Mr. B joined in. We talked about music, tempos, and even preparation and execution of ballet steps. It seemed that I had his ear and my mouth and heart seemed to delight in our conversations. Before I knew it, *The Spellbound Child* taping was over. We were finished, and it was time to bid Mr. Balanchine farewell. He wished me good luck and thanked me for being a part of the production. I felt a bit let down and I knew I would miss him. In retrospect, I think I was very drawn to his way of working. He made me feel like an autonomous adult and a protected child all at the same time. I do not think that I realized until that time how much anxiety I lived with daily at the Dance Theatre of Harlem.

The next few weeks, back home at DTH, we were busy preparing for our engagement at the White House. The company would be dancing at a state dinner in honor of British Prime Minister Margaret Thatcher. Mr. Mitchell counseled us all to keep our hands to ourselves when meeting President and Mrs. Reagan. There were to be no hand-shakes, no hugs, or kisses on the cheek. In reality, the atmosphere was less formal than Mr. Mitchell had led us to believe. The Reagans were happy to shake our hands and came across as genuine and kind. I was pleasantly surprised to find that the President and Mrs. Reagan knew who I was. Their son, Ron, Jr., an acquaintance of mine, was a dancer with the Joffrey Ballet at the time and had told his parents that I would be dancing for them. I also met the Vice-President, George W. Bush, his wife Barbara, and Bob and Dolores Hope. I remember Dolores Hope made me smile with her warm and open charm.

It wasn't long until *The Spellbound Child* aired on the *Dance in America* series. Unbeknownst to me, I had become a bit of a sensation with a new worldwide audience, thanks in large part to the time I spent touring with Alvin Ailey's company. Now, with my guest appearance in Dance in America, many people downtown, both dancers and the audience, were wondering if I was a new member of the New York City Ballet. News filtered uptown to Mr. Mitchell way before it got to me. It was contract renewal time, and Mr. Mitchell did

Mel shaking hands with First Lady, Nancy Reagan at the White House, 1980.

not offer me the same one-year contract that was standard for everyone else. Seemingly out of the blue, in the middle of a rehearsal, Mr. Mitchell said that he was sick and tired of investing so much time and energy into his dancers only to have them stolen from him. He cited the recent filming of the movie, *The Wiz*, for which nine company members disappeared, never to return. They were fired, due to the fact that they had gone to work elsewhere and had not given the Dance Theatre of Harlem credit as company members.

    I had not yet made any concrete plans to leave, but Mr. Mitchell could apparently see the writing on the wall even before I did. It was no secret that I had been unhappy for most of the last year. Instead of proposing the one-year contract that he offered the other dancers, he offered me a five-year contract to ensure that I would not leave. I believe he thought that I should be flattered, but I was not. I told him I could not sign that type of a commitment. He told me to think about it, and that I would not be receiving a paycheck until the contract was signed. That was it. An alarm went off in my head and my heart. I was sick and tired of being controlled and manipulated. I had had enough of Mr. Mitchell and his ultimatums. At twenty-seven years old, I was no longer young in the professional ballet world. In my mind, there were only two realistic options at that point: going to Broadway or making a complete change by retiring from the dance world and going back to college.

    By this time, Ronald Perry had left the American Ballet Theatre for Maurice Bejart's company, Ballet of the XX Century, and suggested that I come over to Europe and audition for Bejart. But by that point, I was sure that I did not want to leave the United States. Oddly enough, Mr. Ailey's words still repeatedly whispered themselves to me: "Your mother would not want you to go live in a foreign country." I had started to think seriously about Broadway. Ever since dancing at the Kennedy Center Honors for Agnes, I had been receiving offers. I had turned them down so far, because the thought of dancing the same choreography every night just did not appeal to me, even for four times the money I was currently making. Now that I was miserable even though I was dancing different choreography each night, Broadway was looking much more interesting to me.

    I shared my frustration with my new *The Spellbound Child* friend, Susie Freedman. According to Susie, I must have made a lasting impression on Mr. B, because, once the project was over, he constantly asked her about me. "How is 'Miel'?" he would ask her. For several weeks, Susie repeatedly asked me to come down to the New York State Theatre and take company class. "Mel, Mr. B asked about you again." "Mel, Mr. B wants to know where his 'Dark Angel' is and how he is doing." And finally, "Mel, Mr. B wants you to come see him. He wants you to come take company class." Finally, Susie invited me to come see the Second Stravinsky Festival and perhaps speak with Mr. B. Up until that point, I thought Susie was just being kind, and flattering the narcissistic part of my nature. My frustration with my current situation at the Dance Theatre of Harlem was the main reason I finally acquiesced to Susie's requests. Just the thought of seeing and speaking with Mr. B again calmed me. My feelings of frustration had grown to the point of misery, so much so that I had become desperate to find a new home.

It was wonderful to see Mr. B again. Being in his presence made me feel secure and protected. I told him that I was seriously thinking about leaving the ballet world and either going straight back to college or possibly giving a nod to Broadway first. Mr. B was appalled and invited me to take company class the following week.

In retrospect, I guess it was only a matter of time before I would go down to the New York State Theater at Lincoln

NYCB's Susan Freedman, as the Tea Cup in Dance in America's – L'Enfant et les Sortileges, 1980.

Center and take company class with the New York City Ballet. I was not nervous, as I had so many old friends from my North Carolina School of the Arts days in the company – Peter Frame, Peter Schetter, John Bass, and Bruce Padgett, to name a few. My new friend, Susan Freedman was my best cheerleader, constantly telling me that I would be great and that Mr. B loved me. Without Susie, I do not think I would have had either the good fortune or the nerve to audition and join the company.

In Susan Freedman's words:

Working on L'Enfant et les Sortileges with Mel was wonderful. We had an immediate affinity for each other; we just had such a good friendship right from the start. Since there were just the two of us dancing, our rehearsal sessions with Mr. B were very private and personal. Mr. B saw Mel's capabilities from the very beginning. He always looked at the dancer, not their color or nationality. I think Mr. B saw that both Mel and I could act, we could both play a character. That's why we were chosen for Sortileges. Mr. B knew exactly what he wanted. He was very specific. He was always willing to work around people's deficits because his goal was always to make everyone look their most beautiful.

I did try to be a support system for Mel, just as I would do for any new dancer joining the company. Everything has its own destiny. It was simply Mel's time to join the company. I think he was too much of an asset for Mr. B to have let him get away. He just had so much to offer the company at that particular time that I believed it was inevitable that he would get in.

The day I took company class was a sunny, but cool, late-October day. New York in October is beautiful. The air is cool and crisp, and it smells wonderful. Gone are the high temperatures and humidity, and the horrible rotten-garbage odors of summer. The weather tends to be perfect and the whole atmosphere in the city is mixed feelings of several things – relief that the miserable summer heat has finally ended, excitement for the future and from the beautiful feelings, sights, sounds and smells that accompany the beginnings of the autumn season, and excitement for the upcoming fall ballet and holiday seasons. In New York in general, and especially in the ballet world, Autumn is most definitely the best time of the year. How could I feel anything but exhilaration on my way to the New York State Theater that day? I was nervous, but only for the newness of what was ahead of me. I already had good friends in the company and I trusted that they would vouch for the veracity of my character with the other dancers. Somehow, I already knew that I would be just fine.

Peter Martins taught the class. Peter, a principal dancer in the company, had joined as a principal. He was from the Royal Danish Ballet, and Mr. B had hand-picked him because he felt that Peter had something very special to offer the company. And he did. This was how Mr. B operated. Even though the majority of the dancers in those days, just like today, were "born, bred and raised" in his school, the School of American Ballet, there were still some dancers that Mr. B hand-picked and personally contracted, who came from outside his specific sphere of influence. I would be one of the very last dancers that Mr. B would hire who did not come from his school. Valentina Koslova and her husband, Valerie Koslov would be two other dancers from the outside to be hired in Mr. B's final years.

The first thing I noticed when I walked into the fifth-floor rehearsal studio at the New York State Theater to take company class for the first time with the company was that the dancers were all dressed in their own personal styles, unlike at the Dance Theatre of Harlem where we were all expected to adhere to Mr. Mitchell's idea of appropriate dress. Here, there were T shirts, all in various states of re-design, with necklines cut out, hems slit and tied up, sleeves cut into a cap-style or cut out completely. Safety pins adorned the center fronts and center backs of many of the women's leotards, ruching them into more flattering and stylish designs that, at that point had yet to be picked up by the major dancewear companies. Runs in leotards, tights and legwarmers were the common thread holding all the re-designed work-clothes of the New York City Ballet dancers together. Only Suzanne Farrell seemed to have a design not yet dared to be picked up by anyone else – her soon-to-become signature look – a fringed scarf strategically folded into a triangle which, when wrapped and tied around her waist, hung down over her rear-end like a tight but beautifully asymmetrical short skirt.

I felt quite conspicuous in my pristine, black tights and white t shirt, white socks and white shoes, known in the ballet world as "the uniform," worn by male students in professional training programs worldwide. I had purposely picked out the uniform that morning, thinking it would make me look disciplined and professional, but at that moment I felt that my clothes, much more than my color, were making me stick out, but not necessarily in a good way. Looking in the mirror, I was horrified to realize that I looked like a student, not a professional dancer from another ballet company.

Peter Martins, who would become Artistic Director of the company much sooner than even he could have expected, taught a clean and elegantly-refined class. However, it was a class in which few did the steps as given. I marveled at this because I assumed it would be much more like company class at the Dance Theatre of Harlem than company class at Alvin Ailey. This was Mr. Mitchell's home. I assumed that this was where he had gotten his ideas as to how class should be run. Obviously, it was not.

At the end of the class, Mr. B, who had been quietly watching part of the class from the door, asked me to do a few steps, including the dreaded *double tour en l'air*. Try as I did, I could not do one *double tour*. I landed on my derrière more than once. I could see the company members' expressions reflected in the mirror. Many seemed to have confused expressions on their faces. I could see their thoughts: "Why on earth is Mr. B so patiently giving this guy the time of day?" "Where is his technique?" "Did he leave it at home?" "Mr. B is so patient and kind." "I wonder what the new guy's hair feels like to touch?"

Mr. B simply said, "Don't worry. We have school to teach you that." He did not seem worried in the least about my lack of technique. He commented that my left foot was better than my right foot. Finally, he asked me to do a manége of *sautés* and *jetés* that I knew would allow me to save face with the other dancers after my dreadful *double tours*. I definitely worked those jumps. Afterwards, Mr. B told me to get dressed and come to his office.

As I walked down toward his office, there were people along the way with welcoming smiles of congratulations. They seemed to know something that I did not. I met Mr. B's secretary, the very-efficient and patient Barbara Horgan, who sent me right in. Mr. B's office was in the middle of a re-decoration. He had wonderful photographs on his wall of many celebrities – Fred Astaire, and Bette Midler, to name a couple. In the office, I commented favorably on one of Mr. B's chairs. He gave it to me. Just like that. This is exactly how Mr. B was. He was generous and loving. I count the three years I got to work with him before his death as three of the best years of my life.

During our talk, Mr. B gave me a contract to be a corps de ballet member. The contract was for more money than I had ever expected to be paid as a dancer. Mr. B told me that I would move up quickly, but that I needed to "go back to school." He told me to go take classes at the School of American Ballet, the school he had founded and built into the training ground for his dancers. He said the school would make my technique stronger. I was twenty-seven and had been honest with him about my age, despite Miss de Mille's words repetitively sounding in my head: "Don't tell them your real age. It is better for you if you say you are younger than you are." The last thing I thought I would be doing at this point in my career was going back to ballet school, but there was something so hypnotic about Mr. B that I, like everyone else, would do exactly as he told me to do.

Mr. B asked Barbara Horgan to get a contract ready for me, and as I was leaving, he told me to take my time and read it over. I told him that I would need to give Mr. Mitchell two weeks' notice, and that during those two weeks, I would be in Japan on tour with the Dance Theatre of Harlem. I think it was at this point that Mr. B asked me about my contract with the Dance Theatre of Harlem. Once again, I spoke before I allowed myself the luxury of considered thought. "Well, technically, I am a Principal. I do principal roles in all your ballets that we do, but I don't currently actually have a signed contract. Mr. Mitchell told me that I needed to sign a five-year contract a few weeks ago because he was sick and tired of losing his male dancers to other projects and companies. He told me I would not be paid until I signed it, but I have not signed it yet and I have not been paid."

Mr. B just stared at me. To me, this state of affairs at the Dance Theatre of

Harlem was just "business as usual," in Mr. Mitchell's world, but Mr. B did not look happy. Later, when Mr. Mitchell confronted me about airing our business to Mr. B., I wondered if Mr. B. had called him about it. How else would Mr. Mitchell know what was said in our private meeting? It seems that Mr. B. was protective of his dancers, even those who had not yet become members of his company. A few minutes later, when I left his office, carrying the chair he had given me, Barbara, as she handed me the contract, said, "Look it over. Bring it back to me on Monday." I guess three days was all the time she felt I would need. She was right. It was more than enough time.

After meeting with Mr. B, I realized that I was late for rehearsal at the Dance Theatre of Harlem, but I was so elated over the morning's activities that I did not care. Mr. Mitchell was out of town, so I knew it would be a few days before the news that Mr. B had offered me a contract, got to him. When I arrived at rehearsal, the dancers gave me a hard time for being late and missing company class, until I pulled out my new contract and showed it to them. Everyone was flabbergasted. "But, you can't even do a *double tour*!" was probably the most-repeated reaction to my new-found reality. "Wait until Mr. Mitchell hears. Are you ever gonna be in trouble," was the second reaction. As fate, or my good luck would have it, Mr. Mitchell was down in North Carolina at my alma mater, the North Carolina School of the Arts, that very day receiving an honorary doctorate for his outstanding achievements from the very school he had disparaged by telling me "They don't know how to train black dancers," when I first arrived at the Dance Theatre of Harlem seven years before. I knew there would be hell to pay when he returned. I also knew that I would give my two week notice immediately and that I would be joining the New York City Ballet.

In former NYCB principal dancer, Peter Frame's words:

> *I had graduated from the School of the Arts and landed in New York City with a scholarship to the School of American Ballet, bestowed upon me by Violette Verdy. Once again, I found myself in another world within this world, now amongst the great ballet masters of that era and dancers beyond compare.*
>
> *Within a year, Mr. Balanchine invited me into his astonishing New York City Ballet where there was no sense of time for me but, just being enthralled and lost in the moment and hypnotized by amazing choreographers, choreography, a resounding orchestra, Madame Karinska's exquisite costumes, performances in New York State Theater, unexpected opportunities and seemingly*

endless performances from Suzanne Farrell, Peter Martins, Patricia McBride and so many, many more gifted dancers. It was a never-ending fairytale.

One day in between rehearsals with NYCB, I was sitting in the audience watching a rehearsal and one of my friends came over to me and said there is a friend of yours back stage who wants to see you. He said his name is Mel Tomlinson. It must have been eight years since I had seen Mel last and off I went backstage scrambling through the row of seats with my mind racing, and there Mel stood in his full glory, quietly postured in a most coy and disarming manner which, as always, caught me off guard.

I said, "Mel?" "Yes brother," he responded.

We went on and on for some time catching up at record-breaking speed. Then he uttered, 'Mr. Balanchine invited me to dance with your company.' This, he stated in a very proper, but beguiling way.

"What?" I said. And like my first encounter with Mel back at NCSA, I just didn't know how to respond. I truly thought he was playing with me in a big way. I was excited but, I had a tendency to be a bit gullible when I was younger, a lot actually, and my friends had a heyday playing games with me. I was easy fodder for Mel.

Vera Zorina, narrating George Balanchine's Persephone.

The oh-so-familiar song and dance went on between the two of us for some time and then I realized I had to go to a rehearsal. We parted for that moment so excited in our reunion, but I just did not know if Mel was pulling my leg. Mel kept reminding me that he would see me tomorrow in company class and that I better be in my best form.

The next day, in company class, I quickly discovered that he was indeed now part of Balanchine's family as he walked into class donned in one of his signature, stunning unitards, of course, designed by none other than Mel himself. Mel knew how to make an entrance and it wasn't hard to be captivated by his strikingly sculptured, lean physique and powerful presence.

MY LIFE AT THE WHITE HOUSE - PART ONE, SPELLBOUND

There we were now reunited and dancing for Mr. Balanchine and what a glorious and joyous ride we had. Soon after Mel joined NYCB, Mr. Balanchine created the ballet Persephone, narrated by the legendary Vera Zorina, in which Mel danced the role of Pluto opposite the most stunning Karin Von Aroldingen. The elaborate costumes and sets created a rather mythological scene that was absolutely brilliant, and Mr. Balanchine's choreography captured Mel's unique qualities so beautifully, like a storybook creature come to life before your eyes. I was always inspired by Mel's effortless, powerful and confident stage presence. And his performance in Persephone was magical and memorable.

Lourdes Lopez, Peter Frame, and Mel Tomlinson in Kammermusik No.2 by George Balanchine.

In those fleeting years in the company it was wonderful how many ballets we were cast in together; Mr. Balanchine's Agon, Four Temperaments, Midsummer Night's Dream, and Kammermusik No.2, Jerome Robbins' Concertino and Glass Pieces, John Taras' Concertino and Peter Martins' Ecstatic Orange. We were cast in Agon together for the Live from Lincoln Center Performance which remains personally a most memorable and cherished experience.

Mel never took this opportunity to dance for Mr. B. for granted for one second, always grateful, humble and so inspired by Mr. B's hand chosen artists, whom he spent so much time to cultivate and nurture. Mel had a reassuring compliment for everyone and wasn't shy about expressing it to all the dancers. I would say most sincerely that Mel's presence in NYCB was an asset for so many. Wherever Mel was, there was joy and laughter to be had by all.

It did not take long for Mr. Mitchell to hear the news and respond. I was at home on Long Island at the Perry's house when I got the call summoning me into his office. Terrified, I insisted that there be someone else there. At this point, I do not even remember who it was, but I think it was probably his secretary who joined us. It was an awful meeting, full of manipulative, guilt-laden arguments and threats. How could I be so disloyal as to discuss internal Dance Theatre of Harlem contract business with outsiders? How could I so casually take a contract from the New York City Ballet without first discussing it with Mr. Mitchell? Had I not learned anything from my year with Alvin Ailey? What made me think that I, of all people, could or would even have the remote possibility of fitting in at the New York City Ballet? How could I possibly think that I could dance down there? How could I be so disloyal? Don't you know you are letting down the whole company? Letting down your friends? Your family?

The whole conversation was ridiculous. I knew I would be just fine. I had friends dancing in that company who had known me and accepted me for who I was from way back in my North Carolina School of the Arts days. At that time, my blackness was much more of a novelty than it was now, seven years later. Mr. B was not hiring me because of my color, of that I was sure. And even if he was, to be totally honest, that was all right with me, too. I was joining the New York City Ballet. I did not care at all why I was being hired. At that point, I felt more confident that I could prove myself and my special talents to Mr. B and everyone else at the New York City Ballet, than I felt I could ever do with Mr. Mitchell. I had spent years trying to prove and re-prove myself to Mr. Mitchell and I felt that he had let me down repeatedly.

"You will not leave without teaching every part you know to Eddie and the others. And you will dance in every ballet over the next two weeks in Japan," said Mr. Mitchell, rising from behind his desk, signaling the end of our meeting. I just stared at him, speechless for one more very rare moment in my life. He thought he was punishing me by making me dance! To this day, I do not understand, except that maybe he thought this would weaken and exhaust me to the point that I would be a mess when I started at the New York City Ballet. Little did he know that Mr. B had already told me to go to the School of American Ballet for a time and that his plan was to introduce me to his world during the Spring season, which was months away. Little did I know that things would not work out exactly as Mr. B planned and that I would end up being introduced successfully to the New York City Ballet audiences much sooner, and without any improvements to my technique.

Chapter Nine

My Life at the White House – Part Two
Performance of the Year

The last two weeks I spent at the Dance Theatre of Harlem turned out to be spectacular. My impending departure from the company I had called home for the better part of the past seven years, was bittersweet to say the least, as I had joined the company in 1974 when it was a fledgling, five-year old upstart. In my six years there, I had been both a witness and a part of so much magic. We had toured the world. I had danced with black ballerinas, whom over the passage of time have been proven to be some of the greatest ballerinas of all time, black or white. Our audiences had grown both at home and abroad. We were treated like royalty wherever we went. All these things were tremendous accomplishments for any young ballet company, but we were a young Black ballet company, so I will argue that the accomplishments probably meant even more to us. Mr. Mitchell and Mr. Shook had created the environment, and the vision, that was to make all of it our reality.

Both AGMA union rules and basic common decency said that I would need to give the company two weeks' notice before leaving. As it happened, the Dance Theatre of Harlem would be spending those two weeks touring Japan, the cities of Osaka and Tokyo. This would be the first Japanese tour for the company. I was excited to be a part of something so historic for any ballet company. None of us had ever been to Japan so we had no idea what to expect. After a fourteen-hour, overnight flight, we arrived in a very different world.

Mr. Mitchell was true to his word as far as the amount of dancing I was given. In fact, due to some last-minute injuries, I ended up cast in every single ballet, sometimes only having a short pause in which to use my quick-change abilities. I had grown to love quick changes, now that I had them down to a science. I danced everything in my repertoire. I even finally got the opportunity to dance the "Golden Slave" in Fokine's *Scheherazade* when Eddie Shellman became injured. Dancing so much was not a problem for me at that point. I was still riding high on the adrenaline burst that joining the New York City

Ballet had given me. My feelings about myself and about dancing in general were more positive than they had been in a long time. I like to believe that in his heart, Mr. Mitchell allowed me to dance so much because he trusted that I could deliver and that I would not let him down. Teaching my parts to other dancers as time allowed during the tour was not easy, but I found the time. There was little time for sightseeing. I was happy to honor my commitments to my fellow dancers. They had been my family for many years and I knew that I would still be a part of that family even when I made the final move to the "White House," the nickname some of my friends had given to the New York City Ballet now that I would be joining that company.

The theaters in Japan ran like a finely tuned Swiss watch. The backstage crews were highly organized, catered to our every need, and consistently delivered incredible accuracy in all that they did. Our audiences were attentive and quite well-mannered. They seemed quite anxious to see us and very open and accepting of our American version of this classical art form. I must say that their method of appreciation did come as a surprise to all of us. They did not clap when we expected them to do so. Instead, they stomped their feet as their way to show how much they enjoyed our performances. Their very sincere applause was truly thunderous. Both inside and outside the theater we were treated royally, like stars. I felt so proud to be a part of the company and to be able to represent the United States with honor and grace.

Unfortunately, a silent drama, akin to a Sunday night soap opera, was also taking place. There was an obvious "coldness" that Mr. Mitchell had toward me and my closest friends in the company. At any other time in my tenure at the Dance Theatre of Harlem, this would have filled me with terror, for, like so many director/dancer relationships, ours had always been that of strict parent/frightened-into-submission child. However, at this point things had changed for me. For the first time, I had no fear of Mr. Mitchell. At twenty-seven, I was a man-child who had taken a stance of independence and near defiance. It was a position that most teenagers go through when making that separation from their parents. The closest I had ever gotten to going through this with my parents was when, at nineteen and leaving for New York, I told Mrs. Tomlinson that she would never beat me or my younger siblings, or, she would have me to contend with. Looking back, even though I was quite late to this particular party, I think that this was one of the most important steps in my becoming a fully functioning adult. My character was beginning to evolve as I looked to an even more challenging future. So much confidence came with the signing of that contract with the New York City Ballet. My main objective on this final tour with the Dance Theatre of Harlem was to rise above the pettiness, but also to maintain my health and strengthen my technique. I knew I was not nearly the strongest technician at the Dance Theatre of Harlem, and would certainly not be considered a strong technician at the New York City Ballet. I had always depended a lot on faith and my passion for what I was doing. Now I wanted to consciously build my technique so I would be stronger and even more stable as a dancer. I resolved to stay busy, healthy and happy during those two weeks and not to fall victim to any negativity.

My friends and I did manage to find a little time for sightseeing and shopping. I found the most magnificently ornate kimono, elaborately adorned in gold and silver trims. It cost a whopping $500 USD, which, for me was a huge amount of money, especially in 1980. I bought it, and immediately began wearing it around the theater as a warm-up robe. Unfortunately, it was a wedding kimono and some of the crew and producers took it that I was mocking their culture. Mr. Mitchell had to break his silence with me so that he could reprimand me and tell me not to wear it. I took it off right away and apologized for my mistake. I felt terrible that I had hurt anyone's feelings. I took it home with me and would display it proudly when I moved into my own apartment. I did wear it again, much later, in New York, to a costume event.

Through all the drama, I found strength in my fellow dancers. We simply enjoyed dancing with and for each other, probably for the last time. I think we all instinctively knew that I would not be coming back this time. They were my family and as dancers, they understood my drive and my yearning to grow as an artist. I felt their love and encouragement and that was all I needed for closure. They threw me a surprise farewell party in one of the hotel rooms. We laughed and remembered all the good times, and, of course, the struggles we had encountered on our journey together. We even re-enacted some almost-forgotten past happenings that were not so funny at the time, but now, through the passing of time and our combined sense of sportsmanship we found a way to laugh at it all. Mr. Mitchell was the only member of the Dance Theatre of Harlem who was not present. Although my outward attitude was dismissive of his absence, on the inside, I felt it keenly. He and I would never have an official goodbye, something that I have always regretted. I know I must have come off as arrogant and dismissive to Mr. Mitchell and everyone else. It was my defenses kicking in. I was as scared and nervous as I was excited about my impending future, and I needed to show confidence so as not to show my very real terror. In my heart, what I really wanted was for Mr. Mitchell to be happy for me and supportive. I would have loved to have left knowing that I could have called him for advice in the future as my mentor. I had learned a great deal from him. Problem was, I just did not know how to tell him that. It was almost six months later when I finally wrote to him and told him how I felt.

In thinking about my departure from the Dance Theatre of Harlem, I realize now that everyone is replaceable. At the time, I felt that Mr. Mitchell had not used me to my fullest potential. Also, I felt that there were things that I could do that would not be easily replaceable. You could call my attitude "the arrogance of the innocent." I think to a certain extent that Mr. Mitchell felt that way, too. This may well be why he was so upset with me for choosing to leave. However, we were both wrong. Ballet is an art. To borrow a phrase from both my Christian roots and Ernest Hemingway, it is a "moveable feast" of creative, sometimes irreverent, breathtaking beauty that is constantly in flux. No two moments are ever the same, whether created by one artist or several at different times. I am grateful to have been a part of the Dance Theatre of Harlem in the days of its youthful innocence. Those memories will stay with me always.

The two weeks flew by. Suddenly, I found myself at home in Great Neck, Long Island, exhausted both from jet lag and dancing for so many days in a row. I was looking forward to a few days of recovery before I was to start my classes at the School of American Ballet. It was not to be. My second day at home, the phone rang. It was Barbara Horgan, asking me to please hold for Mr. Balanchine.

"Miel, are you back? I know you must be a little tired, but I need to ask you – do you know Agon?" Mr. B asked, already knowing the answer to that question.

"Yes," I said. "I know the whole ballet -- score and all. I have been dancing it with Lydia Abarca. Is there any particular part that you are interested in?" Mr. B then told me that Peter Martins had injured his back, and that he, Mr. B, would like to see me do the pas de deux. So much for training at the School of American Ballet for a while and being presented to the public in the spring. I was a bit nervous, but would be going in the next day, Monday -- the "dark day" in the ballet and theatre worlds -- to rehearse with Mr. B, Peter Martins, and a young principal dancer I had yet to meet, but whose reputation had preceded her – Heather Watts.

For thirty-five years, I had no idea that Mr. Balanchine had told me a little white lie. While working on this book, my co-author, Claudia Folts, asked Heather Watts for confirmation as to how our first *Agon* performance had

March 1981

Dear Mr. Mitchell,

I hope that you do not think that I am the insensitive ungrateful brat that I may appear to be – for I am not.

I'm more that grateful for the opportunity you lent me in working as a guest artist with the New York City ballet and Mr. Balanchine. My work with him was and enriching experience and a direct reflection of ~~Although the choreography could have easily been executed by you~~ – injured knee ~~and all~~. I'll always admire the the strength which is you and the generosity which you've shared with me and my career and ambitions towards being a dance artist.

what he's taught you what you've taught me

This may sound a bit far fetched – but we as people find it hard to say thanks and be sincere – especially one man to another and even more so student to teacher. But as one person to another and a friend always, I Thank you

Sincerely yours,
Mel A. Tomlinson

Draft of Mel's letter to Arthur Mitchell, expressing his gratitude for all Arthur had done for him, March, 1981.

come about.

In Heather Watts' words:

> *He (Mr. B) wanted a black man and said so to me and Peter....he said, "You are good Peter, but you aren't black. Please take Miel through it with "Hedder" for me.*

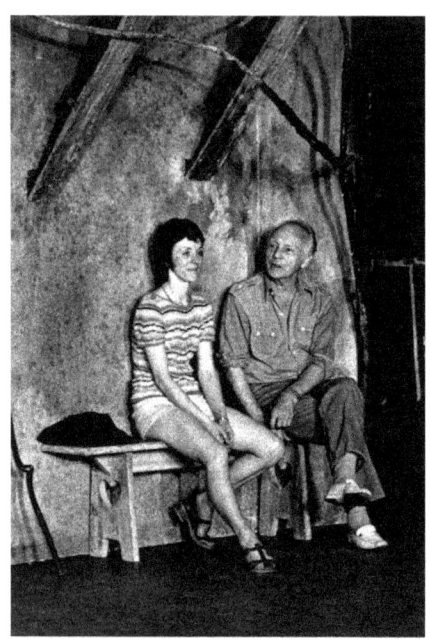

Ballet Mistress, Rosemary Dunleavy with George Balanchine. Photograph: ©Steven Caras, all rights reserved.

I would be dancing the pas de deux from *Agon* with Heather. It was 1981. Heather had been with the company for ten years and had been promoted to principal dancer two years before. She was among the last dancers that Mr. B would promote to principal. She and Peter Martin's rather tumultuous ten or twelve-year relationship preceded my meeting them both, but I had heard all about their legendary public fights. I arrived at the theater early on Monday morning. It was so quiet there on a dark day, almost desolate. I rather liked the quiet. It allowed me to focus completely on warming up and getting myself ready. I had never seen a New York City Ballet rehearsal before, so I had no idea what to expect.

Rosemary Dunleavy, the ballet mistress arrived with Heather and Peter. As we were saying our hellos, Mr. B arrived. First, he introduced me formally to Heather and then he asked the pianist to play the pas. I gave Heather the once over. She had a reputation for chewing up partners and spitting them out. As I looked at her for the first time, that was certainly hard to believe. She was so delicate-looking. She did have very wide shoulders, but she was small-boned and quite thin, with a long, tapered neck and a pretty face with big, innocent-looking eyes. She looked more sensitive and ethereal than evil-bitch-from-hell. I took her hand as if I was in total control – after all I had done this ballet for years at the Dance Theatre of Harlem. Arthur Mitchell was the originator of this role and had taught me every nuance, and my former partner, Lydia Abarca had filled in details from the female dancer's point of view. I'm not sure how I would have felt at that moment, had I known the truth, that Peter's back was not injured and that Mr. B was looking to re-create the black/white dichotomy of his original work.

We took our places for what I knew was, in reality, an audition of sorts. Heather and I walked on with a shared, quiet elegance and questionable state of expectation. Neither one of us knew what to expect from the other.

Most of the time, one knows the person he or she will be dancing with at least as acquaintances, before the first rehearsal. There are always a few surprises when you start rehearsing a new ballet even when you know your partner.

I have always loved the entrance to the pas de deux in *Agon* because of its

Mel, with Heather Watts in the pas de deux from Balanchine's Agon. Photograph: ©Steven Caras, all rights reserved.

abrupt pause just before the dance commences. I hoped that Heather would simply trust me and let me do my job. I led her through her paces, remembering a story Mr. Mitchell had once shared as to how this pas de deux had come into existence. Mr. B had started choreographing *Agon* before his then-wife Tanaquil LeClerq was stricken with polio. He took off some time, a year's leave of absence, to be with Tanny and assist her while she tried to recover. When he returned to the company, he was inspired by his time with Tanny and finished creating this ballet, with Arthur Mitchell and Diana Adams dancing the pas de deux, reflecting his actions and his love. The word *Agon* means "conflict" or "competition". I'm sure there was much conflict in Mr. B's and Tanny's life while they fought that insidious disease and what it had stolen from their life together. Tanny's inability to make her legs move is reflected in the stark, control-oriented choreography.

It was also the 1950's and artists have always been the catalysts of change. On the surface, the black/white, male/female conflicts of *Agon* were reflective of the times, and Mr. B put them right out there, on a public stage for all to see. However, I also wonder if the literal dark/light of the male/female skintones was meant to reflect, either consciously or unconsciously, the darkness he felt over Tanny's fate, and his (and everyone else's, for that matter) perception that

Mel, with Heather Watts in the pas de deux from Balanchine's Agon.
Photograph: ©Steven Caras, all rights reserved.

she was a beautiful angel.

I moved Heather gently and with great regard for what I saw to be a rather petite, frail body. While not large by any means, the girls I had been used to partnering at the Dance Theatre of Harlem had muscles you could see and they just looked strong and powerful. Heather appeared to be so delicate. I was wrong. At one point, Mr. B stopped me and told me to start farther away from Heather and to come in to catch her at the very last minute. I was not prepared for this instruction, but I did it. Mr. B knew exactly what he wanted. It almost felt like he was showing me off to Peter. He told me to throw Heather, to stop being so careful with her. He assured me that her strength was supernatural and promised me that she would not break or fall. Once again, Mr. B was right. Heather was amazing, even though I was still a stranger to her. I am sure she had been looking forward to dancing with Peter, but she did not let on or have a bad attitude. She was kind and completely professional. She seemed to go out of her way to help me to feel as comfortable as possible in such a new and unique situation.

When we finished the pas de deux, there was complete silence. I had completely exhausted myself through a combination of jet lag, sacrificing caution, and simply dancing with someone new to me. Mr. Balanchine was thrilled. His eyes lit up, and he seemed renewed and overjoyed, as if he had found something that had been lost. He said that it was as he had first created it and he had not seen it that way for many years. It was all lines, angles,

Mel in rehearsal for Agon with Heather Watts.
Photograph: ©Steven Caras, all rights reserved.

tension and a certain degree of elegance.

Mr. B seemed quite revived and did not hesitate to show his pleasure. I felt his pride and was happy that we had pleased him. All told, the rehearsal only lasted about thirty or forty minutes.

Mr. B informed us that there would be a stage rehearsal in a couple days, following company class and that we would be performing it the following Friday night. I would not see the rest of the cast until the stage rehearsal, but Mr. B did not seem worried.

On the stage rehearsal day for *Agon*, I arrived early for company class and did my own warm-up before the class. I wore one of my custom-designed unitards, made for me by Evelyn Miller at the School of the Arts. No more "dancer-boy uniform" for me. I felt that I was out from under Arthur Mitchell's control, but, at the same time, I felt so grateful to Mr. Mitchell for teaching me all the details and nuances in *Agon*. After class, we all left the fifth-floor rehearsal studio and went down to the theater on the first level of the New York State Theater at Lincoln Center. There, I first found out who else was in the cast. I also met the conductor, Robert Irving, for the first time. He greeted me with genuine warmth and kindness.

Agon Curtain Call. Heather Watts and Mel Tomlinson.

We began the rehearsal with the four men facing upstage. We had to stop on the very first note. Mr. B told me that I was early. I had begun on the breath – "and one," whereas the other men were waiting for the "one." I was confused, and my mouth started talking, mainly because I was trying to sort out my confusion. I explained to Mr. B that that was how the score was written and that Mr. Mitchell had taught it to me. Robert Irving, the conductor, jumped up joyously, saying, "Finally! Someone who knows music. I have been saying that for years." Mr. B just smiled a little smile, but told me to start on the one since there were three other men starting on the one and only one of me. He never got defensive, and certainly never behaved in anything but a quiet, easy-going manner. He always listened to everything that was said. Even when you did not get your way, it was fine because you could not help but feel that your thoughts had been respected. Mr. B promised to fix it at another time, but I don't think he ever found the time to do so.

My fellow male cast members were Victor Castelli, Jean-Pierre Frohlich, and my old NCSA friend, Peter Frame. There were eight women in the cast, too, all of whom I did not yet know, except for one, my friend, Susan Freedman, from *The Spellbound Child*. It was a relief for me to know that both Peter Frame and Susan Freedman were in the cast. They were two people who loved me and only wanted the best for me. It gave me strength to know that they were there. The rest of rehearsal went off without a hitch. I could tell that everyone was waiting to see how Heather and I did in the pas de deux. Mr. B was in his place in the downstage right front wing. He wore a look of approval and accomplishment. He was happy with his new dancer, who just happened to be black. I am sure he was thinking back to the days when he had first worked with Arthur Mitchell. I remember hoping in my heart that Mr. Mitchell was proud of me and wishing he would come see this performance and give me some feedback. We ran the whole ballet once. Heather and I danced as if we had been dancing *Agon* together our whole lives.

Friday evening, without a clear warning to the audience, the curtain opened to silence and wonder. There I was, tall and very black, and without the fanfare of an announcement that I would be filling in for the much-beloved Peter Martins. Not only was I new to the company, but I was filling in for an audience favorite, and dancing an audience favorite, with another audience favorite. I was definitely not Peter Martins. I turned to face the audience and the challenge began, without so much as a breath from anyone until after the pas de deux was complete. The wings were full of dancers all trying to get a better view. However, Mr. B was not in his place. I had heard from other dancers that he was always in the downstage right front wing. He was not there. I found that to be a bit unsettling, but I made it through remembering his blessings from the stage rehearsal. When we finished, the house erupted in more applause than I could ever have imagined. I do not remember exactly how many curtain calls there were, but there were so many that they had to delay the start of the second ballet. It was so exciting. I had done *Agon* many times before, but had never experienced this. And most of it was for Heather and me. Heather even pushed me out in front of the curtain alone a few times, saying, "They want you, Mel!" As I bowed repeatedly, I looked up to the fifth balcony, remembering one of my amazing teachers from the North Carolina School of the Arts, Duncan Noble, and how he had taught us to be sure to thank every single person in the audience.

Afterwards, choreographer Jerome Robbins came backstage looking for me. He congratulated me and told me that he wanted to use me in his new ballet, *Gershwin Concerto,* and to come to rehearsal the next day. Robbins always had his finger on the pulse of the audience. He was a master at choosing to use the dancers for whom the audiences were hungry. He was so nice and positive that night backstage. I had heard that he was a very difficult taskmaster. How hard could it be to work with him, I thought to myself, a question I never should have asked.

I went home that night elated, but exhausted. I was still suffering from a bit of jet lag, but I hardly noticed. I was disheartened that M. B had not been in the wings nor had he come backstage afterwards, leading me to believe that he had not been there at all. Old insecurities reared their ugly heads and I took it to mean that he did not care. I comforted myself with the knowledge that so many of my friends from the Dance Theatre of Harlem had come to the performance. Peter Martins, seeing them cuing up for tickets before the show, and recognizing them as dancers, had invited them all in for free to see me. The next day, the New York Times dance critic, Anna Kisselgoff, proclaimed our performance of *Agon* to be "….one of the most dynamic and electric in years." All I could think was, "Wow, talk about an introduction to the New York City Ballet audiences!" Reading that review took my breath away.

As soon as class was over that morning, I took that review and headed for Mr. B's office. He was there. Waving the review in his face, I said, "Why weren't you there?" I was more than a little annoyed that he had not been there to see it.

Mr. B answered, "Miel, I was not well last night. I have been under the weather. But I knew it would be wonderful." That was the first inkling I had that Mr. B's health was not as good as it should be. I'm sure his closest confidants knew the state of his health, but I had no idea that there was a serious illness brewing. For the next three years, I would feel complete at the New York City Ballet. I had found yet another wonderful home. And Mr. B was the best father figure next to my own father that I could have asked for.

It was the beginning of a whole new life for me. Long ago, when I was first at the North Carolina School of the Arts, I had learned quickly to seek out the most talented, brightest and most beautiful of all the students. You are judged by the company you keep. Over the years, I had expanded on this knowledge to the point that, much as I hate to admit it about myself, I held a bit, let's be honest, quite a bit, of arrogance in my soul. I had learned to wear blinders when it came to many people if I did not perceive them as having anything special to offer to the world or specifically, to me. I was at a point where I was in danger of beginning to take myself too seriously and "believe my own press." Jerome Robbins would take care of that for me. He had a way of making sure that you did not lose touch with who you really were, at least in his opinion, a lowly human capable of making huge, very stupid mistakes. With me, it could even be argued that, on top of being a lowly human and stupid, he made sure that I would not forget I was black, not for one second, and it was not pride in my heritage that he was making me see. It would be very hard to maintain a sense of arrogance when working with the racism and verbal abuse of Jerome Robbins. He became my next Mrs. Tomlinson.

I regret that I have more negative things to say about Jerome Robbins than positive things. In life, we earn some things, while other things are simply deserved by the very nature of our beings. Jerome Robbins deserved his reputations; both that of his evil viciousness toward his dancers, and that of his willingness to give his audiences everything they wanted and more. The audiences adored him for that. The dancers, not so much. There is an old story that, years before during a Broadway stage rehearsal, Jerry backed up and fell off the stage, suffering a concussion while the dancers watched without warning him. I think that story says it all.

Although my relationship with Jerry was never smooth or comfortable, I am very grateful that I got to work with him. He was a musical genius and, looking back, I am astonished to realize how much I learned from him and how much good came out of his abuse. I have always believed that Jerry's work was so incredibly three dimensional that it was not necessarily simply his ballets, but the artists with whom he chose to work who gave his choreography life. Not every good dancer can do justice to his works. He always made sure to know his dancers very well. It was like he had a sixth sense, kind of like those extra eyes I still believe that Mrs. Tomlinson had in the back of her head.

The New York City Ballet has always been and always will be a family. Jerry was a large part of that family. As with many families, no one wants to talk about the bad things. The wagons get circled and the ranks close whenever a family member elects to talk about "family business" publicly. It is not my intention to air any of this very-important-to-me family's dirty laundry, not that there ever was any. But Jerome Robbins was a large part of my life at the White House. I had trouble from the very beginning with his ethics and his cold-heartedness. I truly believe that many times he went out of his way to maintain his reputation through his cruel and disdainful treatment of his dancers.

Yet, we all loved him. After all he worked closely with Mr. B so he must have met with Mr. B's approval. To this day, I simply cannot understand how someone as kind and supportive as Mr. Balanchine could ever condone, much less approve of Jerome Robbins' ways. Was it enough for Mr. B to like and respect Jerry as a choreographer? Did his brilliant accomplishments negate his abusive behavior in Mr. B's eyes? Or was it simply the fact that his box office receipts went a long way to help pay the expenses? I wish I knew the answers to those questions. As near as I can tell, Mr. Balanchine's and Jerry Robbins' relationship was similar to that of my own parents. I never did understand how or why my father put up with Mrs. Tomlinson.

There was a time when Jerome Robbins danced for the New York City Ballet. It has been said that he even had a special place in his heart for Tanaquil LeClerq. Everyone knows that Jerry was gay, but sexuality is always complicated. It is entirely possible that he may have loved Tanny. Who knows? Maybe he simply wanted what he could not have, someone who perhaps could have given him more power and attention. Tanny was beautiful, both inside and out, completely breathtaking.

I define evil as the misuse of power. That is the simple description of exactly who Jerome Robbins was. He was so far beyond the definition of a taskmaster. I did, however, notice that he never treated the principals in the same way that he treated the soloists and corps de ballet members. The principals were in positions of power and could refuse to work with him if they wanted to do so. I believe that his behavior at that point in his life was that of a cowardly bully. He took the arrogance of associating himself with the best, brightest and most beautiful much farther than my arrogance ever allowed me to take it. It is one thing to like living within the most popular group. It is completely another thing to do exactly that while belittling and abusing those with less power and authority.

I had crossed paths with Jerome Robbins much earlier, in 1975, while dancing with the Dance Theatre of Harlem. Mr. Mitchell took two casts of men down to American Ballet Theatre to learn *Fancy Free* from Jerry. There was a lot of ego and testosterone in the rehearsal hall that day. You could cut the tension between Jerry and Mr. Mitchell with a dull knife. True to his reputation, Jerry was not patient with us at all. In fact, he was quite rude right in front of the American Ballet Theatre dancers. It was completely emasculating, especially for Mr. Mitchell and the first cast. At the time, it did not faze me, as I was new and in the second cast. I did not realize what was going on and other dancers had to explain it to me later. I was simply young and naive. I felt like I was just along for the ride.

Finally, all of Jerry's "dark" verbiage and references became too much for Mr. Mitchell and we left the rehearsal and returned to Harlem. The situation seemed to prove Mr. Mitchell's words that Harlem was where we belonged. At that time, I had not yet been exposed to the political side of directors and choreographers. I did understand racism, but to me, it was just the way white people thought about black people, more a fact of life than something I thought one could do anything about. Mr. Mitchell had been facing racism in the ballet world for many years. He already knew that it was more than just the way white people thought. It was a rough introduction and lesson for me. Growing up in the projects, I rarely was exposed to white people as a child. My first real exposure had been through ballet and I had not faced this kind of racism. Both Jerry and Mr. Mitchell were from a different generation and thus a different mindset than the one that was my initial introduction to the ballet world.

The Dance Theatre of Harlem did not get *Fancy Free* at that time. It was later, when I was in New York City Ballet, that DTH finally received the okay to dance it. They did already have the rights to do Jerry's *Afternoon of a Faun* at that time. Lydia Abarca danced it with Ronald Perry. The work was deep and honest and Mr. Mitchell's coaching was spot on. I fell in love with that ballet, but never got to do it for the Dance Theatre of Harlem. It was only in the repertoire for a couple of years. I am guessing that there was a fee that needed to be paid to Jerry whenever it was performed and the company ran on a small budget at that time. Mr. B gave Mr. Mitchell the rights to do any of his ballets that he wanted for free. Mr. B and Jerry were very different people.

The more I made inquiries about Jerome Robbins, the more I wondered what made him tick. Where did his genius and creative gifts come from? Why was he so mean? Was his cruelty truly a necessary part of the Jerome Robbins experience? I learned that he read music incredibly well and understood nuances that many did not. He had been quite a musical prodigy as a child. He began his career as a choreographer with *Fancy Free*, while still a young dancer with Ballet Theatre, in 1944. It was the early 1940's. The music, composed by the then unknown Leonard Bernstein, was as fresh and relevant as Jerry's choreography. By all accounts, Bernstein and Robbins apparently made a great team. I also learned that Jerry had choreographed several pieces, including "The Small House of Uncle Thomas" in the *King and I*, that presented anti-slavery sentiments. How could someone who had made anti-racist statements in his work, later behave in such racist ways? Was it possible that I was misunderstanding his behavior? For a long time, I chose to believe that I was misunderstanding him.

Jerry loved and was inspired by New York City and had great passion for New Yorkers. In that way, he had similarities to Woody Allen, but the similarities stopped there. I never found Jerry to have a sense of humor, dry or otherwise.

Being from the South, I have always been used to addressing adults as "Mister" or "Miss," but it became obvious that I had little respect for Jerry, as I called him "Jerry" from the beginning. I do not believe many respected him, and any respect he got came from pure terror. We all called him "Jerry." I do not think he cared what we called him.

I had heard stories that Jerry was known for "borrowing" steps from other choreographers, including some of his *West Side Story* choreography. I have no idea if this is true, but I did see Jerry at the Brooklyn Academy of Music, one time in the audience to see some new works by Ulysses Dove. The next day in rehearsal, I recognized some of the combinations of steps from the night before.

I was nervous about my first rehearsal with Jerry. He was so nice to me backstage after the *Agon* success. Surely he would be civil to me after that performance being considered one of the top performances of the year by Anna Kisselgoff. The new ballet he was working on was a tribute to Gershwin,

Jerome Robbins could easily devastate his dancers with verbal abuse.
Photograph: ©Steven Caras, all rights reserved.

entitled *Gershwin Concert – Concerto in F*. As it happened, Jerry had no more of an idea about what to do with me, than I had any idea of what to expect. He already knew what he was doing with Maria Calegari, Chris d'Amboise, and a very young Darci Kistler. I had heard that Jerry loved versatility and passion in his dancers, as well as excellent technique. I figured that, like most choreographers, he would adore quickness in learning and interpreting what was given, two traits that were very much a part of me. I knew my technique was nowhere near excellent, but hoped that my quickness and memory would make up for it.

As the rehearsal went on, I began to feel his impatience and his frustrations with me. I felt like an unloved step-child. Finally, Jerry brought me into the ballet about half way through the second movement. I was beginning to think he had changed his mind about using me, but he was simply choreographing the ballet to excite his audience, and since I was "flavor of the month" at the moment, he brought me in at strategically the perfect time. He was a master at knowing when and how to use his dancers.

There were so many times when I watched brilliant dancers leave Jerry's rehearsals emotionally crippled and reduced to agonizing tears. He showed himself to be very difficult, and often impossible, to please. Having the knack for finding a person's weaknesses and then pouncing on them came naturally to Jerry. I had grown up with this behavior from Mrs. Tomlinson, but I was older now, older than many of the other dancers, and no longer willing to allow

Mel with Lourdes Lopez in Jerome Robbins' Gershwin Concerto.
Photograph: ©Steven Caras, all rights reserved.

myself to be emotionally brutalized by anyone's ignorance and ill-tempered displays of power. From Jerry, I learned a lot about the insidiousness of racism. Jerry used racial slurs to try to control me, asking me for "Mammy hands" or "Al Jolson hands" when looking for a certain step. More than once he told me to make sure I was on time. "You know how YOU people are – always late."

After one very intense rehearsal, as I was leaving the studio, I was met by author, Greg Lawrence, Gelsey Kirkland's ex-husband, who was writing a book about Jerry, that would be entitled *Dancing with Demons*. He asked if he could interview me. I told him that now would not be a good time because I had just had a run-in of sorts with the man. As I started to walk away, I thought, "Oh, what the heck. Why not?" I told my truth at that moment and when the book came out, I found myself on the back cover, the first to be quoted, "If I die and go to hell, I won't be afraid of the devil because I have worked with Jerome Robbins." I am sure I lost a lot of friends and fans with that quote, but, once again, it was my truth. What I was quoted as saying on the inside of the book was just as blunt. I would not change a word.

I was upset many times, but I refused to allow Jerry to see me in that state. Never did I walk out of rehearsal in tears. The racism card that he constantly played with me hit me where I was most vulnerable. At the time, I was one

Sean Lavery, Merrill Ashley and Mel in Jerome Robbins' Concertino.
Photograph: ©Steven Caras, all rights reserved.

of only three black members of the New York City Ballet out of a hundred dancers. Being black in a white world could be difficult enough at times. But for Jerry to constantly hammer at the core of my very being without any regard whatsoever to the hurt he was causing finally became too much. He knew I was upset when I arranged a meeting with Mr. Balanchine.

The ultimatum I gave them was this: either Jerry's attitude towards me changes, or I leave. Mr. B was concerned. I had his attention. He concluded that I should be taken out of all of Jerry's ballets except the ones he had created on me. This would mean that I would not have to suffer through as many rehearsals with Jerry. In turn, Jerry would tone it down a bit.

To Jerry's credit, I must say that he did know how to motivate me, even if any and all discussion with him could strike terror in my heart. I remember the day he informed me that he was putting me in the pas de trois, *Concertino*, with two of the best technicians in the company, Merrill Ashley and Sean Lavery.

"You better step up your game, Mel, if you are going to dance with them," he said, staring at me with eyes full of absolutely nothing. My countenance never wavered even though my heart was pounding and my breathing felt shallow. The ballet was a hit and even became poster material for outside of the theater. I have always loved a challenge, and Jerry always gave me that.

Much later, after I left the company and was teaching in North Carolina, Jerry called me and asked if I was in shape and if I remembered my role from *Gershwin Concerto*. He had a way of insulting me pretty much with every breath. Of course, I remembered it! He created it on me. It felt like he was insinuating that I might not be capable of remembering it. I went back and did the ballet for him. It was his contribution to the American Dance Festival that year since he had not done a new ballet for that festival.

Years later, I would see him two more times. Once was in Boston. At that time, I was a principal dancer with the Boston Ballet. Our director, Bruce Marks, wanted to acquire the rights for the company to perform *The Concert*, one of Jerry's most-loved ballets and a true comic masterpiece. Jerry was in Boston to see the company in performance so that he could decide whether or not to allow the company to dance it. I was not dancing that night, and I caught his eye just as he was about to enter the theater. He was not looking so well. He asked me if this company was just as good as the New York City Ballet. I answered him honestly with my truth, and said, "No." Without another word, he made an about face and headed back to New York. I was stunned. He had taken my word without even staying to see the company himself.

The last time I saw Jerry was shortly before his death. I was visiting friends at the New York State Theater. I found myself in the elevator, heading down to leave when the elevator doors opened on the next floor down and Jerry entered.

"Babe, I know we have had our differences and I apologize. I love you, please forgive me and I want you to do well in North Carolina," he said. He spoke through very glassy, teary eyes. I was stunned yet again by this enigma of a man. He then asked if I knew the steps and parts to his ballet, *Concertino*. "Of course, I do! How could I forget it?" I asked. He said he wanted me to stage it for him in Paris. Unfortunately, that request was never realized because he passed soon after. But I am so grateful to have had those few minutes with him. He gave me both a new relationship with him and closure at the same time. I realized that I had great respect for this brilliant but frightening man. Everybody has a Jerry story. In retrospect, I now know that I am better for having worked with him because I am very strong and resilient, two qualities that tend to develop from the difficulties we face in our lives. Jerry will not be forgotten.

Chapter Ten

My Life at the White House 1983-1986 – Part Three
Losses and Endings

As I stood next to his casket, looking down at the familiar face that, even in death gave me so much comfort and peace, I could not help but reflect on the death that had been all around us for the past three or four years. It was May 4, 1983. Mr. B had been dead for five days. So many friends, ballet family and fans had arrived at the Russian Orthodox Cathedral of Our Lady of the Sign on Park Avenue at East 93rd Street, where Mr. Balanchine had worshiped, to say our final farewells.

Although I was early to arrive, I was late due to the large crowds outside. At first, I feared I would not get into the church to pay my respects, but the staff spotted me and ushered me to the front. I am told that Peter Martins and Lincoln Kirstein stayed outside in the courtyard for the entire three-hour service to make sure that every one of Mr. B's dancers would get to be inside of the church for the ceremony. These two men, who probably felt the loss even deeper than anyone else, were more concerned about the feelings of Mr. B's "children" than their own deeply-felt loss.

Lincoln Kirstein, Administrator and General Manager of NYCB, confers with George Balanchine.

Lincoln Kirstein, had co-founded the company with Mr. B. He was the Administrator and General Manager of the New York City Ballet. Lincoln believed that all contemporary balletic innovations had to be based in traditional classicism to have credibility. He was much more interested in what could be done using those classical ballet traditions than what had already been done using them. I believe he really "got" Mr. B. It made total sense that he would financially back someone of Mr. B's caliber and help build such a great company and school.

He had first seen Balanchine's work early on, in Europe in the 1920's, when Balanchine was the hot new, young choreographer with Serge Diaghilev's Ballet Russes. It was several years later, in 1933, that Lincoln would convince Balanchine to settle in the United States. I believe that Lincoln knew that he had found an artist worthy of support over the long term, someone who would bring a new, freshly American view to the world of ballet. He helped Balanchine found the School of American Ballet (SAB), first in Hartford, Connecticut, in 1934, then moved the school to New York City, first to the East Side at East 59th Street and Madison Avenue. The school would move a couple more times, including to Broadway and West 82 Street, and finally ending up at its current residence in the Rose Building at Lincoln Center, with state-of-the-art, beautifully designed studios. SAB now has a modern dormitory as well, for students from both near and far, who come to the School, leaving their families and all that they know in hopes of one day joining one of the greatest ballet companies in the world. Lincoln was another brilliant man of vision and generosity. Even though he had lost his good friend and colleague, he was concerned with the feelings of the dancers on that bleak, spring day.

Any event involving George Balanchine was always an event of major proportions and public attention. His funeral service was no different. The church was ill-equipped to handle the masses of people who arrived to pay their respects to this brilliant man, a man who had been to all a great choreographer, but to the chosen few, those of us in his New York City Ballet immediate family, so much more. He had been a father figure to us all; a friend and confidant; someone who could fix any problem and make everyone feel like they were the luckiest person in the world simply for being in his presence. We all knew that we had been invited to live our lives on a higher plane when we were accepted into the New York City Ballet. Now we were all at such a loss. How would we go on without him?

I stood just inches from his motionless body and fell silent in prayer and thanksgiving. I had lost a friend and mentor and I waited to be touched by the radiance of his soul. I glanced behind me and saw dignitaries from all four corners of the earth. There were so many pale, sad faces and bodies dressed in black that held on to the memories of the moment. It was one of the most magnificent send-offs that I had ever witnessed. I was suddenly overwhelmed with pride for Mr. B and realized that God had called him into yet another service. It was with that thought that I found an inner peace that would sustain my emotions and provide comfort for my loss.

I would love to say that back at the theater on this very sad day, that work went on as usual, but I cannot. The work went on, but certainly not as usual. Who felt like dancing? People were quiet and obviously sad and upset. It felt wrong to be there, at the theater preparing to perform that very evening after spending three hours saying goodbye to Mr. B at his funeral. Lourdes Lopez, one of the company's amazing technicians, who now directs the Miami City Ballet, and I were to dance *Kammermusik #2* that evening. Lourdes's energy and faith literally pulled me through. We became each other's strength that night. We danced as if Mr. B were present in his place in the downstage right front wing and dedicated our performance to him. I wanted to thank him for all that he had done and all that I expected he was going to do. I had given him my total trust. His efforts had revived my career and my love of dancing. Mr. B really saw and understood me more than any other director at that point in my career had. He had recognized my need to dance as well as my need to love and be loved. Like everyone else in the company, I loved it when he stood in the first wing downstage right and watched his creations on stage. He knew his dancers, their abilities, their weaknesses and strengths, their personalities and their love for his work, the music, and the audiences that he had developed. We all wanted to please him. His presence in the wings always added a certain security in our delivery. He was interested not only in the reception of his ballets, but in the dancer's interpretations and translations. Many people still want to deify him, but I knew him to be a mere mortal who happened to be gifted and had the courage to realize his gifts. So many of his gifts appeared to come easily to him, but I know for a fact that a lot of it was born of sheer determination, hard work and long hours of restlessness. He was quite adept at gathering the right people for the right jobs. Mr. B knew how to delegate and placed trust in the people with whom he worked. We all wanted the same result – Art. Mr. B gave us art in the highest form, reflecting his childhood memories and his classical ballet training in Russia, and yet, forging new artistic territory. He was very true to his homeland's traditions and customs, and seemed to me to be fueled by the promise of sharing those sacred traditions with the world by enveloping them within his new, American mindset.

What I loved most about Mr. B was his approach to all forms of dance, with the thought that ballet as a foundation would support his current views on movement and execution. He collaborated with composers, musicians, friends, and even his own dancers – John Clifford, Edward Villella, Jacques d'Amboise, Jean Pierre Bonnefoux, John Taras, Jerome Robbins and Peter Martins, to name a few. He seemed to know innately how to assist and offer the fruits of his experience without taking over the work of others. His passion appeared to surpass his very presence and there will probably always be those who try to figure him out and try to emulate him. In the end, all that is really left are our memories and a few instructions. I am in awe of the ballet masters and mistresses who have worked hard to maintain his original intent within his work, even with the changes and developments in and of ballet technique over the years. They, along with the dancers who were his muses will forever have my ear as I continue to try to absorb and pass on, all that I can from his teachings, even now, so many years later.

I am sure that everyone has personal stories about Mr. B. Mine are all quite personal and in a way sacred to me. I will hold fast to them forever. He made me feel special, as if I had something to offer and even more to gain. He placed me amongst a family of dancers, each of whom he had groomed and prepared for their own greatness. We were now one. I remembered once arriving quite early for a rehearsal to find Mr. B in the studio playing the piano. Very quietly, I entered and started my warm up. As I was stretching, Mr. B stopped playing and said, "Miel, don't. We have girls for that. No need for you to do that." He then invited me over to sit with him at the piano. I immediately noticed that he was missing one of his ring fingers. I had never noticed that before. Without thinking, I reached out and gently touched his hand and asked what had happened. "It was when I was married to the Indian," he said, meaning Maria Tallchief. He said it was an accident while cutting the grass where they had lived out on Long Island.

I also remembered the chair he had given me that first day in his office. I thought of other times when I went to his office with various problems and he always made them seem easily surmounted. Once I went in, concerned as to his reason for having me in the company. Was I there because of my color, or because of my special gifts? In his mind, did he view me as an artist or as an "only-est," that is, a sole Black man in the "White House?" Mr. B told me I was his "Dark Angel," but the superficiality of my color was not the reason I was there. He explained how I was an important part of his garden as were all the dancers, and we were all different flowers. I remembered how calmly he listened to my hurts and upsets concerning Jerry Robbins. My memories were comfort to me at that moment. I was so happy that I had the opportunities that afforded those memories, and took comfort in the knowledge that I would always have them.

I did my very best to comfort my fellow dancers with my spiritual strengths and optimism. Many of them did seem to gravitate toward me as if they instinctively knew that I was the one who had the ability to give such comfort. I prayed with them and held more than a few hands, wiped a lot of tears and tried to prepare my fellow dancers for the responsibilities of living up to Mr. B's legacy that we now faced.

Mr. B's death was not the first that any of us, even the youngest members of the company, had dealt with over the past few years. The uncompromising realities of death had been slowly insinuating themselves into our daily lives for some time now. The so-called "gay disease" had been systematically taking our friends, many of whom were much younger than my thirty years. Even some of my teachers had become ill. It was a deadly plague, to be sure, but we were still quiet about it, not having any idea how to react to so many sudden losses. It was only within the last year that we had noticed that some rare diseases, pneumocystis pneumonia, and Kaposi's Sarcoma, to name two, were showing up more and more and were taking the lives of so many talented, young gay men. This was not "normal," this constant facing of death at our young ages.

As I had gazed at Mr. B for the last time that morning, I realized that his was a normal death. He was seventy-nine years old. He had lived a long, extremely fulfilling life. He had married four times. He had built one of the best ballet companies in the world, and had choreographed great works of art on great artists. He had worked in film, television, Broadway, and had traveled the world. George Balanchine had lived, really lived, and was so deeply loved by so many. Looking at him, I knew that we could rejoice and celebrate his life. I knew that the legacy he had left was so strong, so powerful, that it simply could not do other than continue and grow stronger. I knew that we, his children, his disciples, would be fine. He would take care of us in death as he had in life, so strong was his spirit and his legacy. Looking back now, I believe that this understanding was the beginning of ministry for me. The seed was watered and began to grow that day at Mr. B's funeral.

In a way, death has always fascinated me. I had grown up believing it was a necessary part of life; a passage into a future that we, as yet, did not fully understand. Having lost my beloved grandfather when I was six, my thought was that death was expected. One would lead a full life and then move on. With this understanding, I was able to be a comfort to many of the dancers, a few of whom had not dealt with death in their young lives yet.

We all had known that the day was upon us when we would suffer the loss of one of the world's most prolific choreographers; a genius. Mr. B had been in the hospital since the previous November due to complications from a neurological illness. He would succumb to pneumonia. Just a month before, in March, the Board of Directors had named Peter Martins and Jerome Robbins Co-Ballet Masters-in-Chief of the company. Even knowing that Mr. B no longer held that title was not enough of a warning to any of us of what was to come. We knew, but we did not know.

I remember when I received the early morning phone call from John Taras, one of Mr. Balanchine's long-time ballet masters/repetiteurs informing me that Mr. B had transitioned to his next life. At that moment, I knew I needed to be there, at the theatre. I readied myself for class just as I did each day, as if nothing was different. But everything was different. I felt empty and heavy-hearted.

Numbly, we all arrived at the theatre, each one feeling the same pain. It was like taking class with the lights out. Everything not only felt dim that day, but everything was dim. Our collective light had gone out. I cannot even remember who taught the class that day, nor can I remember anything about the class except that everyone looked the same, stoic with deep despair showing through the tear-stained cracks. Our hearts were just so heavy, full and empty at the same time. We were all confused and heartsick. A loneliness pervaded.

As I began to explain earlier, the shadow of death had been hanging over the arts community for several years now. No one spoke of it, probably, I believe, out of fear of opening the floodgates. Looking back, I believe we all subconsciously knew that something truly heinous was taking place, but we were powerless to control it or fix it, so we turned a blind eye to it for a long time. Many beautiful, young lives were being cut short, before their lives had had a chance to fully flower. This scourge of a plague would continue for many years, growing and spreading. None of the powers in the political world at that time would do anything about it. Many would call it God's wrath and say that the gay community brought it on themselves. It would take public knowledge of heterosexual men, women and children contracting HIV before anyone would take it seriously and start the long, arduous process of researching for a cure. In the fifteen or twenty years before HIV and AIDS were acknowledged to affect everyone, many beautiful souls suffered and died needlessly, and often alone, having been abandoned by their families and friends. The effects on the ballet world were huge. Whole generations of brilliantly talented male dancers were lost. It was the generation following that of great superstar Mikhail Baryshnikov, my generation, and the one immediately after mine. For a good twenty years, there would be a tremendous shortage of male dancers. At the time, the late 1970's and the early 1980's, finding out you had HIV was a virtual death sentence. Very few recovered. Back then, I knew of no one who recovered. At the New York City Ballet, we would lose some of the most brilliant, talented, kindest young dancers – John Bass, Tracy Bennett, Tony Blum, Deni Lamont, and Rick Hoskinson, to name a few with whom I was friends -----and so many other dancers from all over the world. More often than not, they would get sick and suddenly simply disappear, sometimes going home to their families to die, many others facing death alone. We would hear of their passings much later, often months after their funerals had happened and they had been laid to rest. I believe that the companies that toured heavily were hit the hardest; I lost several friends at the Dance Theatre of Harlem and at the Ailey company. Touring was an adventure in so many ways; and up until that time, we were young and naïve enough to believe we were invincible.

It was at that time that I first started asking my partners to use condoms; I had never bothered before. I became more selective and careful with whom I became involved, as did everyone else I knew. The casual sex era was not over, but a consciousness of thought before action had begun to emerge. I believe that the saddest thing of all was that often, families would cover up a loved one's real cause of death because the shame was more than many could withstand. Years later, I would face this within my own family. In reality, no one actually dies of AIDS. It is the complications from opportunistic infections related to AIDS that kill. When you take the time to really think about it, death comes to us all in exactly the same way, AIDS or no AIDS: we die when our hearts stop, figuratively and literally-speaking.

During my time at the New York City Ballet, we suffered more than our share of loss, not just from complications due to AIDS, but from every other manner of death as well. The first that I remember was the death of Ronald Bates, our stage manager, followed shortly thereafter by the untimely and tragic death in a car accident of a beautiful, very young corps de ballet member, Michelle Bailey. When I first saw Michelle, I saw one of the most breathtakingly beautiful creatures that God ever created, then reclaimed. Looking back now, it takes my breath away to realize that she never got to experience the years of life, both good and bad, that I have experienced. This makes my heart ache for her.

All death is heartbreaking for those left behind, but the death of so many young people who had not even begun to really live their lives was devastating. It took its toll on us all. Probably one of the hardest deaths for everyone was that of Joseph Duell. Joe would fall from his fifth-floor apartment window on a frigid Sunday morning in February, three years after Mr. B's death. He was only twenty-nine years old. Joe was a perfectionist, working and striving his whole life to reach his goals. He was a principal dancer in the company and much loved by everyone due to his kind, loving personality. He was also a budding choreographer, and I was lucky enough to have been included in his work, *Creation du Monde*, which I danced with Maria Calegari. Everyone knew that he was harder on himself than anyone else could possibly have been on him. Only Jerry Robbins could find a way to be harder on Joe than Joe was on himself. Joe was the only principal dancer that I ever witnessed being completely disparaged and emotionally destroyed by Jerry. I witnessed this at rehearsal the day before Joe's death. Unfortunately, none of us had recognized the agony that Joe must have already been enveloped within. If we had, every one of us, Jerry included, would have embraced Joe in a protective love and held on unceasingly until the agony dissipated and his crisis subsided. Jerry knew our weaknesses and he knew that he could often get our best out of us by hitting us where we were most vulnerable. He knew that Joe had been struggling with depression, but I do not think that Jerry or anyone else knew just how deep Joe's agony ran. He had recently had his engagement to Maria Calegari broken. No one expected Joe's suicide. We lost many beautiful artists/soldiers in those years. The glue of the company seemed to weaken with each passing.

Joseph Duell, left, with Maria Calegari and Mel rehearsing Creation du Monde.

When dancers retire from the New York City Ballet, the company always gives them a beautiful public send-off – a final, farewell performance heralded as such. There is one thing that I believe we, as dancers, all have in common; it is our desire not to be forgotten. I believe if those who passed, especially from untimely deaths, knew they were going in advance, they, too, would desire not to be forgotten. As their sisters and brothers, and Mr. Balanchine's children, I believe that we all owe each other that honor.

It took a while following Mr. B's death, but eventually the company found its' footing under the newly appointed director, Peter Martins, who co-directed with Jerome Robbins. I must admit that I, along with others, was surprised when the announcement came in March of 1983, a month before Mr. B's death, that Peter was to be at the helm. I had honestly thought that the job would go to Suzanne Farrell, Jacques d'Amboise or Edward Villella because they were all true disciples of Mr. B and knew better than most what his wishes were. Peter had been one of my fellow dancers. He had joined the company after first making his reputation as a principal dancer in the Royal Danish Ballet. I had made my debut with the company by filling in for Peter, thinking, under Mr. B's purposeful misguidance, that Peter was injured. He now had rather big shoes to fill and it would take time for him to become completely comfortable within those shoes.

I must admit that I had issues with Peter suddenly becoming my boss. I did not respect the idea of Peter becoming director because I was still very protective of the memory of Mr. B. Mr. B had believed in me in a way that no one else had. He respected who I was as an artist and allowed me to make his ballets my own. I was not alone in these protective feelings towards Mr. B. Everything would now be different, and I would need to learn to adapt. It was very difficult for me to believe that Peter could keep the company going in the same or even a remotely similar way as Mr. B had. Peter was a beautiful dancer, so clean and technically perfect. He was also a physically beautiful man, tall, with wavy blonde hair and bold, ruggedly handsome features. Where Mr. B had vision, Peter had a perfect, classical ballet body and technique. They were as different, in my mind, as an architect and an engineer: one had the vision to design near-perfection; the other had the skill to be or build near-perfection as inspired by another's design, but not the vision to elaborate on and share a vision that should have been behind his mind's eye but was not.

Looking back now, from my much-older and hopefully wiser viewpoint, I can see that Peter's appointment was the next step in the New York City Ballet's evolution. Mr. Balanchine's vision will always be there, in the background, alive in the hearts of his dancers and the audience through his choreography. Peter, more the engineer than the architect, has taken the company to a stronger place technically, with dancers, most of whom having trained through the School of American Ballet.

Some dancers and staff from the past feel that the technical abilities of today's Balanchine dancers bastardize the intent of Mr. B's choreography through over-use of the dancer's technical capabilities, but I do not always agree with this assessment. Even Mr. B was aware that his choreography would change and continue to morph once he was gone. Whether he would approve or not does not matter to me. Mr. B set certain pieces of art in motion and in order to continue, they will change as the times change and as the lives of the audience changes. The mere fact that his works have survived his death and continue to thrive, albeit with changes and tweaks added by the personalities of all currently involved in the dissemination of his work, is a testament to the very power of his vision. Many things that were believed to be beautiful in the past in one light change and morph, often into something completely different. What was considered near perfection in a bygone era, seems, to some, to be ridiculous or downright ugly in the present.

Everything changes, especially art or at least the perspective from which it is seen and examined. Recently, I watched myself and Heather Watts on a YouTube video of us performing *Agon* back in the early 1980's. Immediately after watching it, I watched another YouTube video of Arthur Mitchell and Diana Adams, the original dancers on whom Mr. Balanchine first set *Agon* more than twenty years before I first danced it with Heather. It was so different. Everything was different, from the nuances of the movements to the energy of the performers. In their respective time, both pairs of dancers were considered brilliant in the same parts. So many of the differences had to do with the very aliveness of the personalities dancing the parts as well as the evolution of ballet technique. The collective energy of the consciousness of the particular time in history was also very important to what was portrayed. We all take and give to the art according to where we are in our own lives and how the collective consciousness of our particular world's time views the art. In retrospect, I think that Peter's technical abilities were the beginning of bringing the company to where it is today, a company of dancers with amazing technique. It is a beautiful company of which I am still very proud to have been a part. But I do miss the exuberance of personalities that ruled the company during Mr. B's tenure.

Peter Martins, 1983. Photograph: © Steven Caras, all rights reserved.

Ballet companies are nothing if not families. New York City Ballet was no different. From the very beginning of my time there, I realized that this magical place was just like any other family. The first thing that should be born of family is that sense of joyful security one gets from the feeling of belonging and knowing one is loved and appreciated. As in any family, there is a pecking order with siblings. There are, of course, sibling rivalries and disagreements, too. At the New York City Ballet, I remember that I loved the fact that the programs always listed the dancers in alphabetical order. It was the "parents'" way of keeping the sibling rivalries to a minimum. I think what has always shown through any rivalries, in my opinion, was the fact that all the dancers supported each other both on and off the stage. The sense of family was always so evident and real to me. It gave me the greatest sense of security to belong to this amazing family.

With Mr. B gone, many of us were at a loss as to how to fill the hole in both our collective and individual hearts. I tended to try to fill mine with becoming attached to the ballet masters and mistresses in the same way I had been attached to Mr. B. Rosemary Dunleavy, in particular, seemed to offer me strength, guidance and encouragement at those times when I felt most lost and confused. She was the strong shoulder that many of us leaned on, as she was a tie to the past, to Mr. B. Rosemary brought comfort and compassion to those of us who needed it. She was not afraid to stand up for her beliefs. There were many other behind-the-curtain, unsung heroes: stagehands, wardrobe personnel, administration, marketing, lighting designers, physical therapists, orthopedists, masseurs. The list goes on, but to me, Rosemary stands out because of her consistently strong belief in the company and each of the dancers. She often helped me to be able to put the rigorous training and discipline of things into a proper, non-melodramatic perspective, something with which I very often have needed help throughout my life.

I think dancers tend to stay quite childlike into adulthood in some ways, often because the normal rites of passage into adulthood are missed because of the very-strong authority figures with whom we work. Looking back, I can see that many of us never seemed to get beyond that need for parental figures who offered a strong sense of security and guidance. We tended to need someone whom we viewed as more of an adult than we considered ourselves to be; someone who could help to fill that void left by Mr. B. It seemed to me necessary to exist in that child-like state so that I could allow the innocence of my journey to spew forth from my heart and the sweat of my brow during my performances.

I knew that while he lived, I would be protected and loved unconditionally by Mr. B. It is that sense of support that makes it possible to be courageous enough as an artist to share your vulnerabilities with the audience and thus become more human and more alien at the same time. Our selfishness, as well as our generosity, are both highly-developed as artists, just as those two traits are highly-developed and evident in young children. It is a dichotomy that is both simple and deeply confusing at the same time.

I wish with all my heart that I could say that I was as happy dancing with the New York City Ballet after Mr. B's death as I was before his passing. Unfortunately, I cannot. Mr. B had been the only choreographer/director who really knew what to do with me. I had charisma. I had strong stage presence. I could move my body in ways that were completely foreign to even the most highly trained ballet dancer. Double tours still eluded me. I yearned to be cast in the highly technical pieces, like *Symphony in C*. With Mr. B gone, I began to feel very alone. In my heart, I came to know within a short time that I would not be moving up any farther and there would be no more new ballets set on me. Peter Martins was not the visionary that Mr. Balanchine was. My life had suddenly regressed back to the days of frustrated choreographers asking themselves, "What are we going to do with Mel?" As the weeks and months stretched into years, I found myself only doing the same short list of repertoire, and doing those pieces at the most two to three times a week. My spare time stretched itself out into long days of working out, gossiping with friends, doing photo shoots as a nude or nearly-nude model, and wishing for yet another change to occur in my life. It started to feel like my best years as a dancer just might be behind me.

During my third year at the New York City Ballet, several months after Mr. B's death, I was in Denmark with the rest of the company, when I found out I had been awarded the prestigious North Carolina prize, a $10,000 award given to an artist of merit from the state. At a café for breakfast I was with some of the dancers, when one of them found it in the *International Herald Tribune*. I was flabbergasted, as I didn't even know there was a North Carolina Prize, much less that I was a nominee for it. Later that day, at the theater, I received my first telegram. It was from Lincoln Kirstein, congratulating me on receiving the honor. This marked the end of that period in my life when it seemed that every time I turned around something special and magical was happening to me. From that point on, I began to feel passed over, no longer 'flavor of the month.' Just a short time before, while we were in London, Andrew Lloyd Weber invited me out to dinner and offered me a part in his newest show

MY LIFE AT THE WHITE HOUSE – PART THREE

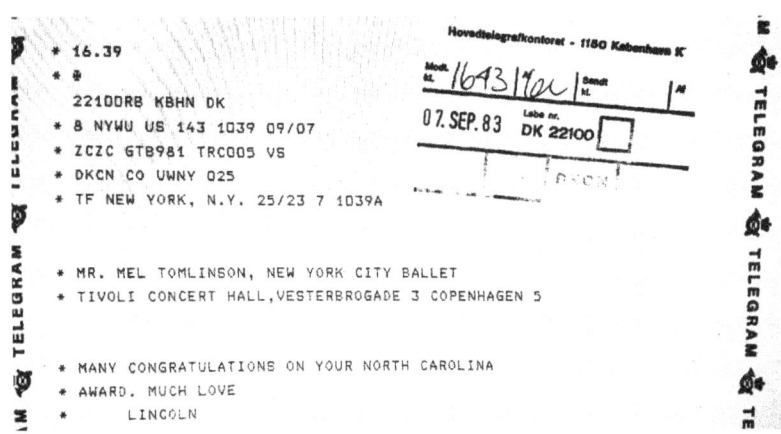

Mel's first telegram was from Lincoln Kirstein.

called *Cats*. I turned him down, but I was beginning to wonder whether I had made a mistake. Maybe I should have taken him up on that offer.

That year following Mr. B's death, I looked back on my earliest days in the New York City Ballet. They had been such exciting days. I had developed an instant following of balletomanes after that first performance of *Agon* with Heather Watts. Mr. B referred to me as his "dark angel" and was using me in all of what he termed his "dark angel" ballets, *Orpheus, Persephone, La Valse*. I had moved up from corps de ballet to soloist in only five months with the company. I felt sure that had Mr. B lived, I would have moved up to Principal and would have been given the opportunity to do many more ballets, perhaps even *Symphony in C*. Suddenly, I felt forgotten, more like an unloved stepchild than one of the cherished children. With each passing month, it became more and more obvious to me that my star had dimmed with Mr. B's passing. I became certain that Peter had no plans to use me further. After almost a year and a half, I started to think seriously about my future. I decided to write a letter to the company, specifically to Peter about my feelings.

It was around this time that Robert Lindgren, my first director and the dean of my alma mater, NCSA, reappeared in my life. I was so happy that he had come to see me dance. Unbeknownst to me at the time, Mr. Lindgren would eventually leave the North Carolina School of the Arts and turn his duties as Artistic Director at the North Carolina Dance Theater over to Salvatore Aiello, so that he could, in turn, take over from Lincoln Kirstein at the New York City Ballet and School of American Ballet when it was time for Lincoln to retire. Mr. Lindgren would have only a short tenure at the New York City Ballet -- six years -- for several reasons, including a heart attack and quadruple bypass as well as differences in management style with Peter Martins and others.

I confided my unhappiness to Mr. Lindgren, and told him that I was seriously thinking about leaving the ballet world and going back to school. He suggested that I think about applying for his old job as the Dean of Dance at the North Carolina School of the Arts. I was quite taken back by this suggestion. At first, I could not imagine being in that position. However, the more I entertained the thought, the more interesting it became. The year before, inspired by Linda Homek, one of the dancers who was going to school at Fordham University across the street from the theatre and majoring in Psychology, I had decided that this idea really appealed to me. I applied to both the University of North Carolina at Chapel Hill and Wake Forest University in Winston-Salem. However, I was just not ready to completely give up on dancing quite yet. Neither school was willing to allow me to work outside of the traditional

```
                                                September 14, 1984

New York City Ballet
Lincoln Center
New York, New York

     Dear          ,

            The intention of this letter is to inform - not to notify.
     I am aware of the size and talents that compose New York City Ballet.
     I am also cognizant of my personal past experience as a dancer who
     has performed many of Mr. Balanchine's great works: AGON, FOUR TEMPERA-
     MENTS, BUGAKU, CONCERTO BAROCCO, SERENADE, ALLEGRO BRILLANTE, SQUARE
     DANCE and DIVERTIMENTO No.15.
            It saddens me to know that I danced more of his works before
     joining NYCB than I'm presently involved with now (either as second
     cast or as understudy).
            Unfortunately, I am moved to the written word or plea, as it
     may appear, for participation and/or visibility as an artist who is
     here to be a part of the company rather than being a part from it.
            It would be to the best of my mental, emotional and physical
     being to be taken into careful and judicious consideration. If
     there is a problem with my work, please tell me.
            Empathetic toward the changes that are inevitable during a
     period of transition-
                                                I am graciously yours,


                                                Mel A. Tomlinson


     cc: four (4)
```

Copy of Mel's letter to NYCB asking to be given more to do as a dancer in the company.

classroom setting and advised me to put my school plans on hold until I was ready to commit to the university in the same way that I was committed to dance. I felt sure that one day I would study psychology. I was at a point in my life where I really wanted some answers as to why my mother had been the way she was, and why I believed and felt some of the things that I believed. It occurred to me that if I was the Dean of Dance at the University of North Carolina School of the Arts, a part of the same university system as the Chapel Hill school, maybe I could work out my schooling.

Mr. Lindgren suggested that I go down to Winston-Salem and teach at the School of the Arts for a year in order for both me and the school to assess my abilities. While I was still at NYCB, I started to collect recommendations from everyone I could think of in a position of power, Lincoln Kirsten, Agnes de Mille, and Philip Hanes to name a few. Agnes de Mille, who probably knew me better than most, stated in her very upfront, honest way that she did not think I would be tough enough to be the Dean. She did not believe I possessed the leadership skills to manage the opportunity. Of all the recommendations and advice that I received, I love and treasure hers the most. It made me think hard about myself and my weaknesses when it came to my social and business skills. Since I would be teaching on the staff for a year, I would have some time to assess and hopefully strengthen my skills. While teaching that year at NCSA, Agnes wrote me a letter letting me know about two of the questions that she had been asked by the search committee but felt she could not adequately answer. She always was so thorough, going above and beyond both in her honesty and willingness to give me every chance for success.

I have always followed my intuition in making important decisions about my life. I seriously doubt that I will ever change that "formula" for it has always been in my best interest. One needs to be careful not to wear out one's life's welcome mat when there is the possibility of furthering your growth and holding on to your senses and sanity elsewhere. It is always better to be in charge of your own future, than to have your future decided for you. I will forever be grateful to Mr. Lindgren for giving me a sense of direction and purpose at that point in my life. Once I had that, the rest fell into line very easily for me. I gave the New York City Ballet a full year's notice that I would be leaving. I did not do this, as some of my friends assumed, in order to garner sympathy, or to give the company time to come up with any new parts to entice me to stay. Once my mind was made up, it was done. I think I needed the time for several reasons. I wanted to spend some time watching my favorite teachers teach with my eye toward becoming a good teacher. I wanted to have plenty of time to organize the move and find a new home. I also wanted to really enjoy what, at the time I was sure would be my last year dancing professionally. There was one more reason. I would be thirty-three when I left. There was much significance for me to leave at that age. It was "the Jesus number." It just seemed to me that it would be a good time, the right time for me to make such a huge change in my life. I would leave after our summer season in Saratoga.

It was 1987. I had "found" myself at the New York City Ballet. By that, I mean to say that I found out who the real Mel A. Tomlinson was. My life had become very real as I had begun to express my opinions, both in my personal life and in my work. I don't know how I would have fared had I joined the New York City Ballet at a younger age. I probably would not have been able to stand up to Jerry's abuse if I had been younger and in a less adult frame of mind. Early on, when I joined the company, I bought a T-Shirt that said

AGNES DeMILLE PRUDE
25 EAST 9TH STREET
NEW YORK, N. Y. 10003

January 11, 1988

Mr. Mel Tomlinson
3812 Heathrow Drive
Winston-Salem, NC   27127

Dear Mel,

    I talked at length with the chancellor this morning about you and the situation. As an artist you cannot be bettered. How much experience have you had in executive work and how much experience have you had in judging and controlling human beings? These questions I couldn't answer. I think you must make this quite clear to the people who are looking for a replacement for Bobby.

    All good wishes for the new year!

Affectionately,

Agnes de Mille

Agnes George de Mille
AGdM/dec

Letter to Mel from Agnes de Mille advising Mel on what he needed to do when applying for the Deanship at NCSA.

"Property of NYCB." I had worn it with pride. However, one day, when I was thirty-two and trying to sort out my future, I suddenly looked at that phrase very differently. I remember realizing that I only really belonged to God and He had never considered me "property." I flashed back to earlier days where some instructors taught with sticks and public displays of verbal abuse. I realized that I was a grown-up who had finally grown up, and I would never be "property" again. When you cannot change the things around you, it is time to change yourself. It was simply my time to go.

I do have a few lingering "what ifs." What if I had stayed? Would I have eventually moved up to Principal as my "replacement" Albert Evans did? What if Mr. B had not passed? I will never know the answers to these questions.

The company gave me two beautiful farewell performances. The first one was in Saratoga. At the end of the evening, I was given a standing ovation by the audience, and then presented with a giant teddy bear, on stage by six-year-old Matthew Drouin, the son of my dear Saratoga friends, Jacques and Mary Drouin. It was a magical, memorable evening. My second final performance was during the fall season in New York City. I had already "officially" left, but the company felt that we owed it to our audience. Both the performances were wonderful but bittersweet for me at the same time. I am not sure that I realized how many wonderful friends I had in the company, all of whom I had come to love dearly. For the first time, I realized that leaving this time was much more like leaving the School of the Arts so many years before. I was heading into the complete unknown this time. My life in the next ten years would be much more of an unknown than I could ever have guessed.

*Mel and Jerri Kumery in Balanchine's Who Cares?
New York City Ballet. © Fred Fehl, all rights reserved.*

Chapter Eleven

The Prodigal Son and His Ballerinas

The day had finally come. For so long, it had seemed distant, almost like it would never become my reality. As I walked back into my apartment to get the last items I needed to finish loading the double-parked rental van with all my worldly possessions, my phone suddenly rang and I remembered that I had not yet called the phone company to inform them that I was moving. There just seemed to be so many details to attend to.

"Hello," I said, still distracted by all the details I had to finalize. It was my doctor. He was one of the few openly "gay doctors" in New York, at the time, specializing in gay patients and issues particular to us. His office was located in Greenwich Village, the area of New York City that had been home to so many gay people and businesses for several decades. He was calling with the results of my most recent HIV test. Like most gay men who I knew in 1987, these tests were becoming a regular part of our lives. As I half-listened while still thinking about all I needed to get done, he told me that I should not be alarmed, but my test had come back "false positive," whatever that meant. I was not alarmed, not at all. I was barely paying attention. My overly-promiscuous days were long behind me, and back then I had no idea that the incubation period before becoming seriously ill could be as long as nine or ten years. In fact, no one knew that in those days. The incubation period was believed to be fairly long, by that point, around five and a half years, but no one yet knew that it could be as much as a full decade. I was quite sure that I could not possibly have contracted HIV in the past five and a half years, as during that time, I had been almost completely focused on my career at City Ballet. Almost - I was careful, always careful. HIV and AIDS had loomed at the back of every young, gay man's brain for years now. Like watching what we ate, it had become a "normal" part of our lives. The collective belief, even in the gay community, was that AIDS was out there, but it happened to someone else. The bathhouses had been closed-down finally after much fighting over whether or not to close them. Word was that the baths were where one picked up HIV due to so much promiscuous, homosexual behavior. In the gay community, the baths represented a sort of freedom to be who one was – a sexually-active gay man. This was important to a community that had long been forced to hide and lie about our truths. Aside from what the baths represented, they were also financially important to the gay owners of these businesses who were making a killing by allowing their customers to take the huge risk of possibly catching a killer disease which they knew was running rampant inside their businesses. The anti-gay powers-that-be in the New York City government were also happy to keep the baths open. After all, they reasoned, it kept the homosexuals out of the bushes in the parks.

In 1987, the truth was only just getting out to the general public that HIV/AIDS had gone beyond the world of promiscuity. The Reagan administration and those in charge of the blood supply had been swearing for years, since 1981, that all was safe for everyone except those promiscuous homosexuals, even though they had absolute proof that the blood supply was tainted with the disease, and transmitting it to around 25% of those who had need of a transfusion and/or to the hemophiliacs using factor VIII, to help their blood to clot. Heaven forbid they should sacrifice some money in the name of stopping such an evil, virulent disease.

"I'd like you to come in, Mel, and let's re-do the test," the doctor said, reiterating that there really was nothing to be concerned about.

I told him I was about ten minutes away from getting in my rental van and leaving New York City forever. "Yes, yes," I promised, "I will see someone as soon as I get to North Carolina." That was the last time I thought about it for nine years. Out of sight, out of mind.

Denial is one of the most powerful things in the world. It can keep a child from remembering the horrors of abuse. It can keep an alcoholic from knowing he is addicted. It kept me from admitting that something truly heinous had possibly invaded my body. At the time, I did not know that the HIV virus could live in your body for so many years with no symptoms. I think my denial was so complete that I decided that since I had never had any symptoms I could not possibly be sick. I'm not proud of this. Looking back, I am sure that sub-consciously I was terrified of the possible truth and that had a lot to do with my new-found sense of responsibility to my partners. During my six years at New York City Ballet, I had very few sexual encounters and was always careful to use condoms responsibly. I was older and looking for real love.

It was during the year that I spent with the Ailey company in 1976-77, when I first remember becoming aware of AIDS. It was not called AIDS then and HIV had not yet been discovered. The scourge began, officially, according to the Centers for Disease Control, on June 5, 1981, but we in the arts communities all were aware of it well before then. There had been whispers in the gay community about GRID – Gay-Related Immune Deficiency since the mid to late '70's. Too many small groups of young, gay men were getting strange, rare diseases like Pneumocystis Pneumonia and Kaposi's Sarcoma. To the many in mainstream American Christian religions, the so-far-unspoken-at-that-time opinion was that it was God's retribution for "choosing" a homosexual lifestyle. Being an active Christian, I had to allow myself to think about that possibility. I negated it quickly because the God I knew so well was loving, not vindictively evil. In those days, to many, being homosexual was considered abnormal, and no better than choosing pedophilia. It was considered a bad choice made by bad, or badly misguided, people. As the reality of life and death took root in my person during the late 1970's, I began to ask my partners to wear condoms, and I became even less frequent in my conquests. I knew what I liked and had long since come to terms with my homosexuality, but I knew that I had to be even more selective with whom I was liking it.

I remember when I first joined the New York City Ballet. There is so much pressure being the "new boy" in a ballet company. One of the first things everyone in the company wants to know is if you are straight or gay and what you might be bringing to the table. I am sure that with my being black and coming from Harlem there were even more than the usual questions that had to be answered. I was not just new. I was also different, very different. There had not been a black male dancer in the company since Mr. Mitchell left in 1966. In the same way that Mr. B liked to touch my hair, the dancers also wanted to know and understand what I was all about.

Our world was still very segregated in many ways. At the time, white people did not go above 96 Street unless they were passing through on the way to Westchester, or getting off the subway at Columbia University, an Ivy League school. There were still signs at some subway stops in Harlem warning that it was not safe to get off there. Those warnings were mostly for white people even though they did not specifically say so.

As a black man, even simply changing clothes at the New York City Ballet was awkward in the beginning. I always sought privacy. Some male dancers can be quite forward with their intentions. I remember one day, in particular. I was getting dressed in the boy's locker room at the School of American Ballet before a class with Stanley Williams. I was putting on my dance belt when

I felt a hand on my backside. I slapped it away only to realize it was Rudolf Nureyev. He was always quite forward with me whenever our paths crossed, having followed me around backstage when I was with the Dance Theatre of Harlem, both in New York and on tour in Paris. Mr. Mitchell had protected me at the time, telling Rudolf to back off and leave me alone. I was every bit as clear with Rudolf as Mr. Mitchell had been and I thought that was the end of it. I was not the least bit interested. It did not matter to me that he was a superstar. He made one last attempt while I was in Paris with the New York City Ballet, changing place cards at a formal dinner so that he could be seated next to me. He spent the entire dinner flirting with me and asking me what I was doing after dinner. I had to be even clearer, practically rude, telling him in no uncertain terms that he was barking up the wrong tree. I knew other dancers who would have jumped at the chance to be with him because of who he was, as well as several who were with him for the same reason. For me, that simply was never enough. I was not physically attracted to him and, more importantly, I felt no emotional connection to him.

By the time I had gotten to the New York City Ballet, I had learned that it was not always the wisest choice to get involved with other members of the company. Workplace romance was most often not in anyone's best interest in the ballet world as well as the business world. Unfortunately, in the ballet world, our work lives were never simply nine to five. They tended to be ten in the morning to eleven at night. In our world, there was little chance to meet "outsiders." I think I had a fling the first week I was at the New York City Ballet, mainly because everyone seemed to be trying, and, to be honest, only because I was the new boy and certain questions just need to be answered in a ballet company. Other than that, I had very little to do with the dancers and patrons there.

So much of what Mr. Mitchell had said to me about being black in the "White House" had stayed with me and I was not going to allow myself to be known for the wrong things. I was there to dance and was a bit too old at that point to play the games that I may have indulged in when I was a novice. The same was also my truth later at the North Carolina Dance Theater and the Boston Ballet. My desires were plentiful, but I did not act on many of them.

During the long drive to North Carolina, I had plenty of time alone with my thoughts. I thought about the wonderful dancers I had danced with over my twelve-year career. I especially thought about the ballerinas. To me, they were the magic. It had been drummed into my head from that first year at the North Carolina School of the Arts that my job was to support the ballerina and make her look beautiful. Throughout my career, I was always happiest to stay behind one of the many beautiful ballerinas with whom I had the honor of dancing. Mr. Mitchell repeatedly told us that the better we made the girls look, the better we looked. He made me realize that I could be the hero. I loved that feeling. I also found it kind of interesting that when I came out as gay, I was better able to communicate with my female dance partners. Our relationship seemed to me to become more professional, but more personal at the same time, because that man/woman sexual attraction was taken off the table, allowing us to more easily communicate our needs as dance partners.

I danced with so many beautiful women. Most were beautiful both outside and inside. Dancing with another person, one-on-one, is all about communication. To be successful, two must become one, very much like a marriage. The sooner in the rehearsal process that you can find this connection, the better. If you do not find it, then it is impossible to bring your audience into the fantasy that you are creating because it will not feel truthful. It will have no depth of feeling; no depth of connection. You might succeed in being beautiful, elegant, technically-precise, but you will not succeed in creating art. This is the difference. It is why great art is not, and never should be, treated as sport.

As I drove along, I remembered my very first dance partner. I had only been studying ballet for a few months, off and on, with Betty Kovach in Raleigh. Betty was the first person to "discover" me, though the press has always given Agnes de Mille that distinction. Betty was not famous like Agnes. She was a local ballet teacher in Raleigh, North Carolina, but she saw something special in me. Betty paired me with a local dancer, who, to me at the time, was a seasoned dance professional. Her name was Patsy Collins. I remembered being happy and a bit overwhelmed at the same time. How was I to handle, partner, or even make physical contact with a female, especially one who was a little bit older than me and much more mature. I remember listening so carefully to her every direction. I did my part; I did not let her fall. We performed at WRAL-TV, a local television station in Raleigh. Patsy wore a black unitard and I wore what I did not know at the time would be the first of many hated white unitards I would wear throughout my career. Thinking about this, I wondered if this might have been Patsy's first time dancing with a partner, too. There were very few boys dancing ballet in Raleigh at the time. At any rate, I am grateful that Patsy was so kind to me and so very patient. Her attitude and communication skills set me up to have enough confidence to go into many unknown situations as a professional.

When I was at the North Carolina School of the Arts, I was lucky to partner with several wonderful dancers. The first two, Stephanie Ely and Kathy Kroll, were modern dance majors, the same as me at the time. Both were strong, musical modern dancers. Stephanie went on to dance in Martha Graham's company. Kathy, I fell in love with for a short time. She was my first heterosexual love in the dance world.

When I moved to the ballet department, I was paired with some more wonderful dancers. The one I remember most is Julie Jordan, a powerhouse technician who was also quite blessed up top. She was vivacious and so strong that I believe that she did not even need a partner. She was, however, a very patient, kind person, and made me feel like I was doing a good enough job. As with all students, I made my share of mistakes, but my journey continued; and I was able to shed all my inhibitions along the way: worries about my age, my race, my lifestyle, my strength, even my aura, and the way I smelled. I always made sure to be clean and I wore cologne. The girls asked to work with me and that went a long way to helping me to become a confident partner. I loved the idea of being photographed with beautiful women. Maybe that went back to my insecurities and jealousy of my older brother, Dexter, who was so handsome and charismatic and always had girls fighting to be with him.

On Agnes de Mille's Heritage Dance Theatre tour, I partnered my classmates, Cynthia Penn and Regina Reynolds, two of the most gorgeous and smartest black girls on the tour. To this day, if we were to meet, I believe that our friendships would stand as if no time had gone by.

I have already talked about how I met and danced with Karen Brown for a Southeast Regional Ballet Association festival. It was because of that first partnership that both Karen and I were offered a place at the Dance Theatre of Harlem. When I first arrived at the Dance Theatre of Harlem, Karen and I immediately started working together to learn everything by understudying all the principals in the hopes of getting cast. We were new, and well-aware that there was a pecking order that had to be acknowledged and respected. Finally, the day came that I was taken away from Karen and asked to prepare to dance with the breathtakingly alluring Lydia Abarca. She was the unspoken ballerina of the company and an obvious favorite of Mr. Mitchell's. I do not know the details of what happened with Derek Williams, her partner before me, but I suddenly replaced him. I still cannot believe my luck when I think about this. Lydia taught me the ins and outs of how to be an even better partner and how to maintain eye contact. She would very softly say, "Stop looking at your friends. Keep your eyes on me." It was definitely not hard to do, for she was one of the most beautiful women I have ever seen. Eye contact is so important when it comes to partnering. I also learned from Lydia that a whisper between partners could be reassuring and comforting in terms of communicating with your "significant other."

I also danced with three other incredible ballerinas at the Dance Theatre of Harlem, Stephanie Dabney, Virginia Johnson, and M. Elena Carter. Stephanie was always fun, as her energy and mindset matched my own so well. She was a performer who knew how to keep the audience's attention every minute. She went on to become renowned for her interpretation of the "Firebird." Like me, Stephanie would be diagnosed with AIDS in the early 1990's and would spend years fighting many insidious infections. She would live much of her life from a wheelchair and also, like me, would be an AIDS twenty-plus year survivor.

Stephanie Dabney, Dance Theatre of Harlem's original Firebird. Photo by Martha Swope.

Virginia Johnson was tall and elegant, and so smart. She was always thoroughly prepared in every way for rehearsal and performance. Working with her, I would feel secure and strong. Virginia would go on to a second career as the first Editor-in-Chief of Pointe Magazine. It was no surprise to me, years later, to find that Virginia was Mr. Mitchell's choice as his replacement as Artistic Director of Dance Theatre of Harlem. I know that the company is in good hands.

My all-time favorite ballerina to dance with will always be the late M. Elena Carter; ballerina, friend, comedian, technician. She was a real person with personality and confidence. She will forever reign at the top of my list of ballerinas. I have neither seen nor worked with anyone better. Dancing Balanchine's *Concerto Barocco* with Elena will be eternally emblazoned in my heart. We took a lot of calculated risks that worked because we took them together. The world lost her much too soon to cancer.

At the Alvin Ailey American Dance Theatre, I was originally hired because Mr. Ailey was looking for a new partner for Judith Jamison, but I ended up partnering several other amazing dancers there as well. I remember being surprised when I first met Judy that she was not as tall as she appeared to be on stage. The magic of her charismatic stage presence and movement creates

Eddie Shellman, left, and Elena Carter, Center, with First Lady, Nancy Reagan.

that illusion. She was very welcoming and made me feel as if I had known her for years. She was completely professional in her preparations and rehearsal. I discovered that she was quite "the beast" of a consummate artist on stage. She danced circles around me. I often found myself thinking, "Judy, let me be the man, please!" I had truly met my match and I loved it. I love a challenge so dancing with Judy was something to which I always looked forward. She kept me one hundred percent present when we danced together.

Sara Yarborough was an island girl, complete with her own set of attitudes and approaches. She was always nice, but demanding, and tried hard not to ever appear needy. Sara's sound ballet background made partnering her a walk in the park. It gave us both more room to be actors as opposed to dancers working toward technical excellence. I could feel the abundance of freedom in our work together. I was to find out much later that Sara first told a certain choreographer with whom I was to dance the "Firebird," about me, setting the stage for my employment years later.

Donna Wood, another great Ailey dancer who I used to think of as Judy's double, definitely held her own. She was closest to my height of all the ballerinas with whom I have worked. Her lines went on forever and it was obvious that she enjoyed movement and moving. Of all the girls I have partnered, Donna was a bit more to move around. She was extremely tall, big-boned, and liked her food. She was not fat by any means, but with her height alone came added weight that did make one work a little harder.

Partnering Sarita Allen was a breeze. She was smaller, lightening quick, and always on her leg. She was so much fun to dance with, but our best times were spent off stage, especially when we partied all night in Brazil.

Last but certainly not least at Ailey was the unforgettable Marilyn Banks. She was hell on wheels and everyone loved her. We danced together in a ballet choreographed by fellow North Carolina School of the Arts Alum, Rael Lamb. Sometimes Marilyn could be all over the place, but I knew how happy she was that she was able to dance with me. Our partnership, and our friendship was an adventure and my happy pleasure. I loved her youthful energy and approach. She was also a very giving tour roommate, making for a passionate, though short-lived partnership off stage as well as on.

During the last six years at the New York City Ballet, I had the opportunity to work with many beautifully-trained dancers. I must talk about Heather Watts first, as she was one of my most endearing partners ever. It was with Heather that I danced for the first time at the New York City Ballet, filling in for Peter Martins that fateful performance that Anna Kiselgoff called "….one of the most dynamic and electric in years." Heather was always quite sure of herself and willing to take risks. She was an audience favorite as you could always expect excitement from Heather. It would not be a dull or predictable performance if she was dancing. During those years, Heather was thought to be the "tough girl," but I saw right through her act from our first rehearsal and gained her respect. She had my respect from the first five minutes of that first *Agon* rehearsal. She had a slight curvature of the spine that made partnering a bit awkward at times, but she functioned quite well with it. She was no doubt the strongest and most fearless ballerina in the New York City Ballet back then. She always amazed and inspired me and made me and her audience want to see, and know, more.

The first Balanchine ballerina I danced with was Susan Freedman, whom I had become great friends with on the set of *The Spellbound Child*. Susie was and still is a beautiful woman, and

Susan Freedman as Coffee and Mel as Chocolate in Balanchine's, "The Nutcracker.

one of the kindest, warmest people I have had the pleasure to both know and dance with. Stunningly beautiful, she was both leggy and elegant, making the audience wish they were in my place.

Suzanne Farrell was always an enigma to me. She was a principal dancer, a star ballerina, and always seemed to be a bit of an island unto herself. She had her own friends, a small group, and kept to herself. I was intrigued and a little nervous, I must admit, when I found myself on the schedule to dance as her "Dark Angel" in *La Valse*. Suzanne danced with ease and without effort. She knew where everything was or was supposed to be; the music, the props, the costumes, and, of course, the dancers around her. She had total control and commitment, a true ballerina. There was always an aloofness to Suzanne, on or off stage. It worked. It was hers and it was part of her own special magic. I was in awe of her always and just a little intimidated.

Merrill Ashley had probably the most perfect technique of anyone with whom I had ever danced. Her proportions were perfect, from head to toe and she was all muscle. I found her body to be a bit boxier than most, but she was so strong that she did not need any help from me. She was built for speed and perfection. Merrill was also a kind and generous teacher. At one point, I was asked by artistic director, Salvatore Aiello to guest with the North Carolina Dance Theater. My friend, Karen Brown, who was still dancing at the Dance Theatre of Harlem at that time, wanted very much to be my partner for *Allegro Brilliante* in my hometown of Raleigh. I was not convinced that Karen's technique would do that ballet justice, and had planned to ask either Heather Watts or Lourdes Lopez to dance it with me. Karen was adamant that she could and would handle *Allegro Brilliante* well. I asked Merrill if she would coach Karen and told Karen that if Merrill thought she could handle it, then we would dance it together. Merrill was a brilliant, generous coach and Karen not only surprised me with what she could do, she surprised herself. I was so proud and honored to dance that ballet with Karen, one of my best friends.

When I danced with Darci Kistler, she was still a young colt, only sixteen, but an extremely talented one. She knew what she wanted and was determined to have it. She was very young and I attribute her demanding personality and arrogant neediness to her youth. At one point, she told me that there was no need to hold her so much, insinuating that she was stronger than those girls uptown with whom I was used to working. I must believe that her attitude was the arrogance often equated to youthful innocence. I did not let her antics or her attitude bother me. I was older and I like to think at least a little wiser. She was an amazing talent who went on to have a stellar career. I look back and am very happy and honored that I got to work with her.

Dancing with Vera Zorina, one of Mr. B's wives, and Karin Von Aroldingen, Mr. B's confidant, made me a little nervous. They were seasoned professionals who had no trouble voicing how they felt, or what they wanted and needed. They both had Mr. B's ear, so I completely deferred to them, doing whatever I needed to do to make them happy.

Maria Calegari, one of the feisty redheads, who I remember fondly, was my partner in Joseph Duell's *Creation du Monde*. I will never forget my reaction on stage when Maria purposely grazed my crotch with her hipbone. I completely lost my concentration. Maybe she thought I needed that to maintain my character. Maria was always musical. Her timing was perfect.

When I partnered Maria, there was very little for me to do. She and Valentina Koslova, though very thin and tiny, were so muscularly-built that I had to use more muscle and thought before even attempting to lift them. I made sure to do my weight-training exercises whenever I was working with them, not because of their weight, but because they were deceptively powerful.

Kyra Nichols was another one of my favorites to watch and with whom to dance. She was arguably one of Jerry's most adored ballerinas. Her work was almost predictable because of that unwavering technique, so rock-steady and reliable. I witnessed her strength and control even when she faltered. Thinking of her reminded me of something that Mr. Mitchell taught me. He advised us men to watch the girls in class for their timing and the way they danced. This, he told us, would make us much better partners.

I found Stephanie Saland to be the most physically beautiful woman in a company full of physically beautiful women. Her deep-set eyes were inviting and almost mesmerizing. She gave the appearance of being a big thinker, but I am not so sure about that. Stephanie had trouble learning and maintaining choreography. However, when she finally got it, she danced the hell out of it. I think my biggest disappointment while at the

Stephanie Saland, dancing Balanchine's Divertimento #15. © *Steven Caras, all rights reserved.*

New York City Ballet was that although Stephanie and I learned and worked hard at *Bugaku* we were never cast to do it because Mr. B died during that time.

I was very lucky to be paired often with Lourdes Lopez. We, along with Patricia McBride, "Patty-Mac," as I nicknamed her, and who regretfully I never did get to perform with, were often the first to arrive to warm up before classes. Patty was always so kind to everyone, warm and easy-going. She did not have a mean bone in her body. I loved to watch her make an exit from stage. With those amazing eyes and that charismatic personality, she took every single audience member with her right through the wings and backstage.

Lourdes was always a true professional, willing to take on any role with total commitment and verve. Her technique was flawless. She had a solid, down-to-earth, secure personality, and a humility that was just so welcoming and honest. I suspect that it probably serves her very well these days as Artistic Director of the Miami City Ballet Company. She was a dark-eyed, lovely young woman that I took great pleasure in escorting on stage. I will always be so grateful that it was Lourdes with whom I was scheduled to dance that sad evening following Mr. B's funeral. Lourdes and I also had great fun performing together at Studio 54, dancing a John Taras ballet there together.

Judith Fugate displaying her amazing strength and power.
© Steven Caras, all rights reserved.

The one dancer in the New York City Ballet that I thought was going to be a chore to lift and partner was Judith Fugate. Judy was not that tall, and she appeared to me to be fleshier than most of the others. As it turned out, next to M. Elena Carter at the Dance Theatre of Harlem, Judy Fugate was my all-time favorite partner. Everything she did was perfect. Her preparations for all the jumps and take-offs were gracious, with appropriate warning and perfect timing. I could not have asked for, let alone received, a better partner. I cannot sing enough praises about this ballerina who also happened to have the smallest and most beautiful feet I have ever seen. Judy was complete. She had a real, and very lovely personality, and elegant artistry. Her supple, hyper-extended knees made for beautiful lines. She was flawless and consistently worked hard.

I learned something important from each of these amazing ballerinas. I had, and still have, great love for them all. I appreciate their loveliness, confidence and most of all their beauty and artistry. I thank each of them for the opportunity to dance with them because each of them were such important parts of the lessons for my artistic journey. Thanks to them, when I teach pas de deux classes, I do so using what I refer to as the "Light-Touch Technique." It is all about developing our ability to communicate need, thought, touch and response.

During the drive to Winston-Salem, I also thought about my family. I had spent years trying not to think about them. Of course, I visited during holidays, and I always included my family whenever I received an honor or was involved in a special performance. When Heather Watts and I danced at the opening festivities of the Stevens Center Theater in Winston-Salem for my alma mater, invited by Robert Lindgren, my family was honored, put up in a beautiful hotel and delivered to the theater in limousines. Dancing on that Gala was such an honor and such a high for me. To see my family, but especially Mrs. Tomlinson, arrive in limousines dressed to kill, to see me perform was such a highlight for me. As it happened, it was one week before Mr. Balanchine passed. I remember musing how many incredible highs in my life were followed by incredible lows. My life was to continue to follow that path.

I also remembered the time when I was honored in Wilmington, North

Mel arriving to perform at the opening of Stevens Center, in Winston-Salem, NC, with his sister, Ellen, and other family members. Photo courtesy of UNCSA.

Carolina, by Governor James Hunt and he presented me with the $10,000 North Carolina Prize for my contributions in the arts. My family was treated like royalty and put up in a gorgeous hotel penthouse. At that time, a journalist from the *New York Times* came down to Clayton, North Carolina, with me to meet my family and write about them.

There were so many things that had come about for my family because of my career. I was Bill Cosby's double in *"Leonard, Part 6,"* a comedy about a secret agent (Cosby) who used dancing ballet *en pointe* as his secret weapon. It is arguably not only one of Bill Cosby's worst movies, but is considered one of the worst movies ever made, by many sources, including Roger Ebert's list of most-hated films, and the Golden Raspberry Awards. Even Cosby denounced the film publicly in the weeks before it came out, and he was the writer and a producer, as well as the star.

This was way before any of Cosby's current sexual scandals. I knew nothing of any of that, though I will say this: I was asked to watch the door during what I believed were consensual trysts. During the filming, he offered to share his trailer with me. Ten years earlier, I had been in *A Piece of the Action*, another one of his movies, directed by Sydney Poitier and reviewed favorably by critics. We talked quite a bit and he asked me about my family and offered to call them to say hello. I think my mother almost had a heart attack when she picked up the phone and found Bill Cosby on the other end. Mrs. Tomlinson talked about "Bill" for years after. These exciting opportunities were a double-edged sword for me and my family. Though exciting, they tended to cause rifts between us, with my family seeming always to assume that I had become arrogant and my feeling that jealousy on their part was keeping us separated.

Marjorieline and Tommy Tomlinson, Mel's parents were getting older.

I knew that Mrs. Tomlinson had not changed over the years. She was still the same bitter woman who had raised me, although, according to my father, when I was not around, all she could do was talk about me and how proud she was. He said she constantly bragged about me to anyone who would listen. I cannot for the life of me remember a single time when she told me she was proud.

I knew my parents were both getting older and neither was doing great health-wise. They were both consumed with serious health issues. My father was now completely blind due to glaucoma. My mother had developed Type-2 diabetes and had many health issues, due to the fact that she still drank Pepsi like it was water, and smoked heavily. My youngest sister, Janie, also had diabetes, Type-1, and her health had greatly deteriorated. She, like my father, had also lost her sight.

Marlon, my younger brother, by this time known only by his nickname, "Hazard," had already started his life of petty crime and drugs and was well-acquainted with the revolving door at the local jail. Dexter had his own brushes with the law out in California both before and after getting out of the army. Back in North Carolina now, Dexter had served his time in jail and moved on.

Ellen and Tommina were both married and raising families of their own. Ellen had gone back to school and become the first female in our family to graduate from college. I was very proud of her for this, though I never told her so. I allowed our sibling rivalry to keep me from telling her how I felt. I think I was at a point in my life where I longed to be closer to them all, but had absolutely no idea as to how to tell them how I felt. I wanted to believe that it would be best for all of us if I was closer to home. That feeling of family that I had when I danced at the Dance Theatre of Harlem had been sadly lacking at the New York City Ballet, ever since Mr. B had passed. There was a void in my life and I believed filling it with my family was what I needed.

I must admit that I was a bit nervous about spending the next year teaching on the faculty at the School of the Arts. While I had been gone, some new teachers had joined the staff, the most notorious new faculty member being Melissa Hayden, who had been a principal dancer with the New York City Ballet, retiring at age fifty. Melissa immediately took me under her wing. She considered us to be family since we were both part of the Balanchine "empire." The other newer/younger teachers were either from American Ballet Theatre – Frank Smith and Fanchon Cordell, or North Carolina Dance Theater – Melinda Lawrence and Dayna Fox. All had been wonderful dancers and had the commitment and talent needed to be brilliant teachers.

I moved into a two-bedroom apartment on a golf course, near Melissa's house and worked very closely with her. Melissa was a handful, and like Agnes de Mille, she never held back her personal opinions about anything. I learned so much from Melissa: she taught me about staging ballets, teaching and getting everything possible out of the students, even about judging competitions and choreographing. The most important things she passed on to me were how to work within the political atmosphere of the university system and the importance of serving as a role model for the next generation of dancers. There are many people who will scoff at the idea of Melissa knowing anything about being a good role model. To say that she was tough is an understatement. She was relentlessly tough, but not only with the students, with herself. Melissa knew how to get what she wanted. She knew how to give 300%, in order to make sure she got what she wanted. She could be brutal, but she could also be protective and kind. If you wanted to get her attention in a good way, you had to be talented and, even more importantly, know how to consistently work hard in every single class. Melissa was always honest with her opinions. "Honey....Can you type? No? Well you should learn." "Honey....Can't you count? And one and one and one and one….."

Melissa Hayden, former principal dancer with the NYCB, was a much loved, and sometimes feared, teacher at UNCSA. Photo courtesy of UNCSA.

Melissa's memory for details was off the charts and her keen awareness of others' strengths and weaknesses was astounding. I loved that she did not care one bit about what others seemed to think of her. She was a secure woman, almost to the point of defensiveness, a great person, wife, mother, and a hell of a good cook, but most of all she was a great friend, teacher and coach.

Melissa made dancers. American Ballet Theatre principal ballerina Gillian Murphy is her most well-known student/disciple. She also made a beautiful, young black male dancer named Jerome Johnson, who later joined the New York City Ballet. It is said that if you survived studying with "Millie" you could probably find yourself hirable with nothing more than a visual recommendation. You could tell who her students were by the way they thought and moved. Her presence increased the enrollment of the dance department. Mr. Lindgren had hired her, as he knew what a draw she would be. He and Melissa went way back, having both grown up in Canada and worked together for many years in several companies, including the New York City Ballet.

Once, Melissa and I were taking a class at NCSA. I don't remember who was teaching, but we, and some of the other teachers still took class sometimes. On this particular day, for some reason, Melissa decided to take the barre *en pointe*. She had not been *en pointe* for a number of years. At the end of the barre, we sat down on the floor to stretch out our muscles and Melissa whispered to me, "Mel, I can't move! I need you to pick me up, pretend we are doing a pas de deux, and carry me out of here. Take me to my car and don't let anyone know about this!" I did exactly as I was asked to do, and this is the first I have ever spoken about it.

Melissa had the rights to stage any Balanchine ballet she wanted without all the paperwork and costs. This was great for the School. She used many of these ballets to train her dancers to move quickly and to hone their techniques. I often watched her set these ballets, many of which I knew and had danced. Melissa even cast me in some of the ballets she set for the school. Looking back, I can now see that she, like many people, did not think I was ready to hang up my dancing shoes yet. I was not, but I was also not going to admit that to anyone because after three years of being pretty much ignored by Peter Martins, my confidence in myself as a dancer was almost non-existent. I had convinced myself that I wanted to move on and do something else. It would take Salvatore Aiello, the artistic director of the North Carolina Dance Theater, to change my mind.

I met Sal Aiello while I was dancing with the New York City Ballet. He brought the North Carolina Dance Theater to New York for a short season at the Brooklyn Academy of Music (BAM). I loved everything about the company. The dancers were beautiful and Sal's choreography was incredible. One piece in particular, called "*Satto*," blew me away. After seeing it in a performance at BAM, I went backstage and met Sal. I told him that I would love to dance that piece. Sal said that he would love to have me in as a guest artist to dance *Allegro Brilliante*. I agreed to do it, and Sal would then let me dance *Satto* on the same program. This was the performance during which my old friend, Karen Brown, from the Dance Theatre of Harlem, danced with me. Sal treated us like movie stars and paid us very well.

I remember how wonderful I had felt during that whole experience. I still miss that feeling. I miss the joy that came from moving and performing. It was another piece of my innocence that seemed to have been whittled away. I remember when I first arrived in Winston-Salem wondering if I would ever find that feeling in anything else. I hoped that teaching would bring me that joy.

My first few months back at the North Carolina School of the Arts were a bit of an adjustment. The hardest thing for me to get used to were the faculty meetings. Here I was, no longer a young ballet dancer, but now a thirty-three-year-old teacher, and I had to sit through these very contentious meetings. There were so many talented egos in that room, all trying to talk over each other. Melissa would stand in the doorway, half in and half out while she smoked a cigarette, one second blowing smoke out into the hallway, the next second forcefully expressing her opinions. There were old school and new school differences, as the younger teachers tried to get the older teachers to understand that things were changing in the ballet world and, to be competitive for the few jobs available, our students needed to be more well-rounded. Some of us wanted to offer modern classes in the ballet department and visa versa. This was an unheard-of idea at the time. Interestingly, Mr. Lindgren was having the very same battle in New York at that time at the School of American Ballet. Even though age-wise Mr. Lindgren would have been part of the "old guard" he was always very forward-thinking and would have agreed with the younger teachers about this.

All in all, it was a good year for me. I loved the students, and was close to many of them. I loved being in a position to mentor so many talented young dancers. I spent time with the dancers outside of class, often eating lunch with them in the cafeteria. I felt that I probably knew better than most of the teachers what the students were thinking and feeling. In my mind, that was

NCSA dance faculty and accompanists, early 1980's.
Photo courtesy of UNCSA.

a good thing. I was confident that I would be a great Dean. Unfortunately for me, that was not to be. Many of the faculty members felt that I was too friendly with the students and would not be firm enough to be the Dean. The job went to Susan McGee McCullough, a former Harkness Ballet and Netherlands Dance Theatre dancer who was much better than I at setting boundaries and leading the faculty negotiations on various issues. Looking back, I believe that Susan was the best choice, and I am happy that my life went in another direction.

Chapter Twelve

Diva Days

I won't lie - I was disappointed not to be named the Dean of Dance at the University of North Carolina School of the Arts. I honestly thought I would have that job. Once again, God knew something I did not know. I had little time to mourn the loss of the deanship, however; Salvatore Aiello called me almost immediately and convinced me that my dancing days were not over and that I should join the North Carolina Dance Theater as a principal dancer. I was flattered by what Sal said to me. He made me begin to believe in myself as a dancer again. For the first time in years, I was excited to get back into the daily grind of sweat, sore muscles, and both physical and mental exhaustion.

Aside from being very happy to be dancing again, I was also very happy to be able to stay in Winston-Salem. Over the past year, I had made several new friends, all of whom were very important to me. Some were dancers and choreographers; others were poets and writers. All were teachers of one sort or another and all taught me important lessons.

One of the brightest lights in my life that year was Maya Angelou. One day, out of the blue, I was summoned to Maya's home. "Summoned" is, quite frankly, the only way to describe it. Jim Steele, from nearby Wake Forest University, where Maya was a permanent fellow, contacted me and drove me to her home later that day.

"Maya would like to see you," said Jim, rather like the messenger of a mob boss. When I questioned him as to why, he simply said that Maya would like to meet me.

Maya Angelou, born Marguerite Ann Johnson in St. Louis, Missouri, was one of my idols. Meeting her was a highlight in my life, but to become her friend was more than I ever could have hoped. The day I met her, I was welcomed by her wide, very genuine smile. I was surprised and flattered that she knew who I was and had followed my career. Her seductive, raspy voice captured my full attention right away. Overwhelmed by her intimidating stature, and, at the same time, by her very calm demeanor, I clearly was not on the same level of notoriety as Maya Angelou. I was thrilled to be accepted into her group of friends and acquaintances. Maya chose the people with whom she associated very carefully and purposefully. When she chose to allow me to join her select circle, I felt validated as an important part of the arts world. Maya did not mingle with uninteresting people.

Maya Angelou had an early career as a calypso singer and dancer.

Ushering me in to her lavish abode, she made me feel immediately at home. Her house had three levels. I believe the kitchen was her favorite place. She was a wonderful cook, especially of good old home-cooked southern cuisine. Downstairs, there was a music room, complete with everything one could possibly need to listen to or make music. I was surprised to learn that she was working on a rap song. I had only known of Maya Angelou as a poet and novelist. I was pleasantly surprised to find that she had been a singer, an actress and a dancer. She had even danced with Alvin Ailey as part of a performing duo known as "Al and Rita." The duo did not last long as both had destinies to fulfill that did not include the other. She first became known as a Calypso singer and dancer in nightclubs in San Francisco, and even recorded an album called *Miss Calypso*.

From her dancing past, Maya knew many of the same people in the dance world that I knew. The dance world is so small with, I believe, no more than one degree of separation between dancers worldwide.

Throughout this initial visit, Maya was sizing me up. She wanted to know everything about me, my past as well as my future plans. As always, the minute I opened my mouth, I began talking about myself. I pretty much told Maya everything about my life. Once I started talking about myself, it was virtually impossible to stop. I don't know if I thought that I was so very interesting or if it was that I just like to hear myself speak. I know that I was flattered that someone like Maya Angelou would be interested in my life story. When I finally finished, the conversation became rather serious, as she coached me on how to give a proper interview. She admonished me not to tell everything to anyone, but especially to the press.

Maya said, "If there are ten things about you that you know are true, only give them two or three." In other words, stay in control of the interview so that only the things that one is comfortable with appear in the press. Always hold back a few things for another time. Maya taught me about shielding myself from the pitfalls of being a black celebrity. It was more important for a black celebrity not to be caught in a scandal than it was for a white, because we were expected to be scandalous by the white world, and we must never prove them right. We had an obligation to represent the black community well.

I don't know why, but I told Maya that I, too, was a writer of prose and poetry and would love to have her read a few selections of mine. She simply refused, stating that it would not be a good idea, as sometimes people will inadvertently borrow your materials without realizing what they have done. Not to be dissuaded, I then asked if I could recite just a few of my poems for her. She listened patiently, in a very pensive manner and made no memorable comment that I can remember.

Maya threw a lot of great parties for her friends, many of whom were well-known writers, actors, singers, ministers and even royalty. The food was always amazing and never catered. Maya cooked it all herself as an act of pure love for the people she cared about. She always let me bring a friend, so many of my family members, friends and members of my church got to attend Maya's parties. She made it her business to introduce herself to everyone. No one at a Maya Angelou party was allowed to feel less important than anyone else. This was a woman who never put on airs. She spoke her mind, always without a filter, and could cut you up with her wit and her perfect intellect.

On one occasion, the singer/songwriter team of Ashford and Simpson were there. I couldn't resist asking them about "Ain't No Mountain High Enough," which they had written for Diana Ross, whose rendition brought the song and the writers great fame. Nick Ashford told me that he composed that song in one afternoon while hanging out in Central Park. I was amazed. I realized that the talent part of any artist's equation was the easy, God-given part. It was getting the public to notice that took the time and energy, not to mention the daily consistency and discipline of simply doing the work. I was so inspired as I watched Nick find his way downstairs to Maya's music room to work on a tag for her rap song. What a magnificent collaboration I got to witness that night. The energy in the room reminded me of another great collaboration I once got to watch years before while at the Dance Theatre of Harlem. It was Stevie Wonder and his friends working on the album *Songs in the Key of Life*. There is a collective energy of talent that feeds upon itself and thus nourishes the very heart and soul of art. I always feel so blessed when I get to see another person's genius and works-in-progress.

I would get to perform on stage with Maya just once, during what came to be the first World AIDS Day Celebration. It was also the only time that Maya and I would have a very heated debate/argument as to what I chose to present. I had choreographed a solo about the anguish of succumbing to AIDS. I wanted to dance the solo totally nude, with low lighting to emphasize the nature of the affair. Maya was adamant that I should not dance it nude because, in her opinion, I would be selling myself in a completely exploitive manner to those who so far, respected me. Though I felt strongly that my idea was right for the piece, I let Maya win, deferring to the wisdom of a woman I deeply respected. As a compromise, I wore a unitard, dyed to match my skin tones.

The performance went well and was quite a success. Looking back, it gives me chills because at the time, I had no idea that the choreography I had created foretold the agony of my future ordeal.

I remember when Maya became the Poet Laureate for President Bill Clinton's Inauguration. Her classic poem, *A Rock, A Tree*, ... was wonderful. I remember feeling that I heard some of my poetic thoughts in the contents of her work. I was honored if I did. It reminded me vaguely of my poem, *Autumn Leaves*. I am not insinuating that Maya Angelou borrowed from me. I am saying that we had a special relationship and shared a lot of our personal selves with each other. Maya helped me to open my eyes about expressing myself in other parts of my being aside from dance. She taught me how to share more, and how to care more, and even how to learn about myself through how others

Mabel Robinson teaching at UNCSA mid to late 1980's.
Photo courtesy of UNCSA.

saw me, the *real* Mel, as opposed to "Mel," the personality.

When Maya passed, I did not go to her funeral. I knew it would be a circus of people there to see and be seen and I did not want my last thoughts of Maya to include that. I stayed home and I said goodbye to her alone. I think about her and miss her every day.

My other dear friend from that year of teaching at the school was Mabel Robinson, who was also teaching at the North Carolina School of the Arts. Mabel had a stellar career on Broadway and in film, working as a dancer/singer/actor and as a choreographer. She is best known for her work on the movie, *The Wiz*, as well as *Your Arms Too Short to Box with God, Porgy and Bess* and many other Broadway shows. She and her soulmate, Geraldine Hooper, were my neighbors. Mabel had a thirteen-year-old son named Joe who had been taking the contemporary dance classes from his mother and now wanted to start studying ballet with me. I found Joe to be quite articulate and very engaging. He was beyond his years in maturity. Joe had grown up around adults, specifically, theatre people. He was already a seasoned professional in demeanor.

Joe and I rather quickly formed a bond that went beyond teacher/student and I began to assume fatherly responsibilities for Joe. Mabel did not mind at all.

Mabel Robinson:

> *When Mel and I first met, he was going on to the second plateau of life when you share what you have learned. As he realized his purpose at that time, he influenced my son greatly.*

Mabel was happy that Joe had found a father figure, as his birth father Clerow Wilson, better known as Flip Wilson, had never stepped up to acknowledge and raise Joe as his son. The famous 1970's comedian who invented the TV character, "Geraldine," on his top-rated comedy show *The Flip Wilson Show* on NBC from 1970-1974, had several other children from his marriages. Joe had never met his father or step-siblings. To me, sometimes he looked very much like his mother, but he had the mannerisms and personality of his father. I do somewhat see his father in Joe's physical looks, but well-tempered with his mother's strength of character. His sense of humor and timing definitely were, and still are, that of his birth father. His comedic timing is uncanny. Joe accepted me for me and respected me and my past successes. There were times when Joe defended me against naysayers. As time went on, Joe started referring to me as his father. My heart and my brain knew I had a son. I even allowed my family to know about Joe, my son. I did not tell them that he was not my birth son. Even though they all knew I was gay, I still felt that I needed them to see me as "masculine" enough to create this wonderful son.

Mabel liked that I had taken Joe under my wing. She even re-staged a contemporary piece for Joe and me to dance together for the first National Black Theatre Festival in Winston-Salem. "I Gotta Keep Moving," a piece from a 1972 Broadway show called *Don't Bother Me, I Can't Cope* that was written by Micki Grant and had enjoyed a successful run of over a thousand performances on Broadway. It was an amazing piece about finding the strength and fortitude to carry on. Since the performance was for the opening of the North Carolina Black Repertory Company, and involved several artists of national stature, a critic from the *New York Times* came down to Winston-Salem and reviewed it. It was quite a smash. It is a performance that I treasure on so many levels, but most of all because I got to dance it with my son.

Years later when I became ill, Joe and his friend, Ajani often helped to take care of me. Joe had recently lost one of his good friends to AIDS and he did not want to lose me, too. His need motivated me to fight hard not to let him go through the pain of loss again. I was best man at Joe's wedding. I am the only grandfather on Joe's side of the family, Papi Mel, that his four sons know. I love being a part of the Robinson clan, especially as my lifestyle, and the times in which I lived, never afforded me this type of family experience. I am thankful that I had the opportunity to choose and be chosen to be a part of this wonderful family. As Mabel often says, "We are lucky when we have the opportunity to choose who will be part of our family."

After Joe's first son, Joseph Robinson II, was born, Joe started using his middle name, Kierron, so the family would not have to resort to distinguishing him from his son by calling him "Joseph-Mabel's son." Kierron has grown into a good man who takes care of his family. He works as an electrical technician in Atlanta in theatre and has a wonderful knowledge of the theater, actors and, of course, dancers. I'm very proud of him.

Even though my time as a full-time teacher at the University of North Carolina School of the Arts had ended and I was back to dancing full-time, now with the North Carolina Dance Theater, I still kept a good relationship with the school. Thanks to my strong relationships with my dear friends who also taught at the University of North Carolina School of the Arts, I still taught for them during the summer intensive sessions when the North Carolina Dance Theater was on hiatus.

For the next two years, the company kept its home base at the school in

Winston-Salem. Mr. Lindgren had been offered a job that he simply could not refuse. He would move to New York that year to take over Lincoln Kirstein's duties at the New York City Ballet and School of American Ballet. He chose to turn NCDT over to Sal, who had been the main choreographer for the company for several years at that point.

NCSA was growing and changing quite a bit at that time, making it increasingly difficult for Sal to reach agreements with the school's administration regarding rehearsal space scheduling. Sal became convinced that if the company was to continue to grow, it would need its own space. Sharing with the School of the Arts had become nearly impossible.

The North Carolina Dance Theater had been set up from day one by Robert Lindgren as a touring company. The company had toured worldwide in the past, garnering a reputation as a top-notch ballet company of soloist-calibre dancers. Unfortunately, touring had gotten more and more expensive over the years. By the time I joined the company, it was struggling and no longer did many international tours. Like many ballet companies, the North Carolina Dance Theater was at a point where they had amassed quite a bit of debt. Gas, hotels, food were all much more expensive in the eighties than they had been in the seventies. Paying for all of that on top of livable wages made Sal sure that touring was killing the company.

Sal Aiello and Bobby Lindgren. Photo courtesy of UNCSA.

We toured on an old, blue-painted school bus. The "Blue Goose," as we affectionately called her, was, I believe, acquired by Sal. I think it must have been a tour bus for a group of musicians previously because it reminded me of *The Partridge Family*, a 1970's sitcom TV show about a musical group/family that traveled together on a bus. Our biggest fear was that the "Blue Goose" would someday permanently breakdown somewhere between Winston-Salem and God knows where.

The interior of the "Blue Goose," which had the company name painted on the outside, had been tricked out complete with a lounge area in the back, a halfway decent bathroom and several sleeper births. We could travel comfortably, though not in the style in which I had grown accustomed to while at the New York City Ballet. For me, the days of luxury hotels, airplanes and limousines were now a distant, fond memory, but I did not mind at all. The "Blue Goose" helped us all to become much more appreciative of the simple things that life had to offer. We also learned to appreciate each other more due to the long drives in close quarters.

The bus made plenty of stops along the way for food, bodily relief, and sometimes just to stretch our legs. There is only so much one can do on a bus. We wrote, played word games, listened to music, reviewed choreography and played cards. For me, these were unforgettable times. All in all, there were between sixteen and eighteen of us on any given tour. We were like a huge family, with Sal as our head of the household, a benevolent and loving father figure who made the rules.

The Blue Goose, NCDT's tour bus.

My favorite tour on that bus was a long one. We drove all the way to Nevada. For the first time, I think I really "saw" the country as I had never allowed myself to see it before. Back in the Heritage Dance Theatre days, with Miss de Mille, we had done long bus tours, too, but I was much younger then and spent most of my time talking to Kevin and the other dancers, doing homework, or fantasizing about my future. Now, in my mid-thirties, I had grown to be a bit more introspective. My realities had been different than most of the other dancers in the company, all of whom were much younger than me and had not yet danced with major ballet companies.

Sal instinctively knew what each of us needed emotionally. He was amazing in that way. He treated me like a star, something my fragile ego needed very much at the time. I think Sal worried a bit that I would grow weary of the level at which this company worked, lived, and traveled. Sal had danced with the Harkness Ballet back in the days when Rebecca Harkness behaved as if she had all the money in the world, lavishing luxury on her dancers in the form of trips to the Bahamas, plastic surgery, growth hormone shot trips to Switzerland, porcelain-capped teeth, and first-class tours to Monte Carlo and all the top capitals of Europe. He instinctively understood that traveling on a blue school bus might be a bit of a let-down for me. In reality, it was not a let-down at all. I felt loved and appreciated by my director, by all the dancers and by our audiences. More important, I felt completely sated artistically, something that I had yet to feel anywhere else. Salvatore Aiello and the North Carolina Dance Theater gave me what I had worked and longed for my entire dancing life. I felt like Dorothy returning home from Oz. There simply was no place like home, and I was home.

At some point, I do not remember exactly when, the "Blue Goose" took her final breath. It appeared that the cost of needed repairs had a lot to do with its lack of continued use. She was sold on State Surplus for $250, and spent the rest of her life transporting seafood from the coast to Raleigh.

As I've already said, the company had built its reputation from touring. In 1982, the National Endowment of the Arts named the North Carolina Dance Theater as the country's highest-rated touring company. Most of the company's budget from its inception had come from touring. The company did not travel in style, especially in the beginning. The hotels we used were third rate at best. Touring, even in the best of circumstances is difficult. When it is your life 24/7, it can be exhausting and takes its toll on the dancers both physically and mentally.

Sal had done his share of touring, first, as a soloist with the Joffrey and Harkness Ballet companies in the 1960's, and later as a principal with the Royal Winnepeg Ballet in Canada. None of those companies traveled the way the North Carolina Dance Theater did. I believe that Sal wanted more for all of us. He became convinced that touring costs were getting worse and worse and there was no way to upgrade the tours to a more comfortable status. I believe that these worries were Sal's alone, as the dancers, including me, were so happy to be working for Salvatore Aiello that we would have followed him anywhere without a second thought. This is high praise coming from me, as the North Carolina Dance Theater was not a union company and I have always been very much pro-union. Dancers are in a position where they have no power. It is a business with a 96% unemployment rate. With so many dancers waiting in the wings for their chance to have a job, individual working dancers are not considered to be the major asset in any ballet company. AGMA, our union, is very necessary. I must admit that being non-union, Sal did get away with a lot with which he would not normally have gotten away. We often arrived at a venue, jumped off the "Blue Goose" and went straight into the theater for a performance. The younger dancers did not know that many times they were being asked to do more than what was appropriate. Even to me, someone who knew better, it was absolutely alright because it was Salvatore Aiello doing the asking. I could see Sal's vision. It was infectious. I wanted to see the company grow and thrive as much as Sal did.

The thought of having a home that could support two full seasons a year for the company, the way the larger professional companies were supported appealed to Sal. He knew that would never happen in Winston-Salem. The city was just not big enough.

From the company's earliest years, some "powers that be" in the city of Charlotte had expressed an interest in having the company move there. Exactly how it came about, I do not know, but Sal announced that we were moving the company to Charlotte. The decision to make the move seemed quite sudden to me. None of the dancers, myself included, had any idea how much debt the company had amassed, or that money was owed to some very generous - and patient - city leaders in Winston-Salem. It was not until much later, after the move, that the Winston-Salem Journal published articles detailing the company's fiscal woes.

Many of the dancers who had been with the company for years chose not to move to Charlotte. Some felt that it would be a good time to make some changes themselves. Sal hired quite a few younger dancers fresh out of the school. These were dancers at the beginning of their careers who were willing to work for apprentice wages. As a result, the company that originally moved to Charlotte was not as strong, or as large, as the previous version of the company had been. Sal relied on the use of my name to help raise money for the company. I was fine with that. I believed then and I still believe that Sal was one of the finest choreographers of the 20th century. I was happy to help him in any way that I could.

Sal hoped to set down roots in Charlotte, at first exploring the idea of joining forces with a top ballet school in the city, the Charlotte City Ballet School.

In co-author, Claudia Folts's words:

> At the same time that the North Carolina Dance Theater was planning its' move to Charlotte, the Louisville Ballet Company was negotiating with the Charlotte City Ballet to join forces in a sister-city collaboration. The local newspapers tried hard to turn it all into an ugly competition between Louisville Ballet and North Carolina Dance Theatre, with Charlotte being the grand prize. Those of us involved in the process did not care at all about competing with each other. We all wanted what we perceived was in the best

interest of Charlotte. Eventually, under pressure from those with financial clout in Charlotte, Louisville Ballet pulled their offer. Charlotte City Ballet, knowing that a ballet school simply cannot be expected to shoulder the financial burdens of a professional ballet company, chose not to join forces with North Carolina Dance Theater. Sal ultimately started his own school, originally called "Dance Place." His vision included seeing the school grow into a fabulous training ground for serious young dancers. The school would feed the company in the same way that the School of American Ballet fed the New York City Ballet. He became convinced that this school would make enough money to support the company financially while they built community support and grew without the exhaustive burden of touring. It was a naïve and radical, new idea for the company, an idea with which Robert Lindgren, the founding director, was not entirely on board. Mr. Lindgren had already moved to New York and taken over from the retired Lincoln Kirstein at the New York City Ballet. He was still a board member of the North Carolina Dance Theater at the time, but after the move, Sal decided new blood was needed. It was then that he also decided to change the spelling of the word "Theater" to "Theatre" in the company's name. Mr. Lindgren was not entirely happy with any of this, but he still believed in Sal as the brilliant choreographer that he was.

The company's first home in Charlotte was a broken-down building with no heat. The use of the building had been donated by a local commercial realtor, but we would not have it for long, as it soon sold and was razed for a gas station/convenience store. We were all glad to get out of there. It was so cold and rained as much inside that building as it did outside.

Spirit Square Center for the Arts, Charlotte, NC.

We next moved downtown, "Uptown" in the local Charlotte Chamber of Commerce's lexicon, to a small arts center called Spirit Square Center for the Arts. Built from a rebuilt, small church, Spirit Square was quaint and beautiful from the outside main theater entrance, and plain, boxy, and rambling from the rear, parking lot entrance. It housed the offices for Opera Carolina, the Charlotte Symphony, an Actors Equity theatre company called Theatre Charlotte, and the studio of an NPR-affiliated radio station. Spirit Square had recently been renovated and there was a great deal of ostentatious marble and red carpet. The dance studios were very small, one with no windows, and neither offered much room to move. There were two theaters, a depressingly cramped black box that we used as a rehearsal and class space, and a tiny theater in the main part of the church that had beautiful stained-glass windows and no wing space whatsoever. It was obvious that those in charge in Charlotte considered marble and red carpet to be more important to an arts center than proper studio space or usable theaters. The saying, "lipstick on a pig" comes to mind. This should have been an omen of how tough things would be for the company for the immediate future. The money people in Charlotte at that time cared more about the superficial than the substance. North Carolina Dance Theatre had many critical adjustments to make.

Salvatore Aiello, Artistic Director of North Carolina Dance Theatre, early 1990's.

I did not care about the difficult working conditions in the least. Sal respected me as an artist and a human being, and made me feel that I was not only a part of the company, but a sort of "investor" in its existence and future. He knew that there would be no way for him to match my salary from the New York City Ballet, so he gave me a second job, that of Education Director, and thus a second paycheck. I organized the outreach programs to the local schools and to schools in the cities to which we toured. We were still touring in those early days in Charlotte. It was my first "normal" non-artist job. This job proved to be a wonderful experience that helped me when I was ready to make the transition to my first job after my dancing days were finally over. It was because of Sal that I became aware of my own need to contribute and give back to our ballet community that had given me so much. For helping me to see beyond myself and my own needs, I will be forever grateful to him.

Except for Mr. Balanchine, I have never worked for as talented and humble an individual as Salvatore Aiello. Sal was not physically a big man. He stood about 5'8" tall, and possessed exotically beautiful, swarthy, dark features. Sal was born in Herkimer, New York, and started his ballet training in his hometown at the age of seven. He was a natural talent. It is said that in his dancing days, Sal's movement quality was incomparable. In fact, friends of mine who joined the Harkness Ballet after Sal's time there tell me that he was a legend to them, along with fellow dancers Lawrence Rhodes, Helgi Tomasson, and Christopher Aponte, to name only a few, as all the teachers there spoke so highly of their abilities as dancers.

Working for Sal was the first time in my life that I felt like a "DIVA," each and every day. I had my personal diva moments with Agnes and Arthur, and at Alvin Ailey and the New York City Ballet to be sure. However, none of them let me forget that each morning I would have to start the process of proving myself all over again. Sal never treated me that way. He made sure that everyone knew that I was "the diva of the company," and that I deserved their respect. I loved it. At last, I got to believe my own press completely, not just occasionally with non-dancers. I had principal dancer status at the North Carolina Dance Theatre, and Sal expected the other dancers to treat me with respect.

During those early days in Charlotte, the main company dancers were incredibly eclectic, strong artists and real "down-to-earth" people. The main

The North Carolina Dance Theatre, early 1990's.

company was very small as there was so little money. There were more apprentices than main company members. The apprentices were a talented group, but they were not yet fully formed dancers and needed more training. The days of being considered a company of top notch soloists were all but gone. Sal was a mentor to all the dancers. Everyone put their full trust in him, not because he told them to do so, but because he exuded a confidence and knowledge that was calming and reassuring. He was completely charismatic and hypnotic. We all wanted to believe in him and wanted to watch his dream become reality. He seemed to have such a clear vision of what he wanted the company to become.

Sal was a workaholic and expected his dancers to be the same. He ran a tight ship. I always had the feeling that he knew everybody's business; that he knew each dancer's personal story. Most of Sal's works were group-oriented and that made for a feeling of equality among the dancers. The first piece that I saw, for just two dancers, was his astounding *Satto*. It was danced by two of the company's superstars of the 1980's, Pearl Potts and Edward Campbell. It was part myth, part majesty and quite simple in its makeup. As the elements wind and earth, the dancers were intimate, yet tastefully separate in their presentation. The whole dance took place on a diagonal path of light. As the light dissolved, so did the dance, and the suspense in which Sal had placed his audience. It was insanely memorable; a combination of Sal's unique, childlike creativity and adult wisdom. Most, if not all of Sal's works were successful and sound. They were what I like to call "keepers."

Jerri Kumery, Ballet Mistress of the North Carolina Dance Theatre had been a member of the NYCB.

I remember noticing that Sal almost always had headphones on, listening to music while he dreamed of what he would create next. I do believe that Sal pulled a lot of his inspiration from the musical scores, but I am sure that his main muses were his dancers, as well as his own past.

About six or eight months into our time in Charlotte former New York City Ballet dancer Jerri Kumery joined us as Ballet Mistress. I had danced with Jerri at the New York City Ballet. We danced Mr. B's *Who Cares* together.

Jerri was, and I am sure still is, one of the finest ballet mistresses ever. I do not know how Jerri and Sal knew each other, but it was obvious that their love and respect for one another was undeniable. Jerri was still in amazing shape. She had a gorgeous body, with long, supple legs. Her back was simply breathtaking. She was the perfect teacher for the company, but especially for the women. Since she was young, in her early to mid-thirties, communicating with her was easy and very comfortable for the dancers. Jerri had the amazing ability to remember choreography instantly, retain it forever, and communicate it clearly to the dancers. We all followed her instructions without hesitation. She had Sal's ear and his heart. After Sal's untimely death, Jerri became the keeper of the rights to all his works. These days, Jerri is Ballet Mistress for Richmond Ballet as well as a repetiteur for the Balanchine Foundation. She also stages Salvatore Aiello's ballets, and runs the website for his ballets. There was a regalness about Jerri, but also an honesty and great compassion. It did not take long for all of us to realize that Jerri could communicate with Sal better than anyone else, and we would go to her if we felt that we needed to voice something to Sal. Being fresh out of the life of a professional dancer, she could sense our concerns. Jerri's aspiration for excellence was manifested through her dedication and respect to the dancers and to Sal. It would be Jerri, along with Sal's partner Tim, who would take care of Sal when he became sick; Jerri who would be there for him to the end.

During my time at the North Carolina Dance Theatre, I danced with many wonderful dancers. The turnover once we made the move to Charlotte was higher than it had been in my earlier days with the company in Winston-Salem. Traci Owens, a principal with the company who was married to company member Robin Franklin at the time, was a very-petite fireball. Height-wise, we were a mismatch, but I loved dancing with Traci and we made it work quite well. Her energy was powerful.

Traci Owens:

> It must have been around 1980 or 1981, when I was about 18 or 19 years old. I was a member of The Feld Ballet, NYC, at the time. The company was on a long lay-off, about three months, so I called Bobby Lindgren and asked if I could guest with North Carolina Dance Theatre during my lay-off. The last month and a week of the contract was a European tour. Four weeks in Italy and one week in London. Word got around that Alvin Ailey's company was performing in London at the same time and that Mel would be dancing. It was then that I learned Mel was an alumnus of the School of the Arts....

and alumni support each other. Those of us who went to the show were sitting in the "nose-bleed" section. The very back row of the top balcony. When I saw Mel, the stage just lit up. He was bigger than life and his presence was incomparable. My memory now escapes me. I have no idea if we went back stage or not to say hello.

Several years passed. It must have been around 1986, plus or minus, and I was now a full-time member of the North Carolina Dance Theatre. Every now and then I would see Mel in the wings at one of our dress rehearsals or performances. He was dancing with the New York City Ballet and I just assumed he was visiting. At some point, he retired from the New York City Ballet and took on a position as teacher at the School of the Arts. For some reason, I don't know why, I didn't think he would continue teaching at the school. It was like putting a wild animal in a cage. Not to say that he appeared wild. To the contrary, he appeared very much in control and a bit reserved. But you could just feel his power and intensity. Mel had too much talent and too much to offer still as a performer to just be teaching.

Then Sal Aiello, our director, had the brilliant idea of making an offer to Mel to join the company. This is when things became very interesting. Mel was hired as principal male of the company. I was the principal female. I am short, 5' 1," muscular and blond. If you look at us side by side....We were not really a match. So in the beginning, Sal put Mel in a pas de deux (can't remember the name) that was perfect for him. This presented his more animalistic side. Then Sal created "Afternoon of a Faun" for Mel and four taller women in the company. This role brought out even more of Mel's artistic creativity. Each performance was different and with each performance he went deeper.

The North Carolina Dance Theatre was such a wonderful company to dance with because we had the opportunity to work with so many great choreographers in so many different dance techniques. One of those choreographers was Rick McCullough, whose choreography was greatly influenced by Jirí Kylián, since Rick was a dancer with the Netherlands Dans Theater.

Rick choreographed a pas de deux for Mel and a beautiful African/American girl named Katherine Thompson in the company. Their body types and heights were a perfect match. I, and another partner, were their understudies. They premiered this piece while we were performing at the Joyce Theater, in New York.

I can't say that I knew Mel very well. We would chat from time to time and I would ask him about his time in New York City Ballet, which was fun, but otherwise, I mostly just observed Mel. I guess I also felt that we would never dance together because of our body types and by now a whole season had passed. I don't remember how or why it happened, but Sal finally put us together in Rick McCullough's pas de deux. It was called, "By Lamplight."

Mel basically taught me the pas de deux because my partner and I had never had the chance to learn all of it because of conflicting rehearsal schedules. Dancing with Mel was magic! Almost every time he touched me I would giggle. I can't explain the feeling. It was simply fun and challenging at the same time. He just made me giggle, all the time. His legs were just so long. He would do a chassée across the stage and be miles away from me. My only step to get to him was a chassée as well. Imagine my little legs trying to get to him...you can understand my giggles!

This pas de deux was one of my favorites to dance with Mel (and, overall, in my career). Mel's "artist" is quite intense and so is mine. On this level, Mel and I were a great match. I so enjoyed this exchange with him on stage.

After this, Mel and I were partnered together in many pieces. One of which makes me laugh to this day! Sal choreographed a piece called, "Homage to Versailles". The women were dressed in short white tutus which extended out a bit farther than usual. They were more like a stiff lampshade. We wore pink tights and pointe shoes and white 18th century wigs. The men wore white ballet shoes, white tights, white tunics and, of course, the white wigs as well. Can you picture Mel? What a trooper he was. All of us felt ridiculous, especially when trying to do pirouettes with these wigs on our heads. And all the while Mel remained the perfect prince and professional. That was Mel. The perfect prince and professional. Not once did I ever see Mel lose his cool or give any attitude. Not ever. Even when there was good reason to do so.

Mel and I also danced Balanchine's "Allegro Brillante" together, and Violette Verdy coached us. Once Mel and I were dancing Lambros Lambrou's "Night in the Tropics," and one of the corps girls dropped a rose from her hair and it landed on the stage as she was exiting. Our pas de deux was next. In typical "Mel" form, while I was going for a relevé á la seconde balance, Mel swoops down to his knee, takes the rose and offers it to me while remaining on his knee. There was a roar of applause. What can I say? He's more than just fun to dance with. He is that prince little girls dream of.

My last season with the North Carolina Dance Theatre was 1989/1990.

I needed to move on to a bigger challenge. So, a few months after the company relocated to Charlotte, I left. I then joined Ballet Austin (Lambros Lambrou, Director) to replace his injured ballerina until the end of the company's season. I had explained to Lambros that I was looking to join a larger company.

North Carolina Dance Theatre was performing in Austin during my time there, and, in fact, I have photos of Mel visiting me in my apartment. After I finished the season in Austin, I moved back to Charlotte where my furniture was stored. I can't remember how it happened, but Mel offered me a room in his lovely home while I looked for a new company. While living with Mel we never saw that much of each other. He was busy doing his thing and I was busy doing mine. We sometimes had profound conversations, but I don't remember much about them. I know Mel in the dance studio and on the stage, and this is more profound than any conversation. I am not a woman of words. I am a dancer. When Mel and I danced we didn't need words. Our souls touched and communicated through the dance.

In May of 1991, I received a call from Robert Denvers, Director of the Royal Ballet of Flanders, asking me to replace his injured Ballerina as "Kitri" in "Don Quichote." It's now twenty-five years later and I'm still living in Belgium.

From time to time I would call Mel on my trips home to visit family in Raleigh. On one of these calls Mel shared with me his hellish experience of falling ill. I was in shock and so saddened by his story.

My father would send me newspaper clippings of Mel when he would achieve yet another milestone or award or something. Mel just continues to achieve, thrive and grow. I'm just happy God decided to leave him with us... to teach us how to be better people all around.

At the North Carolina Dance Theatre, I also got to dance with one of the most beautiful women in the world, Marjorie Grundvig. Looking at Margie was like looking at a "California Girl" commercial. Her face was perfect symmetry, and looking at her was addictive. Margie's roommate, Anita Intrieri, was also beautiful, and had the quickest brain in the company. Anita could pick up anything and then reverse it without missing a beat. She was superbly musical and had a memory that never failed. Unfortunately, Anita had a difficult physical instrument with which to work. I must apologize to Anita for the horrible scene I caused once by refusing to dance with her because of her weight. I was anything but diplomatic or kind and I regret my behavior to this day. Anita, being the consummate professional that she was, stood there and took my cruelty without a word. She lost the weight quickly and became one of my most successful partners. We are still friends today. Anita once noticed that whenever it was time for bows on stage, I would seek out center stage. I did not even realize that I was doing that, but I was. It became a joke between us, as Anita would be sure to point out my need for the limelight.

I danced many of Aiello's ballets and enjoyed every one of them. Of all my directors, Sal is the one from whom I learned the most. He also is the one who gave me the most artistic freedom. He knew my weaknesses, but somehow managed to push me past them. He took a lot of chances with me and the whole company. All his works were well thought out and quite deep in content. Nothing was wasted. Nothing ever looked cheap, even when there was not a nickel to spare. I honestly do not know how he did it. As an administrator, he could be his own worst enemy at times. But he had the faith of Bobby Lindgren, the dancers, and many of the financial powers in Charlotte. Sal tended to have his fingers in everything, from the administration to the finances to the costumes, lighting and sets. Many of his ideas seemed to me to be outlandish at first, but they almost always worked.

The most memorable work that Sal created on me was his *Afternoon of a Faun*. At first, I was skeptical that Sal would choose to do this work that had been done so well by both Nijinsky and Jerry Robbins. It seemed to me to be the height of audacity for Sal, or anyone for that matter, to take this on. However, I could not resist the temptation to explore this part. Sal said the ballet had been waiting for me. Instinctively, I chose to trust him and believe him. I am forever grateful that he trusted me to be his faun.

We took *Afternoon of a Faun* to New York, to premiere it at the Joyce Theater. It was incomplete when we arrived in New York. Sal gave me the liberty to fill in the blanks. The four girls with whom I danced were my heroes. They rolled with the flow, watched me, and totally understood what to do. The work became a huge hit for the company. The girls and I all felt so intimate, like we were personally speaking privately and intimately touching each other while we were dancing. The costumes and sets were stark and revealing. Sal's intent was spot on – clear and deliberate.

Heather Maloy, Jennifer Cavanaugh, and Timothy Yeager, three of the newer, younger dancers in the company seemed to innately know what made Sal "tick" when it came to his choreography. Sal saw this almost immediately and appreciated it to the point that they often ended up assisting in making quite a few of his works. They were youthful and attentive and had a way of keeping Sal focused on all that he had to do. Their love for him was particularly great and his loss was to be devastating to them, as it was to the rest of the people whose lives Sal had touched and changed.

Veteran dancers like Terri Lynn Wright, Traci Owens, Robin Franklin, Diego Carasco, Patrick Badua, and David Bushman as well as those to come a bit later – Kati Hanlon, Mia Cunningham, Ted Sothern, and Barry Leon to name a few, were all a part of what I called Sal's "click," both at work and outside of work. I tended to be a recluse by choice in those days, and only associated with Sal and the other dancers for the most part at work. Every now and then Sal and I would encounter each other coming out of the sauna at the YMCA. We were cordial, but kept walking. At first, I was embarrassed until I came to realize that I had been conditioned by my former directors to believe that co-mingling with the boss was bad. I remembered my encounter in the sauna so long ago with Arthur Mitchell, when I was young and had a youthful crush, and he had told me to keep my mind on the dancing. Now at thirty-six, I was grateful for Mr. Mitchell's wisdom and integrity. I could comfortably be friendly with Sal, my director, without being entwined in a friendship that might muddy the waters of our successful working relationship. I realized that I very much wanted to be like Sal, this man who seemed to always seek out the good parts of life and living. When his light began to fade, it became obvious rather quickly to us all that something was not right.

Around the time that Sal appeared to be weakening physically, the company ran out of money. It would be temporary, but very hard on the dancers. Charlotte was not the financial Mecca that Sal had been led to believe it would be. Our stage manager, Greg Rowland, and I were asked to donate our salaries so that the dancers, who made much less than we did, could be paid. We all donated our time as long as we could, but took other jobs as they became both necessary and available. Sal, not one to ever lose his vision, limped along with Jerri and a group of mostly new, young, apprentice dancers once again. It was around this time that he started the school, originally called "Dance Place." After a couple of difficult years, the company did get back on its feet. I was gone for much of that time, late 1991 through late 1993, dancing in Charleston and Boston.

Chapter Thirteen

Change is in the Air, 1991 - 1993

While I was still a Principal at the North Carolina Dance Theatre, I was occasionally offered opportunities outside of the company. Sal did not try to hold me back, in fact he allowed me to take on guest appearances, because, like most of the wisest people I know, he instinctively knew that trying to keep me from growing artistically would only make me leave for good in the long run.

The first time I ventured out as a guest artist from the North Carolina Dance Theatre, it was to dance with Cynthia Harvey, one of American Ballet Theatre's top ballerinas, in a production of *A Midsummer Night's Dream*, choreographed by Norbert Vesak to be performed with Ballet Florida in West Palm Beach. Mr. Vesak, a Canadian, was a wonderful, quite-well-known, choreographer. I imagine that his connection to the North Carolina Dance Theatre came through either Sal's time at the Royal Winnipeg Ballet, or, possibly from the fact that he and Mr. Lindgren were both from British Columbia. Mr. Vesak had set several of his most important ballets on the Royal Winnipeg Ballet in the 1970's. His *A Midsummer Night's Dream* was originally set on the North Carolina Dance Theatre. Sadly, Mr. Vesak would pass away from a brain aneurysm at the age of 53 in 1990, when he was in Charlotte to attend the 20th anniversary celebration of the company, at which his ballet, *The Gray Goose of Silence* was being performed.

Dancing with Cynthia Harvey was a male partner's dream come true. Not only was she delicate and ephemeral, but she was so strong and confident, had only positive vibes, and practically partnered herself. I was on tour with the North Carolina Dance Theatre at the time of our scheduled rehearsal, so I took a bus to meet Cynthia at the Kennedy Center in Washington, D.C., where American Ballet Theatre was in residence. I learned a lot from Cynthia's musicality and phrasing and her ability to give the choreographer exactly what he wanted. She even taught me how to do *coupe jetés* correctly by giving me a very useful upper body correction.

BEYOND MY DREAMS

The second-time Sal allowed me to accept a guest appearance was when the Charleston (SC) Ballet Theatre's choreographer Jill Eathorne-Bahr, was looking for someone to dance the lead role in her *Firebird*. Sal introduced me to Jill when she was in Charlotte visiting the company. Sal had visited Jill and the directors of the company, Patricia and Don Cantwell, in Charleston to see Jill's *Dracula*. They all became fast friends, as they had much in common. Sal and Jill were both innovative choreographers. Sal and his partner, Tim, were very interested in interior design, and Patty Cantwell is a master when it comes to design and color. The Cantwell home was decorated better than anything one might see in a top interior design magazine. Occasionally, Jill would act as Sal's "beard in a dress" for important meetings and get-togethers for the National Endowment of the Arts and other groups. Even in the arts as late as the early 1990's, the world was not yet an open place.

Charleston was only a three and a half-hour drive from Charlotte, so it made sense for the company's artistic director's to be able to help each other out from time to time. I imagine being a choreographer, especially in the South was, and probably still is, a somewhat lonely job field. It was nice for both Sal and Jill to have a friend/colleague with whom to "talk shop." Sal

Charleston Ballet Theatre performing Salvatore Aiello's Notturno, early 1990's. Dancers, from left: Jennifer Muller, Jonathan Tabbert, Ashley Lazenby Swan, and Peter Swan.

picked up Jill's *Dracula*, for the North Carolina Dance Theatre, and Jill would, in the near future, set it on the company, while the Charleston Ballet Theatre would dance two Aiello ballet's, *Clowns and Others a*nd *Notturno*.

When I first met Jill Eathorne-Bahr, she was sitting in Sal's office, on one of her Charlotte visits. A tall woman with short, red hair, Jill was an instantly personable, likeable woman. Jill would later tell me that she had heard about me from a mutual friend, Sara Yarborough, from the Ailey company. They first met at a choreographer's conference, and Jill invited Sara to Memphis, where Jill was working at the time, to set a solo on her. Later, after seeing me perform, then meeting me in Charlotte, Jill came to the conclusion that I would be the right dancer for her *Firebird*.

"Mel was just such a chameleon when it came to movement. I wanted someone who could move his legs everywhere," Jill reminisced.

She asked me if I would be interested and Sal encouraged me to take this guest artist position. Other than Bejart in Europe, who staged his *Firebird* on Jorge Donn, I did not know of another choreographer to use a male dancer as the *Firebird*, although the critics say the legendary Vaslav Nijinsky, wanted to dance the role *en pointe* in the original Fokine production for Diaghilev in 1910. Like Bejart and Nijinsky, Jill is, and has always been, an innovator.

An incredibly musical choreographer, she had made her home with the Charleston Ballet Theatre in 1987. A tall dancer originally from Detroit, Michigan, Jill studied at the Joffrey Ballet School and the Harkness House for Ballet Arts in New York before prematurely blowing out her knee at about the same time she realized that she was more interested in becoming a choreographer. A severe dyslexic, Jill has always had trouble discerning her right from her left. She could not do it internally, but rather would seek out something in the environment, like a window or a door in the dance studio, to help her keep right and left straight. She has never considered herself to be naturally coordinated either. That makes learning choreography from her a bit of a challenge, but the intricacy, incredible musicality, and innovativeness of her choreography completely makes up for having to deal with her dyslexia issues. She is known for her uncanny ability to choreograph groups of people in amazingly intricate, and interestingly musical ways. With music by my favorite composer, Igor Stravinsky, I was very much looking forward to the experience of dancing the Firebird. I was not to be disappointed.

At first glance, Charleston, South Carolina seems more European than American. It is a small, coastal city of pastel-shaded rainbow-colored townhouses and Civil War era mansions, cobblestoned streets, and a vibrant arts community. Where much of the south's pre-Civil War buildings were destroyed by Sherman's Southern campaign, Charleston was spared. No one really knows why. It is said that Sherman had been in love with a Charleston girl in the 1840's when he spent four years stationed at nearby Fort Moultrie on Sullivan's Island. It is also argued that by the time Sherman had the opportunity to march on Charleston, it was late in the war, and Charleston's economy, as well as it's spirit, had already been destroyed. For whatever reason, Charleston is one of the few southern cities to still retain homes and memorabilia of its pre-Civil War heritage.

Charleston, South Carolina's historic Battery Row Mansions. Photo by Vanessa Kaufmann

Each year, in Charleston, since 1977, the Spoleto Festival arrives for three weeks along with the summer beach season. With it come people from every corner of the world to see cutting edge theatre, dance, opera, and visual arts performed in Charleston's many theatres and outdoor spaces. Charleston is a cosmopolitan city, in the European tradition. No other city in the United States could more perfectly host and honor the vision of Gian Carlo Menotti and Christopher Keene. Their dream was to bring their Festival of Two Worlds to American soil to mirror the already successful festival in Spoleto, Italy.

Coming from the Atlanta Ballet Company, Patricia and Don Cantwell saw Charleston's artistic promise. They knew in their hearts that this was the perfect place to develop a very special professional ballet company. In the late 1960's, they first founded a regional company and were very active in the Regional Dance America movement, specifically SERBA (Southeast Regional Ballet Association), festivals. While Don directed and staged for the company in the beginning, Patty danced the lead roles, having been meticulously trained on full merit scholarship at Balanchine's School of American Ballet in New York.

In 1987, their dream of taking their regional company to the professional level became a reality. Charleston was the perfect place for a small theatrical ballet company specializing in both contemporary ballet and the classics as it had an "old money," educated, and artistically inclined, population. Jill Eathorne-Bahr had been to Charleston to set pieces on the company when it was a pre-professional member of SERBA. Together, Jill, Don, and Patty made a formidable team. Although, over the years, several groups have tried, to date they have been the only ones to successfully conceive, and bring to fruition, the idea of a professional ballet company for Charleston. The company was a highly successful mainstay in the Charleston community for twenty-five years before sadly succumbing to the severe economic downturn in 2012.

It was 1991. North Carolina Dance Theatre was struggling financially. While not yet in the throes of financial devastation – that would come soon enough – the company was struggling to find their place in the Charlotte community. There were definite growing pains involved in changing from a touring company to a resident city company. Having purchased my first home a year or so earlier when the company moved to Charlotte, I had a mortgage to pay. While he struggled to get the company completely on its feet, Sal worked hard to help us find ways to make extra money in order to survive. As it happened, the North Carolina Dance Theatre would be on a lay-off for the three weeks that I would be working with the Charleston Ballet Theatre.

I knew nothing of Charleston or the Charleston Ballet Theatre before meeting Jill Eathorne-Bahr. In my mind, I thought of the Firebird as a jumping role. So did Jill. That worried me, as I was not known for my astounding

Firebird, 1991. From left: Jill Eathorne-Bahr, David Stahl, Mel Tomlinson, Patricia and Don Cantwell

elevation or spectacular ability to jump. I could not help but wonder what Jill had in store for me. After all, the character is a bird. I was supposed to fly. I really have no idea how she did it, but she did. I flew. I wore nothing more than a pair of beautifully fit custom-made dance trunks, designed by Don Cantwell, with a feather in my belt. Only Jill and very few other choreographers successfully got away with such a display back then. Costumes often tend to be integral to the choreography. We were an eyeful, to say the least.

The sets were also designed by Don Cantwell. With my new ability to fly, thanks to Jill, I began to lay the foundation for the character development of the Firebird. I wanted to make sure that my interpretation and execution would live up to the character of the Firebird in the story, and to Jill's vision.

During the making of this production, Jill was hospitalized for eight days due to a bacterial infection, fever and vomiting, causing dehydration, most likely brought on by her penchant for overwork. Jill continued to work from her hospital bed, choreographing and staging various parts of the production right there in her hospital room. When she finally came back to rehearsals, she was dragging her IV along with her. I loved the spirit of this young company. All the dancers, as well as the directors, kept going, kept working, even in the face of Jill's health crisis. Jill put a lot of faith in her dancers, too, expecting them to continue working without missing a beat. From the live orchestra, conducted by David Stahl, playing the Stravinsky score magnificently, to the boldness of Jill's vision of the story, to the complete intensity and beauty of the production, as a whole, and to the beautifully costumed, but half-naked dancers, everything about this production was a huge success. Once again, I had the good fortune to be a part of something very special.

While I was in Charleston, I very quickly became quite close to Jill and the Cantwells, as well as to many of the dancers. Scott Miner, one of the dancers who was originally from Charlotte, became a good friend. I did not know it at the time, but Scott would be one of my most loyal friends, driving up to Charlotte often to visit me when I became sick. Erika Moe Taylor, who was a principal dancer in Charleston, was another one of my favorite women with whom to dance. She had a gorgeous, powerful technique and such dramatic finesse. Erika fast became one of my mentors, too, along with Jill and the Cantwells. I confided in them all that I was worried about whether or not the North Carolina Dance Theatre would survive in Charlotte.

I was, once again, slowly trying to segue out of my performing career. Jill and Patty, wanting to help, first recommended me for a position as a panelist on the National Endowment for the Arts. The panel met in Washington,

D.C. Their task was to distribute grant funds to ballet and modern dance companies. My job was to assist in this process. We read through hundreds of grant proposals, looking not only for artistic worthiness, but for what each company was doing for their local community and for the communities in which they visited to perform. One of the keys to getting grant funds was that a company had to give back to the community in some way. Some started various programs for at-risk students and students from lower socio-economic backgrounds. Others had free or lower-cost tickets for low-income families. I loved being a part of that panel. I learned a lot that would prove helpful for the next chapter of my life.

Jill also talked to her friend Bruce Marks about me. At the time, Bruce was the Artistic Director of the Boston Ballet. He was in the middle of building that company into one of the top professional American ballet companies. Bruce contacted me and made an offer that I could not refuse. I was to be a principal dancer with the Boston Ballet, on the same level as former American Ballet Theatre principal Fernando Bujones, who had recently joined the company. I would also become co-director with Frank Bourman of the Boston Ballet's new Citydance program. Citydance targeted and served the lower socio-economic community. Having just learned of the importance of such projects through my time on the National Endowment for the Arts panel, I was excited to be involved. How could I refuse an offer like that? Looking back, I believe the invitation most intrigued me because I was at the point where I was once again worrying that it might just be time to think about retiring from the stage. When Bruce told me that I would be a principal and have the same status as Fernando Bujones, I simply couldn't refuse. Now I would have one more final hurrah, and at the top of my field. I would finish out my season with the North Carolina Dance Theatre then head back up north, this time to Boston.

The contract was quite lucrative. I would be exclusive to Boston Ballet, and because of the Citydance program, as well as duties teaching in the summer intensive, would have what appeared to be a full 52-week contract. While I loved the security of the contract, I missed the freedom that Sal Aiello had given me. From the very beginning, that old feeling of being "property" reared its ugly head and I felt the same disquiet in my heart that I had toward the end of my tenure at the New York City Ballet. I still had my house in Charlotte. I was renting it out to a couple of the dancers there. In the back of my mind, I think I always knew that Charlotte had become my home and I would one day return there.

I believe that one of the reasons Bruce Marks wanted me for his company was that he wanted to get Balanchine's *Agon* and knew his chances would be excellent with me in the company. However, it did not happen while I was there. Bruce also had me teach company classes when various Balanchine ballets were slated to be performed. I think he knew that I could help the dancers achieve the speed and articulation of movement needed for those ballets.

I was dressing roommates with Fernando Bujones. We got along very well. Fernando was such a nice, kind man. He loved football, and even missed a performance once due to a football game. I went on for him at the last minute – it was Snow King in *The Nutcracker*. The next day, I asked him where he was. "At home watching the game," he said, confused as to my question. He had gotten confused with the scheduling. He and I were both glad that I had been there to fill in.

The only time Fernando and I disagreed was about the tempos of *Allegro Brilliante*. I was livid when he asked the conductor to slow it down. Even though I never danced *Allegro Brilliante* at NYCB, I danced it many times at the Dance Theatre of Harlem, and North Carolina Dance Theatre, and I knew that ballet intimately. I knew what Mr. Balanchine's intent was. I told Fernando, "It is not called 'give me time to do my double tour'. It is *Balanchine*. It must be danced at the proper tempo -- *fast*." Fernando was more concerned about his perfect double tours than dancing the ballet as it was meant to be danced. He got away with it, so I was disappointed in both Fernando and the conductor. It should not have been slowed down.

All in all, Fernando and I became good friends. When one of my students, Alex Ketley, who I had taught at the North Carolina School of the Arts, and was now at the School of American Ballet in New York, needed to be coached in a classical variation for entry into a top-level ballet competition in which students vie for places in both companies and serious, professional-level training schools, Fernando was most generous to help. I choreographed a contemporary piece for Alex, and Fernando set Franz's solo from *Coppelia* on Alex and coached him brilliantly. I think Fernando loved ballet even more than I do. His untimely death, in 2005 from complications of melanoma, while director of the Orlando Ballet, was heartbreaking for his fans, but much more so for all of us who knew him.

I fell in love with Boston from the beginning. It is a beautiful city, full of so much history. I lived in an apartment in a converted brownstone on the westside of town, with my cocker spaniel, Zuri Chantel, named after my youngest sister, Janie Robbin's, stillborn baby. Janie had been plagued with medical issues as a teenager and young adult, most of which were caused by diabetes. She lost her sight, but still managed to be a top student at Johnson C. Smith University in Charlotte.

I wish I could say that I also fell in love with the Citydance program, but I cannot. Actually, it was not the program itself that was the problem. It was my co-director, Frank Bourman. From the beginning, it was obvious to me that Frank had a problem with me. I think that I had a more natural inclination than Frank did when it came to the children in the program. I felt that Frank talked down to them and did not know how to connect, whereas I have always been able to connect with children.

Citydance was started in 1991. Frank Bourman was the original director. Bruce Marks brought *me* in to co-direct in 1992. I'm sure having Mel Tomlinson, a black man, was helpful in establishing the program as both teaching a diverse population and hiring teachers with diversity. The program was organized and extremely well thought out. Each fall, we would go into the Boston area public schools, targeting third graders to join our program and learn various forms of dance. We would hold what we liked to call "try-outs" rather than auditions. Using that word was Frank's idea originally, and was one of the few things that he and I could agree on. "Try-outs" was a word that school children understood. It had the added bonus of not intimidating the children the way the word "audition" did. Those children who showed possible movement talent and enthusiasm for movement would get to spend the next ten weeks in the program. Dance clothes would be provided and the students would be bussed to the studio for their class then returned to their elementary school an hour later.

If, at the end of the ten weeks, they still showed interest, they could continue for ten more weeks in the next phase, a "Beginner Ballet" class. Upon graduating from that class, those who were interested could enter the Boston Ballet School. Financial aid would be available to those who needed it. The program was a great success from Day One and has become the model for many programs across the country.

I think what I love most about children is their unjaded presence. They are honest in their delivery and can see things that adults tend to overlook. They lack that thing that I refer to as diplomacy. They say what they see and many times without filter. I like that and can definitely relate. It keeps me in check. I loved working with the children through Citydance. Unfortunately, Frank Bourman and I never found common ground. I found him to be very calculating and very old-fashioned in his approach to working with the very young. He seemed to patronize them and I am sure the children saw right through him and his phony character. If I could sense his insecurities, I am sure that the children could. I felt that Frank and the school principal were in cahoots at the time, leaving me out of decisions whenever possible.

I was so disgusted with my working situation with Frank, that when Citydance was honored with an Elliot Norton Award, the yearly awards given out to those who make outstanding contributions to the Boston theatre community, I refused to attend the ceremony. Looking back, I think I did it

February 16, 1993

Mr. Frank Bourman
Mr. Mel Tomlinson
CITYDANCE
19 Clarendon Street
Boston, MA 02116

Dear Mr. Bourman and Mr. Tomlinson:

On behalf of the committee for the Eleventh Annual Elliot Norton Awards, I am delighted to invite you both to receive a special honor in recognition of your educational outreach program and its contribution to the future of the arts in Boston. The citation will be presented at this year's Elliot Norton Awards ceremony, which we hope you will attend.

As you may know, the Elliot Norton Awards were established in 1982, when Mr. Norton retired after 48 years as the undisputed dean of Boston Critics. The Elliot Norton Award itself is presented yearly to an individual who has made "a distinguished contribution to the theatre in Boston". Awards are also made to a local actor and actress chosen by our selection committee. In recent years, however, we have expanded the awards to embrace the larger arts community and are especially eager to honor excellence in the fields of dance, music, and arts administration.

Last year's Awards ceremony was truly a tony affair. The ceremony featured, in addition to local honors, the presentation of special awards to nine-time Tony Winner Tommy Tune, Pulitzer Prize-winning playwright August Wilson, and venerable actor Jason Robards, all of whom were present. Our list of special honorees was just as impressive and includes your colleague Fernando Bujones. Elma Lewis, founder of National Center of Afro-American Artists, De Ama Battle, founder of Art of Black Dance and Music, and Ron and Polly Ritchell, artistic and producing director of the Lyric Stage.

This year's gala event will center around Mr. Norton's 90th birthday. The date of the event is May 17th and will be held at Boston's Park Plaza Hotel. We sincerely hope you will give us the honor of honoring you. Please call me at 542-9155 at your earliest convenience to indicate your interest and availability.

Sincerely,

Spring Sirkin
President

Letter to Frank Bourman and Mel announcing their Elliot Norton Award for their work on Boston Ballet's Citydance.

just to infuriate Frank.

All in all, I am proud of the fact that I was part of the beginnings of the Citydance program. I wish I could have done more for that program, but it was not to be. I am proud to say that I had one student from my time at Citydance who went on to a professional career. Her name is Ebony Williams, one of Beyonce's "Pretty Women" dancers. I am very proud of her.

I stayed at Boston Ballet for two years. Just as what so often happened in the past with me, I believe that once the novelty of my special talents wore off, Bruce could not figure out what to do with me. I certainly did not have the technique that Fernando had. Double tours were still my nemesis, and, at thirty-nine, I was no longer young in dancer years. I was always happiest and at my best when partnering. Working with the beautiful ballerinas of the Boston Ballet was the best part for me. I was privileged to work with Carla Stallings (Lippert), formerly of American Ballet Theatre, who was absolutely gorgeous and beautifully productive in all of her executions. She was always very attentive to her partners, as was the statuesque Kyra Strasberg. Julie Bacon, who rode her bike to work on most days, was an inventive, inquisitive daredevil. She was technically astute, with classical lines that were pure and effortless. I found her to be cool as a cucumber and quite the athlete. I adored Adriana Suarez, who, like Carla and Kyra, became a good friend. Last but certainly not least, was the effervescent Jennifer Gelfand who lent her talents to my choreography. She was shorter in stature than the others but she danced bigger and with even more speed and accuracy. This young woman could turn with the best of them, always completely consistent in her execution. Her musical interpretations were always memorable. Working with these beautiful women made my time at Boston Ballet a happy time, despite my discomfort with Frank Bourman. I am happy to have made a few good friends in the company, and have no regrets.

After two years, I suddenly found myself being asked to leave. According to Frank, there was a complaint from a volunteer with the Citydance program that I had made some sexual innuendo that made him uncomfortable. It is very possible, as I do tend to speak before I think and have a very dry sense of humor and quick wit. However, anyone who knows me, knows that I am not serious and would never do or say anything on purpose to make another person uncomfortable. Bruce Marks was kind and very professional when he let me go, but I think that, truth be told, Bruce had grown bored with my special talents and my limitations as a classical dancer. He gave me severance pay and thanked me for my artistry.

I spent one more year in Boston, teaching for the Boston Conservatory of Music. It was a good year, working at an amazing school, but I was ready to go home. The Boston winters were cruel and unforgiving. The South was calling. Once again, I was ready to be home in North Carolina.

Chapter Fourteen

Dark Days: Down the Rabbit Hole
Winter 1995 – Spring 1997

It was during the summer of 1995 when I found out that I was sick with AIDS. It was apparently July 30th, one of those typically Southern, terribly humid days. I was in North Myrtle Beach, South Carolina. Although the temperature was a relatively for much of the South "cool" 86 degrees that day, the humidity was at 97%, making breathing difficult, even for someone who was healthy. I felt with each breath, a struggle that I had never felt before. It was as if I was deeply submerged in water with no hope of finding my way to the surface. With no clouds in the sky, the southern sun was relentless, both for its heat and for it blinding brightness.

For me, it had all started with horrible night sweats about a month before. The sweats were so bad that I had to change my pajamas in the middle of the night every night. I was also losing weight, but that had not alarmed me because I was always on one diet or another. The headaches started shortly after the beginning of the night sweats. I was employed only as a sub-contractor in those days, teaching here and there. I was spending much of my days on the phone, trying to set up guest-teaching jobs. It was becoming more and more difficult to continue to put up with the pain while trying to schedule future employment. My next job was to be a week of teaching at a summer dance intensive being held in Myrtle Beach, South Carolina. Near to the time I was to leave for Myrtle Beach, the headaches had begun to become intolerable.

Gary Taylor, who directed the Myrtle Beach summer intensive with his wife, Rita, was a former student from the School of the Arts. Gary had arrived at the school the same year I returned to teach there, in 1987. After graduating, Gary and Rita had founded the High Point Ballet, a small, regional company in High Point, North Carolina, a town very close to Winston-Salem known for its high-end furniture mart. This would be my third summer teaching at their summer school at the beach, called "Lecon de la Dance." I, along with several other dancers as well as faculty from the North Carolina School of the Arts, Fanchon Cordell, Roscoe Sales, Sheron Price, and Gyula Pandi had been invited to teach the 200-plus students from all over the region who attended. It is funny, but rather unnerving to me that I only remember Fanchon, Gary and Rita as the other teachers there with me that year.

I drove down to North Myrtle Beach from Charlotte, a three-and-a-half-hour drive that, on that particular day, felt more like twelve hours. The headache I had been carrying around with me was at this point so bad that it was blinding me. I will never forget the relentlessness of the sun and what, to me, was intolerable heat that day. I was wearing my sunglasses non-stop, both inside and outside, by that time. I had never felt that kind of pain before. It was the type of pain that made me so very nauseous that it caused me to stop my car to vomit several times during the drive down to Myrtle Beach. The humidity, on top of my fever was completely unbearable. Every breath made me feel even more sure that I was going to drown by breathing in the water-laden air.

I arrived at the Beach Cove Resort, where we would be staying and where the summer intensive was being held. As I remember it, I arrived on the first day I was to teach, a Sunday, with a little bit of time to spare before the class. For as long as I can remember, I have been sure that I arrived and was hospitalized on July 25, but according to everyone else's recollections and records, it was a week later, on Sunday, July 30, 1995.

I remember Fanchon Cordell, former American Ballet Theatre soloist, and one of the faculty members from the School of the Arts, saw me as I entered

The Beach Cove Resort, Myrtle Beach, SC.

the lobby. Being as intuitive as Fanchon is, she took one look at me and knew that something was terribly wrong. Fanchon told me to go lie down for a while and try to get a little rest before my class. I believe I did just that, collapsing in a heap on the bed, although my unbearable headache would not allow me to rest. At least the blackout curtains in the two-bedroom, beachfront condo gave me a respite from the relentless sun.

My roommate for the week was to be Robert "Robbie" Gosnell, an 18-year-old student who had grown up at the High Point Ballet before continuing his ballet education at the North Carolina School of the Arts. He spent his performing career first with Hubbard Street Dance Chicago, then Atlanta Ballet, and finally the Nashville Ballet. I already knew Robbie, having staged a ballet of mine for the High Point Ballet several months prior to the summer school, to be performed first for the board of the Southeastern Regional Ballet Association (SERBA) when the company was applying for membership. Robbie was one of the young dancers from the company who I had chosen to be in my ballet. He arrived the same day I did, flying home the day before to North Carolina from New York, where he had spent the summer at the School of American Ballet, and then driving down to Myrtle Beach with his mother and his sister who was also a dancer.

From this point on, my memory becomes very spotty due first to my illness, and later to all the drugs that I was given to battle the disease. My friend and co-author, Claudia Folts, has helped to fill in the blanks through her memories plus interviews with many of the people who were with me at various points during what I now call my "dark days." From the memories of those who were close to me at the time, I believe we have been able to piece my story together. Much of what has been written from here on out does not come from my actual memories but from my friend's and care-giver's memories. Some recollections will be told in the words of those remembering.

When it was time to leave for the class, I told myself that I could get through anything for an hour and a half. I got up, grabbed my sunglasses, put them on even before opening my eyes, and blindly found my way down to the large banquet hall in which my class was to be held. A Marley dance floor had been laid on top of the close-cropped, industrial carpet, and portable barres had been brought in and lined up throughout the room. I only had the one class to teach that first day, a class of the youngest participants and lowest level so I told myself that afterwards, I would have the rest of the day and evening to rest and recuperate so I would be in top form by the next day when my full-day schedule started. Looking back, I am amazed that I could have allowed myself to believe that I would be okay with a little rest. I kept my sunglasses on as I taught. I told my roommate, Robbie, that I thought I had a migraine and a sinus infection.

I was not one to complain when I did not feel well, something I learned from watching my father as I was growing up. Somehow, I managed to get through the ballet class, mostly sitting down and having students demonstrate. When the hour and a half was finally over, I stood up to leave the class, and remember nothing from that point on, until I awoke in the hospital.

When Claudia and I first began discussing this terrible period in my life, I believed that I had collapsed right after class, melting into a heap on the floor, and was then whisked away to the hospital. I was quite astonished to hear several versions of a very different story.

Robert Gosnell remembers:

Mel was not his usual self, not his bubbly self. I remember getting there and Mel was already there, in the jacuzzi, because he felt like he had a sinus infection. He did teach one class that day, but then he went straight to bed, which I thought was so unusual for Mel. I remember thinking, 'Wow, he must really be sick.' I thought he was wearing the sunglasses because he knew they looked cool and because he was being funny. Mel has always had the best sense of humor. You know, I thought he was just being Mel. I did notice that his energy was down. He wasn't bantering back and forth with me the way Mel does. Something was just off, but I didn't really know what that "off" was.

I remember that he went to the hospital on Sunday, July 30, because my sister's sixteenth birthday was the 31st and we were having a surprise birthday party for her the evening of the 30th. Mel, of course, was invited, to the party, but he did not feel well enough to come. We, my mother, my sister and I, went out to dinner. We were coming back, and saw that there was an ambulance outside of the resort entrance. We went upstairs to get ready for my sister's surprise party. Our rooms, were all on the same floor. When we got upstairs, I saw that the door

Robert Gosnell, dancer and choreographer.

to my suite was open, and I remember thinking, 'What is going on? What's happening?' And that's when I saw the gurney coming out of our suite. And, of course, that's when, me, you know, the normal, dramatic me, Robbie, at that time, freaked out. I remember being very alarmed, yelling, 'What is happening?' 'What is going on?' I completely freaked out. I was panicking, thinking, 'this is not real!'

I guess it was Mel who called 911. No one else was there with him, that I know of, so it must have been Mel. I remember that Rita and Gary Taylor and I went to the hospital with him. We sat there for what seemed like forever in the waiting room and then Karen Brown showed up. Mel must have called her in New York and she flew down immediately, to come take care of him and to teach his classes.

I also remember that after class that afternoon, Rita Taylor, Gary's wife and co-director, talked to Mel about her migraines and gave him something for the headache, probably an Excedrin Migraine. Mel kept turning the air in our suite up and down. He was too hot, then he was freezing. This went on all afternoon. I became convinced that he had the flu.

I just wanted him to get better. At the hospital, we sat in the waiting room for a long time. We were not allowed to go back and see Mel. Eventually, we were allowed to go back to see him, but no one was saying anything about what was wrong with Mel. I don't remember much about the classes that week. I remember Karen taught a good class, but my whole focus was on Mel. Was he going to be ok? That just kept running through my mind. I was young, just eighteen, and that was the first time anyone important to me had been sick like that, the first time someone I cared about went to the hospital.

Sometime during that week, I remember my mom, Gary, and Rita sitting me down and gently breaking the terrible news that Mel had been diagnosed with AIDS. At that time, especially where I came from in the small-town south, very little was known about AIDS or how you got it. I had never known anyone who had been diagnosed with HIV or AIDS. They, my mom, Rita and Gary, didn't want to say anything to me at the time because they knew I would cry. It was too surreal for me to digest at that point. Everyone thought it was an actual death sentence for anyone, including Mel. For many in those days, it WAS a death sentence. I was just not expecting to encounter this reality of life as a homosexual at that point. I was so young, about to turn nineteen. It was a time in my life where I was just finding myself. I was not yet very open with myself as to exactly who I was, a homosexual male. I looked up to Mel. He was special to me because he was the first one to say, "I'm going to give this kid an opportunity to do something." He put me in the ballet he set on the High Point Ballet to be presented to the board of directors of the Southeast Regional Ballet Association. When somebody takes you under their wing like that, you are definitely a little more conscious of your need to do things well.

Mel's illness was very eye-opening to me, emotionally. When I went to visit him in the hospital, I think he could see the fear in my eyes. His reaction was to start cracking jokes with me, bantering again to make me feel better. He comforted me without me really understanding, at that time, that that was what he was doing.

Mel: I find it astounding that I have no memory of any of this.

The next thing I remembered was being in the hospital. I had no idea what hospital, or where, or what had happened. I had no concept of whether or not it was the same day or how long I had been unconscious. I remember being told that the attending physician would see me on Monday. I had been admitted through the emergency room. I guessed that the regular in-patient doctor was off playing golf as it was a Sunday in the South and that is just what doctors and businessmen do.

In Rita Taylor's words:

Rita Taylor, Co-Director, High Point Ballet, High Point, NC.

We did a conference there (Beach Cove Resort) for about four seasons, and Mel was a part of that, I believe, for at least three out of the four seasons that we did it, I would say. It was the last time Mel was there that was the year when he got really sick, and I remember that when he came in to check in at the hotel that he had a really severe headache. He was suffering from the headache so badly that it had delayed him coming in. He was concerned about teaching with it. I think Mel got through a day, maybe two days of classes.

The conference lasted four days, and I think that it might have been the second day that Mel collapsed on the elevator.

(He) was headed back to his room in between classes, and Roscoe Sales, one of the other teachers, called us and said that Mel had collapsed in the elevator. Of course, we called emergency medical services immediately. They came and transported Mel to the Grand Strand Regional Medical Center, the hospital in Myrtle Beach. We followed behind the ambulance in the car to the emergency room where they were doing the assessment. We were back and forth between making calls and trying to get information. Mel had no family there with him initially, so we served as family at the time. We were with him while they asked him questions, and he was going through the process. I think that Mel was there for at least a week. We had to wait at one point for the doctor to come back from a weekend of golf – you know, sweet, southern stuff. We got a diagnosis, it was a couple of days in. Mel was sort of in and out of consciousness, still dealing with a really bad headache. I remember initially telling the emergency doc who Mel was and what all he had done, New York City Ballet, dancing for the Queen…he was quite impressed and seemed to be very concerned about Mel. As a sidebar, he told us, 'You know, I don't really know what this is, but I suspect some kind of meningitis.'

I remember going to his office. This particular doctor also had an office, I guess he was serving as an ER doc at night or something. I went to his practice, because I wanted to ask him about the particulars of the meningitis because I was really concerned about that because of our responsibility for the young dancers at the conference. I was not able to see the doctor at his office, so I wound up circling back to the hospital, and at some point, he was back there again. By then, Mel had been referred to some other doctors. By this time, the doctors were able to help alleviate Mel's pain. I remember bringing Mel a fruit basket because he was craving fruit. He ate one of the peaches, and I remember him saying how good it was not to be in pain, and how good the peach tasted in that moment. I remember that very specifically because he had just suffered so much.

Roscoe Sales' words:

I was at the conference to teach the jazz classes, and was supposed to room with Mel and Robbie Gosnell. I remember that after Mel taught that one class on Sunday, he had no energy. He was just exhausted and went straight to bed. We gave him crackers and ice because he was so nauseous. It was Sunday evening when Mel collapsed and I knew this was something more serious than a headache and sinus infection. We were in the elevator and I had to help Mel down the hall to our room, where he collapsed on the bed and became unconscious. I called Gary and Rita once we got to the room and I put Mel to bed. I told them that something was seriously wrong and they called an ambulance. I filled in the next day and taught Mel's classes, then Karen Brown arrived and took over his classes the next day.

I remember later driving to Charlotte to see Mel with some other dancers from Atlanta Ballet. By that time, Mel had wasted away to almost nothing. I was sure that he would be dead very soon.

Gary Taylor remembers:

Karen Brown came down the minute she heard Mel was hospitalized. She covered his classes and acted as a family member for Mel, as well. Karen was lovely. She stepped in and did great with the kids. Karen arranged for Mel to be transported back to Charlotte.

From Rita Taylor:

A few days later, we drove his car to his home from the beach. Gary drove it, and I followed in my car. I don't believe Mel's AIDS diagnosis was conclusive until after he got back to Charlotte. The doctor used the term "fungal meningitis" with me and said that he believed it was the result of an HIV or AIDS infection. I was honestly more concerned about the meningitis and its relativity to the conference because of the children. We found out from the doctor that it was not a transmittable form of the disease and that our conference members were safe.

There was so little known back then about the long-term effects of AIDS. Mel continued to decline for a long time. Gary would continue to go down to Charlotte to see Mel and saw the decline. At one point, he was sure that it would be his last visit because Mel was just so ill. He was so heavy-hearted about it.

Mel: When I came back to consciousness at the hospital, I remember first noticing that everything was white and my head was still hurting in that totally uncomprehending fashion that I suddenly, instinctively knew was going to be serious trouble. I vaguely remember Fanchon Cordell holding my hand for a long time. It must have been while we were waiting for the ambulance, but I'm not sure, it could have been at the hospital.

The doctor came in and told me they were waiting for test results to see if I had a rare form of meningitis most often related to advanced cases of AIDS. AIDS? My heart just froze. The doctor had said AIDS, not even HIV. He was very matter-of-fact, almost bored. I was sure he had looked at me as if I disgusted him; I was mortified and disgusted with myself. The doctor told me he would see me again in a couple days.

I was terrified, but still hanging on to the denial I had apparently held on to for nine years, but which I, as yet, had no idea I had been holding on to. I suddenly remembered that I had recently had a false positive HIV test in New York. But, wait…. When was I in New York? It dawned on me that I had not lived there for nine years. Between the headache and the nausea and the confusion, I had no idea what was going on. I believe I was in and out of consciousness for several days.

Someone called Karen Brown, my friend from before and during my Dance Theatre of Harlem days, and, also called my family. I do not remember calling anyone, but apparently it was I who called. Having to fly in all the way from New York, Karen still managed to get there before any of my family members arrived. It took them three days to get to Myrtle Beach from Raleigh, North Carolina. I guess they had other things to take care of first. Karen took control of everything from the moment she arrived, taught my classes for the summer intensive, demanded information from the hospital staff, and acted as my spokesperson. My family was not happy with Karen, when they finally arrived because they thought they should be in charge. I was perfectly happy with Karen running things. She made me feel safer, cared for.

Robbie Gosnell apparently took the news of my illness very hard. I never realized before that I was one of the special people in Robbie's life for the sheer fact that I had chosen him to be in my ballet for the High Point Ballet. I guess it was the first time someone had believed in him. I don't even remember Robbie coming to visit me in the hospital. I am glad to find out that I was kind to him and comforted him with humor. By that time, I already had little humor or kindness left for anyone. My despair would continue to escalate in the form of meanness, terrible cruelty and paranoia towards those who were closest to me. Over the next few years, I would take my anger and humiliation out on most everyone with whom I came in contact.

Somewhere along the way, Karen Brown took on Power of Attorney for me. I have no recollection of signing anything giving her my Power of Attorney, but I'm sure I must have done so. I trusted her and had no concerns that she would act in anything but my best interests. She was one of my dearest friends. I knew she would fight for me and that no one was going to intimidate her. Karen was familiar with doctors, hospitals and how things worked within the healthcare system, having grown up the daughter of a prominent

Robert Costello, Mel, Karen Brown and Peter Frame in happier times.

black physician in Augusta, Georgia. I already hated this horrible hospital, the inadequate nursing staff and the rude, homophobic doctor. Karen arranged for a private ambulance to drive me all the way back to Charlotte. My sister, Ellen thought I should go home to Raleigh and let the family care for me. There was no way I was going to do that. I feel sure that I would not be alive now if I had. My mother's shame over my diagnosis alone would have killed me. I wanted to go to Carolinas Medical Center in Charlotte because they were known to be at the cutting edge of AIDS care. For some reason, I was taken to another hospital in Charlotte, which, at that time was just not equipped to handle AIDS patients, and was almost as awful as the South Carolina hospital had been.

Eventually, I got to the Carolinas Medical Center (CMC), under the care of Dr. James Horton, then the Chief of Infectious Disease there. Dr. Horton has since resigned from that position, and is now still on the faculty of Infectious Disease at Carolinas Medical Center in Charlotte, and is also a clinical professor on faculty at UNC-Chapel Hill, where he won the teaching award in 2015. He teaches both the students at CMC and those from UNC-Chapel Hill who come to Charlotte to study internal medicine and infectious disease. He originally specialized in Internal Medicine, which then led him to specialize in Infectious Disease. Dr. Horton came to Charlotte in 1984, after first working in New Orleans, where he saw his first AIDS patient in 1982. He then spent two years in Denver, where he was part of a team, working under a National Institutes of Health grant, studying lymph nodes in gay men. After coming to Charlotte, Dr. Horton was in private practice for six years before joining the faculty at CMC. During the 1990's, Dr Horton was involved in many studies at CMC, working in an AIDS clinical trial sub-unit for the National Institutes of Health (NIH). I instinctively knew I was in good hands.

Dr. Horton wanted to know every detail of my life, the hows, whys, whos, and whens. Although I am sure that much of what I told him about the facts of a gay lifestyle were more detailed truth than he had ever heard before, he never made me feel embarrassed or ashamed. I had already made myself feel those two things in triplicate. I believe that having a doctor who respected me as a person and a patient and did not judge me was very important to my recovery. Dr. Horton has been my doctor now for twenty-one years. He tells me that I am only one of his many AIDS patients who have now survived more than twenty years. According to Dr. Horton, in the beginning of the epidemic, everyone who got sick, died, but those days are long gone.

I believe that I know from whom I contracted HIV. It was nine or ten years earlier, while on tour with the New York City Ballet in Berlin, Germany when I had a short relationship with Rolf Garske, writer and publisher for several international dance-related magazines and books.

Mel, in 2017, with his doctor, Dr. James Horton, who was Chief of Infectious Disease at the Carolinas Medical Center in 1995 when he first took Mel's case.

I was to be the cover story for Dance Magazine-Europe, I believe. We had used a condom, but it had broken and was lodged inside of me. I did some checking when I got sick and found out that he, too, was dying of complications from AIDS. He would pass less than a year later at the age of forty-three. I hold no animosity toward Rolf. We were both consenting adults. We were careful and we knew what the possibilities were. I do wish that he had contacted me and told me that he was sick when he first found out. But, he may not have been aware back then as to just how long he had incubated this hideous virus.

I was back home in Charlotte now and alone with my terror. Every waking hour I was in pain, but not just the physical pain, which itself was earth-shattering, as I had been diagnosed with cryptococcal meningitis, a rare type of meningitis, caused by a fungus commonly found in dirt and air everywhere, and often spread by pigeons and other birds. One of the main killers of people with advanced cases of AIDS, it is exceedingly rare for a person with a healthy immune system to get this rare form of meningitis because a normal immune system will easily fight the infection off. It is not possible to transmit it from one person to another, as it is caused by a fungus found in the soil throughout the world and these fungi are breathed in daily, but do not affect those who are healthy. I was also infected with an insidious, emotional pain that was constant; waking or sleeping it was with me, and it held on with a strength I previously had not known existed.

The worst thing about having an AIDS diagnosis was that suddenly, no one wanted to touch me. The touch of another human is so healing. It is craved by AIDS patients. I dreaded, but came to accept, the fearful look in the eyes of my friends and family. In my heart, I knew that even the people I loved and trusted most, and who loved and trusted me most, would never touch me again.

By now, my dear friend and former director, Sal Aiello was very ill. We spoke on the phone often at this point. He told me to take care of myself and not to try to do too much. Sal also told me to be brave and to continue to hold my head up and be proud of who I was. At first, when I had returned to Charlotte from Boston the year before, Sal had told me only that he had lost a little weight. Because Sal did not talk publicly about his illness, there were rumors floating around. I had heard a rumor that Sal had some kind of heart disease, but when I saw how much weight he had lost, the unspeakable did cross my mind. In fact, Sal had lost so much weight that he was now proudly wearing clothes from the boy's department. Sal and I had always obsessed over weight. We were always on some diet or another, sharing our latest diet secrets. It was a "normal" part of every professional dancer's life.

Sal's energy had always been very strong. Things were different now. AIDS had totally changed Sal's physique, right in front of the company's eyes. Through all the horrible changes and humiliations, Sal had somehow kept his magnificent personality and sense of humor. He was still as bright and witty and fun as he had ever been. I think that I knew even before Sal told me. By the time he did tell me in the early Summer of 1995, I had watched enough friends and colleagues succumb to AIDS to recognize it. Funny, but even as late as June of 1995, I still had not recognized any possible symptoms within myself. By the end of July, only four weeks later, everything in my world had changed. I was not just HIV positive. I was "down the rabbit hole." My world was completely upside down. At forty-one years old, I was dying of full blown AIDS. Sal was fifty-one and would die later that year of pneumocystis pneumonia, a complication of his AIDS.

Somehow, I never for a second thought it could happen to me. I remember feeling so sad for Sal, wondering to myself, "Why Sal?" I believe that sub-consciously I felt that I was protected. It would never happen to me. Denial is such a powerful evil. It is an evil that cannot be seen so it can very easily sneak up on us and grab us without us even having the slightest clue that it has moved in. I did not at that point even consciously realize that nine years had gone by since I got that phone call from my doctor in New York, the day I was moving to North Carolina, telling me that I had a false positive reading on my HIV test. As yet, I still had not even thought about that.

Although I did go through a period of one-night stands in my younger days, I had never considered myself to be promiscuous. Although I must admit that I dabbled in the past, I was not a regular drug user or a drinker or a smoker. I took care of my body, ate well and was super-disciplined. I was a good, God-loving, God-fearing, life-long-every-Sunday-church-going, Southern Baptist Christian, who did my best to live by my Christian faith. I was also a gay man dying of AIDS.

My life was now very different to any reality I had previously known. Where I had always needed to work in the past, I rarely thought about work now. It was a past that seemed so distant, more like a fantasy than a reality. My new reality revolved around being ill. I spent a good portion of my day choking down the sixty-five pills the doctor said were necessary to my immediate survival, and trying to keep them down. Those were the very first days of HAART, Highly Active Antiretroviral Therapy. Before HAART, AZT alone was the main hope for a prolonged life, but many became immune to its affects which is why the HAART "cocktail" of several different drugs was developed. Many of those infected had to deal with horrible side-effects of the early drugs. The newest hope, beginning in 1995, was a sort of cocktail of AZT and other antiretroviral drugs, plus a newly FDA-approved protease inhibitor.

Robert Lindgren, my first director at the University of North Carolina School of the Arts, was working behind the scenes on my behalf. At the time, I had no idea that he had called up co-author, Claudia Folts, then artistic director of the Charlotte City Ballet, and had told her that she would be getting a call from me and that I needed a teaching job. Claudia told Bobby that she could hire me for the Saturday morning company class. I often wonder how many others Bobby called on my behalf. I suspect there were more, but maybe they were too afraid of AIDS to give me a chance. There were a few people I had worked for as a teacher/choreographer in the past who would not return my calls now much less hire me. Bobby gave me Claudia's phone number and told me that she was looking for a teacher. I have no memory of making that phone call, but Claudia does remember it.

Claudia remembers:

During the fall of 1994, Bobby Lindgren was teaching at the Charlotte City Ballet on Saturdays. He had called me and asked if he could come teach as it had been a while since he had last taught. He wanted to get back into the swing of teaching after having spent six or seven years at the New York City Ballet, where he had taken over from Lincoln Kirsten in an administrative capacity. He would be adjudicating for the pacific region of Regional Dance America (RDA) during the winter of 1995 and would be teaching the classes for the member companies and adjudicating their ballets for inclusion in the performances that Spring.

As I remember it, Bobby talked to me about Mel teaching for us back in the late Fall of 1994, the year before Mel got sick. I think Mel has combined a couple of different memories as to that time period. He returned to Charlotte that year, 1994, from Boston Ballet and was doing quite a bit of guest teaching and choreography around the region. As Bobby was one to always think ahead, he knew he would be going on the RDA adjudication tour that winter, and he was trying to help me find a suitable teacher to replace him.

I remember that when Mel called me in January of 1995, he was extremely formal on the phone. He seemed surprised that I even knew who he was, which surprised me. Who, in the ballet world, did not know who Mel Tomlinson was in those days? He and I were not friends at the time, though we had many friends in common. We had not known each other in New York, even though in those days Mel was friends with my roommate, Don Tennenblatt, a brilliant pianist who often played for the New York City Ballet, as well as at David Howard's school. I had even worked at the North Carolina Dance Theatre at the same time as Mel, teaching the women's company class for a few months, the year they moved to Charlotte, filling in before Jerri Kumery arrived to begin her Ballet Mistress duties.

Mel seemed quite surprised on the phone when I told him that Bobby had already spoken to me and that he could start teaching the next Saturday. He taught two or three Saturdays a month that winter and spring. I remember that he was gone sporadically for guest teaching jobs. I think his last class that spring was in May. I remember that he was going to teach in New Mexico, for Patricia Dickinson and then the Myrtle Beach intensive, as well as a couple other places that I do not remember. In May, I told Mel that we would love to have him back in the fall. This was two months before Mel was stricken with cryptococcal meningitis.

In August of 1995, Bobby called me and told me what had happened in Myrtle Beach and that Mel was sick. He asked me if I would consider having Mel come back to teach in the fall if and when he got back on his feet. I told him, "Yes, of course Mel can come back. He and I already discussed it back in May."

Even though Mel was one of the first people I knew in North Carolina to be stricken by this terrible illness, I had lived in New York in the 1970's and the 1980's and had lost many friends, teachers and several roommates to AIDS. I knew that no one was going to catch the disease simply by taking a class from Mel. The dancers all loved him and had looked forward to their Saturday classes with him the year before. I knew they would be very happy to have him back. Unsure of what the reaction of the parents would be, I figured I would cross that bridge when we came to it. Bobby told me that Mel was terribly fragile emotionally, at that time, and very much ashamed. He said that Mel would not call me about teaching, as he was sure I would not want him back, so I would need to call him.

When I called Mel, he seemed shocked that I was asking him to come back and teach. He immediately told me that he had AIDS and asked if that was going to be a problem with the parents. I told him that I already knew, as did everyone else, which seemed to surprise him. The ballet world is so small and people's business travels fast. I told Mel that Bobby had called me and filled me in on what was going on. Mel was very concerned that the parents would shun him. I told him that having him teach would not be a problem. I figured that anyone who had a problem with it would not come to Mel's classes. That Saturday morning class, consisting of both company members and advanced students, was very crowded anyway so I was not worried about it. As it turned out, there was only one parent who had a problem with having Mel teach and she did not bring her dancer to his classes.

Mel seemed surprised that I treated his disease as a minor annoyance rather than the earth-shattering end of the world that it had become to him at the time. Although Mel was not yet ready to see it, I believe that teaching the dancers gave him a glimmer of hope of the possibility that he just might get some semblance of his life back. He taught sporadically for several months, one or two Saturdays each month when he was feeling strong enough. At first, he would drive himself across town to the Charlotte City Ballet's spacious studios. Eventually, he could no longer drive due to a seizure he had that caused the loss of his driver's license. So, either I or Keith Darby, another friend, and former student of Mel's at the School of the Arts, would go to his house and pick him up. Keith was teaching our fledgling boys program at the time.

Over the next year, as his health continued to go downhill, Mel would teach less and less. He would call and say, "I'm in the hospital for a while. I'll let you know when I'm better." I believe that aside from Mel's medical issues, he was not yet ready to allow people to love and care about him again. He had to forgive himself and he had not yet been able to bring himself to do that. I was sure he was depressed, but Mel would deny it whenever I broached the subject. There was a pervading sadness and sense of hopelessness that I could see in Mel. He was so hurt and angry at the loss of his life as he had known it.

Mel: In the beginning, every, single day was steeped in shame. My trip down the rabbit-hole forced everyone who knew me, as well as me, to face my homosexuality full on. Gone were the days of "Mel's gay," which meant only, "Mel is not attracted to women, but he has a great sense of style and a great sense of humor," rather than meaning "Mel likes having sex with other men." No longer was being gay a distant fact that everyone knew but no one thought about because, at that time there were no homosexual public displays of affection, and no official gay marriages. I had contracted a terrible plague merely due to the fact that I had engaged in homosexual behaviors. Every day, when I first woke up, I would feel like my old self for about five seconds. Those few seconds were the single good time in each of my days. Then I would remember my reality and I would relive my shame and humiliation all over again. It would be a couple of years before I would become aware that there were other ways in which to catch this plague and that women, straight men, and children -- even unborn children -- were not immune.

I had virtually no money coming in, except for my disability money, which I was able to receive thanks to Karen's help, and what I was getting for teaching one or two classes a month, so no money could go out. By the time Sal died, in October, 1995, I had already lost all hope and was very close to losing my mind. I was hospitalized at the time so could not go to Sal's memorial to pay my respects. Looking back now, I know I was in a depression so deep and complete that there would have been no way to pull myself back out of it without help. At the time, I had no idea that I was depressed. I was simply living in my new reality. Each time I went to see Dr. Horton, he would ask me how I was, emotionally. "Are you depressed, Mel?" "No," I would say, "I'm fine." And I believed that was the truth.

The loneliness was worse than the drugs. I had gone from a life in which I often had too many people around me, too many choices of things to do and places to go, to a life of almost complete solitude. Before I got sick, I had grown to believe my press and am ashamed to admit that I had become a very arrogant, snobbish person. Part of that behavior had come out of necessity. I was often surrounded by people who wanted to be my friend, not because they genuinely cared for me, but because of my status in the professional ballet world. Since my life had turned upside-down, I was to find out who my real friends were, and that was an eye-opening experience. My arrogance and mean-spirited behavior was to get much worse before it got better, but in the end, AIDS would make me a better person. But those days were still years, and several very-close brushes with death, away.

My days were mostly spent in bed or on my couch. I had no appetite, and would only eat when reminded by something I was watching on TV. For the first time in my life, I did not need one of my crazy diets to look good physically. At that point, I still did my warm up and exercises every day to keep my muscles alive and stretched. I had always been neat and organized, keeping my house clean, my bed made daily, and my kitchen well-stocked. I could not find the energy to take out the garbage or make the bed, much less clean and vacuum.

Two of the younger dancers from North Carolina Dance Theatre, Heather Maloy and Jennifer Cavanaugh, came to visit me. When they saw the squalor I was living in, they took it upon themselves to clean up my house, do my laundry and stock my kitchen. Both no more than twenty-three or twenty-four years old at the time, these two girls came over several times a week to help out. They also made sure I got to my doctor's appointments. Without Heather and Jennifer, who were terrified of my illness but came over anyway, I would not be alive today. They were among the first of several people to step in and literally save my life. It still overwhelms me to realize that it was people who were, in many ways, more acquaintances than close friends or family who jumped in to help me without a second thought as to their fears of any health risks. This became a pattern in my life.

In Heather Maloy's words:

> *I joined the North Carolina Dance Theatre straight out of high school. Having attended the North Carolina School of the Arts when the company was still in residency there, I had been able to watch the company grow. It was the time when the company was getting much attention. They were a touring company of soloist calibre dancers, strong and sleek, and on the cutting edge of contemporary ballet. Mel was one of the principal dancers and we were in awe of him. I was proud and honored to join that company.*
>
> *When we moved to Charlotte, the company fell on tough times for a while, but we were a family and we toughed it out. Sal got sick, with what many of us believed was a heart condition. The fact that he had AIDS he kept completely to himself. I believe that only Jerri Kumery, our Ballet Mistress, knew until almost the end of Sal's life. So when Mel got sick and was candid about his circumstances from the very beginning, we wanted to be there for him.*
>
> *I think the first time we, Jennifer Cavanaugh and I, went over to Mel's it was in response to a phone call. I remember he said he was hungry, but he didn't have any money or any food in the house, but he was also afraid to eat because he felt so sick. We had no idea what to take for Mel to eat. I think we made him some chicken broth and put garlic in it since garlic is supposed to have healing qualities. We didn't even put any noodles in it. So we called Mel and told him we would be bringing this pot of "soup-ish" stuff over. We were just so young and worried about doing the right thing. We tried to get Mel to eat some of it, but it was difficult.*
>
> *Mel was not in a good place emotionally or physically. He was often mean and rude, even to us. He was always lying in that bed. I remember that we would feed his dog and his cat.*
>
> *A few times, Karen Brown would be there when we would arrive. I remember liking her to a degree, but I was also upset with her because, by that time, Mel was upset with her. He had so much paranoia in those days, that it was hard to know whether what he would tell us was real or imagined. Each time we visited, Mel would tell us something different. He seemed to focus his paranoia on Karen at that time, often telling us that she was stealing his things. He said his laptop was missing and his vita-mix blender.*
>
> *Karen had power of attorney, and seemed to have things under control*

whenever she came to visit. She would stock his kitchen and get things organized, but she lived out of town, Atlanta, I think, so she could not be there as often as she was needed.

Before Karen got Mel in-home nurses, I don't know how he was alive at all. He was filthy because he could no longer bathe himself and Jennifer and I had no idea what to do. We were not strong enough to carry him to the bathtub. Sometimes we would arrive and things were just so bad. We felt completely helpless.

Once the caregivers were there, things seemed better for a while. Jennifer and I were so relieved. We still went over to Mel's house to check on him several times a week and took him to his doctor's appointments. Unfortunately, Mel was so hateful to the caregivers, calling them fat, ugly, stupid. It seemed that he had not one ounce of patience or kindness left in his soul. I remember that he would tell us that he hated a caregiver because she was too fat, and the poor woman would be standing right there in front of him. The caregivers were constantly quitting because he was so mean and impossible to deal with. Whenever he would get a really good caregiver, we would beg her not to quit. We would make every excuse we could think of for his horrible behavior. In many ways, Mel had progressively declined into something less than human. There was very little left of that magnificent dancer that we had looked up to when we first joined the North Carolina Dance Theatre.

Probably one of the worst times was the day Mel's family came to visit. Mel called me in a complete panic. "You have to come now," he demanded, "They are going to steal everything. You have to stop them!" At first, I thought Mel was just paranoid yet again, but something made me listen to him. I think it was fear. I could hear it in his voice, feel it in my bones. When I arrived at Mel's house, his sisters and brothers were all there with their teenage children, having also just arrived. The kids went outside to play basketball while Mel's sisters and brothers wandered all over the house, looking at Mel's things. As things started to get picked up, I tried to stop them by saying, "Mel really doesn't want you to take that," or "Please put that down." But they all just looked straight through me.

I felt all I could do at that point was comfort Mel who was pretty much inconsolable. His family seemed to believe that Mel owed them. I think they believed that because Mel had been famous in the dance world, he was rich and should be taking care of them. By this point, Mel's finances had been completely depleted by his illness. He was on over 60 medications a day, many that were not covered by his insurance. It seemed to me that his family had already decided that Mel was dead. There seemed to be little or no compassion or love towards the devastated man laying helpless in that bed.

At least with the homecare nurses more or less in place, Jennifer and I could relax a little. We saw Karen less now, as Frank Smith, one of our teachers at the North Carolina School of the Arts had taken over power of attorney and seemed to have things more under control. We knew that Frank would take good care of things.

Mel spent more time in and out of the hospital and had may appointments for tests, blood, and medication checks. Jennifer and I would take turns driving Mel to these appointments. I am embarrassed to say that one time I forgot Mel at the hospital. Whenever he was done with an appointment, they would put him in a wheelchair in the lobby, with a bowl in case he had to vomit. There, he would wait for whichever one of us was picking him up to get out of rehearsal.

This one time, I completely forgot to pick him up. Rather than have someone call me, as this was before cell phones, Mel just sat there for hours. Finally, late that evening, he called me, telling me he was still waiting and holding on to his bowl full of vomit, as he had been doing since early in the day. From that day forward, he has never let me forget it, always reminding me of my terrible misstep and promising, or rather threatening to put it in his book.

Mel: By the holiday season that year, 1995, I was sure that life could not get any worse. I was so focused on hoping that I would still be alive by the time my birthday came around the first week of 1996, that when I received the phone call from my brother, Dexter, telling me that my father had passed into the afterlife, it was a horrible shock. Daddy had not been well for a long time. My heart was completely broken, as was my spirit when Ronald Perry and Karen Brown came and accompanied me to my daddy's funeral.

Chapter Fifteen

Dark Days: Endless Agony
Spring 1997 – December 1998

Succumbing to the complications of the AIDS virus not only changed me physically and emotionally, it also made me discover exactly which of my friends I could count on. Overnight, I found that I had very few friends and no fans. It happened so fast. One minute I was setting up guest teaching jobs all over the country. The next minute I was dying from cryptococcal meningitis.

I had gotten used to years of having adoring balletomanes writing me notes, and waiting for me outside the stage door. I took it for granted that they would always be there in the same way that I took for granted that all my friends would always be there. Back in my New York days, I was often stopped on the street by fans asking for my autograph. Now no one wanted my autograph. No one was writing me letters. The lives of my friends went on as before, but without me. I was forgotten and I knew it. I could feel my heart sinking a little more each day. No longer "flavor of the month," I knew that I did not matter to anyone anymore. No one wanted to touch me. No one wanted to hug me, or kiss me, or love me. The adoration and applause that had kept me going for the better part of my adult life was done. It was nothing now, nothing but a fleeting memory. For a time, I was not even sure if it had ever been part of my reality. I really did love that life. I was so happy and thankful for that life, thinking and believing that God had singled me out and blessed me more thoroughly than most. I never suspected that it could and would all come crashing down, and would disappear in the blink of an eye.

Alone, desolate, and terrifyingly lonely, for the first time in as long as I could remember; I believed I had no one. I had never felt real love from anyone in my family, except my father, so starved for it as I was in my childhood, I had always needed my fans for emotional sustenance. This scourge that had ruined my life and was not-so-slowly killing me would eventually be my savior, teaching me more about real love than all the ballet fans, fair-weather friends and un-caring family members ever could. But all of that was still several years away. At this point, mid-1997, my life seemed like nothing but endless pain and loneliness.

Almost two full years had passed since I was first diagnosed. I was no longer teaching for Charlotte City Ballet or anyone else, nor was I choreographing any new ballets. I believed I had been picked up against my will and dropped into a very bleak alternate universe. The highlight of my endless days were my doctor's appointments. In the back of my mind, a little voice kept telling me that my purpose in life had been fulfilled and I was now done. I was simply waiting to die.

I was not funny anymore. The days of easy bantering with friends and acquaintances were only a faint memory. When I first started to work with my co-author on this part of my story, I believed that there had only been a year between the time I first got sick in Myrtle Beach and when I went into hospice care. In reality, it was a full three years, four months, and twenty days of relentless pain and loneliness. The fact that I do not have even a whole year's worth of memories during that time, is both a blessing and a curse.

My friend, Karen Brown, was patiently trying to deal with my needs long distance. She would come to town as often as she could, despite the fact that my paranoia and unkindness had to have been extremely difficult for her, but she had her own life to keep up with, too. She did her best to hire new nurses, almost as fast as I made them quit. By this time, I had no money, except for my monthly disability checks, five completely maxed out credit cards that I had long since stopped being able to keep up with, and none of my memorabilia from my career seemed to be left at my house. I was starting to doubt that my memories of a ballet career were even real. They seemed to be nothing more than the fantasies of a severely psychotic person.

Through all of it, Dr. Horton was one of the few constants in my life. He made sure to keep up with every break-through in AIDS treatment. I was lucky to get sick when I did. If it had even been a year or two earlier, I know I would not have survived. The year that I was diagnosed, 1995, was the same year that Saquinivir first became available to the public. Saquinivir was a new protease inhibitor and part of what was called the "AIDS Cocktail." This cocktail, known as HAART, or Highly Active Antiretroviral Therapy, was a major breakthrough. According to Dr. Horton, mixing the available drugs helped to keep patients from becoming immune to any one drug and cut down on some of the side effects. Over the next two years, for the first time, deaths from complications of AIDS dropped significantly in the United States and other developed countries. Dr. Horton said that from 1995 on, AIDS was no longer a death sentence. Patients were no longer dying from opportunistic diseases like pneumocystis pneumonia or cryptococcal meningitis. They were living long enough to die in the same manner as the general public, from coronary heart disease and cancers.

Of course, at the time, I did not know any of this. Having gone for at least nine years without getting diagnosed or treated, had left me in the advanced stages of the disease. My body was already being savagely attacked by cryptococcal meningitis and kidney disease, and I had no immune system left to fight off these scourges. I had my bouts with pneumocystis pneumonia, and a small bout with Kaposi's Sarcoma on my big toe, for which I had to go through radiation therapy. That is why it is always best to find out early if one has a serious disease. It breaks my heart when I hear young people say things like, "What I don't know won't hurt me," because it will, every time. Knowing sooner would not have made me completely well, but I could have most likely avoided the years of suffering from such horribly painful illnesses. I feel certain that Dr. Horton's relentlessness with my care kept me alive more than a few times. I am so grateful to him.

Kevin Self, my oldest and best friend in the ballet world, was now living in New Mexico and teaching at, and running, his wife's ballet school. Kevin called me constantly to check up on me. He and his wife, Michele, even paid my mortgage for two years and flew out to check on me several times. Mr. Mitchell also called me. It meant so much to me to hear from him after how we had left things when I joined the New York City Ballet. I know that I had hurt his feelings terribly when I left the Dance Theatre of Harlem, and that he had felt my betrayal very keenly, but he set all that aside and called to check up on me. Each time I was to hear from these generous, caring people, it was like giving water to a man lost in a completely desolate desert. Their kindness sustained me more than they will ever know.

Ronald Perry called often and even showed up at my bedside. Looking back, I think Ronald probably should have been the main love of my life. He was so much like my father, a strong, very good man. He was also a true friend. There were times when Ronald expressed concern and dislike for some of my other close friends. At those times, I allowed my own arrogance to chalk his feelings up to jealousy. When I got sick, I was to discover that Ronald had been right about certain of those so-called friends all along. I was humbled by his wisdom more than a few times.

Eddie Shellman never called or answered my letters. That hurt me quite a bit. Eddie had been my tour roommate and dear friend at the Dance Theatre of

Harlem. One of the last times I had seen Eddie, he had come to see me dance at the New York City Ballet. I introduced him and his then-fiance', Melanie Persons, also a dancer at the Dance Theatre of Harlem, to Mr. Balanchine. At the time, Eddie was learning Russian and it delighted Mr. B to speak with Eddie in his native language. I thought that Eddie and I would be friends forever, but he seemed to have the "out of sight, out of mind" attitude with most people in his life. I missed him terribly. Several years later, when Eddie had his own troubles, I was the one he called and asked to come to his aid, to teach the summer intensive at the ballet school he and his wife founded in New Jersey. Due to certain legal issues, Eddie was suddenly not able to teach at his own school. I also wrote him a letter of support to the court. I did both of those things with no hesitation, but in all honesty, much as I loved him my feelings were terribly hurt. That is one way to know you truly love someone: when you have been hurt by them and you still help them when needed with no hesitation. I still miss our friendship.

Karen Brown, whom I had known almost as long as I had known Kevin, held my Power of Attorney. I am very grateful to Karen who did manage to navigate the social security system and get me my disability benefits. They were not enough to pay my living expenses and cover all the medications and in-home caregivers I needed, but they certainly helped. I no longer had any health insurance. What savings I had went very quickly.

Although Heather Maloy and Jennifer Cavanaugh were a great help to me, things progressed rather quickly to the point where I needed more help than they could provide. Karen had done her best to get me some more-or-less professional help, two home healthcare workers whose job it was to make sure I took my medicine, ate and was kept clean and relatively comfortable. They pretty much treated me like garbage, showing little or no compassion or respect, while stealing from me. One in-home caregiver even took my dog, Yogi, and my cat, Gypsy, along with some of my memorabilia, my Volkswagen, my TV, and some of my furniture. I have no memory of giving anything to her, but I am told by those who were around at the time, that it was my idea for her to take everything that she took. By a miracle, I was able to get Yogi back from her several years later.

I apparently had added Karen to my bank accounts and credit cards, with right of survivorship, but I have no memory of doing that. I'm sure Karen felt that she was doing things in my best interest, but I had no money coming in and my cards should not have been used to the extent that they were used. I do understand that I must have been a huge burden to her, and everyone else.

I'm sure that it was expensive to try to look after me long distance. Flying and driving in to check on me was more than either of us could afford. Luckily, Karen had a sister, Lorraine, who worked for Delta Airlines and could get Karen "Buddy Passes." I was now hopelessly in debt. I guess both Karen and I naively figured I was dying so the debts would not matter. They were, quite frankly, the last things on my mind.

My sisters, Ellen and Tommina, and my mother came to visit at some point. Ellen told me that Mrs. Tomlinson sat in the living room and wept for me. I vaguely remember her in my room, quietly weeping over me. Once, while I was still under home nursing care, I went to visit her towards the end of her life at the nursing home where she finished out her days. I had been told that the end of her life was soon to come, and she wanted to see me one more time. When I got there, she demanded that I go out to get her some cigarettes. I did not acquiesce. Mrs. Tomlinson then pulled me down to her, and staring me in the eye, unblinking, told me not to ever tell anyone that I had AIDS. Even in my darkest time, and as near to her own death as she was, my own mother cared more about what outsiders thought of her than what was happening to me, her son. This was the moment I knew that this would be the last time I would ever see her, and that I would not attend her funeral when she passed.

Mrs. Tomlinson had cancer, probably caused by her years of constant smoking. During the last year of her life, her lower legs were amputated due to complications from her diabetes. She died at 5:00 a.m. one morning. I knew it before the nurse came in and told me a couple hours later. I awoke when she passed, and I felt her presence there with me in my home. It was not emotional, and there was certainly no sensation of warmth or security or love. She was simply gone, and I knew it. I also knew that I, and probably the whole world would now be able to rest a bit easier.

At her death, my feelings and hurt did not change. I did not attend Mrs. Tomlinson's funeral, but not because of my illness. My sisters and brothers were very upset with me for choosing not to be there. To this day, they believe that it was my lack of forgiveness that kept me away, but that was not it. I alone knew how my mother felt about me, her shame due to my choices as a gay man and the horrible disease with which I struggled. I believe she and I said our goodbyes the last time I saw her when she admonished me never to tell anyone about my disease. By the time Mrs. Tomlinson passed, I was no longer angry with her. I was indifferent to her. I had moved on and simply did not care any longer.

For over a year, my life continued to spiral downward. Heather and Jennifer still came and took me to my doctor's appointments. I was wheelchair-bound for the most part now. The neuropathy in my feet was at a critical point. There were times when I begged Dr. Horton to just amputate them. The desperation I had reached due to a pain that is not possible to adequately describe, was such that even the dancer in me wanted my feet gone.

Once, during a torrential thunderstorm, my next-door neighbor found me unconscious, face down in a mud puddle in my backyard. How I got there, I have no idea. He picked me up, took me back inside, cleaned me up and put me to bed. At the time, I wished he had just left me there to drown.

I did have some "good" days, in which I could walk around some using my cane or a walker, without terrible pain, but I was always, by this point so weak and fragile that I could not support myself for long. I worried that I would slip and fall like an elderly person and break my hips or other bones. Gradually, the wheelchair became my home. I felt safe within its confines.

Whenever Heather and Jennifer came to see me, they always brought me gummy bears, something that I loved and my body seemed always to be able to tolerate. I had stopped answering the phone because no one but my creditors were calling and I had no way to satisfy them. I believe that my credit cards had been maxed out paying my expenses, not by me, but by Karen, who I had given permission, I am sure, to use them. She was doing her best to help me. I had never been one to run up debt. I always thought of credit cards as something one kept in case of emergencies, but until this point in my life, I never needed them. Now, everything about my life was an emergency.

Jill Bahr and Patty Cantwell, my Charleston friends who were so instrumental in helping me get the job at Boston Ballet, took up a collection among their dancers to buy me a new Vitamix, something I needed as my diet was purely liquid at that point.

By late 1997, the pain in my feet had gotten to the point that even a sheet touching my feet was pure agony and walking on most days, was no longer possible. My life became my bed and my wheelchair. I could not bathe myself, and was now wearing adult diapers because, more often than not, I could not make it to the bathroom in time. There would be occasional days of relief, but at this point, at the age of forty-three, my humiliation was pretty much complete. I prayed constantly, asking God to please take me.

Thomassina Craig, one of my friends from my church, took it upon herself to get me to church as often as I was able. She is one of the kindest, most patient people I have ever known, having been there for me through more than one embarrassing humiliation. Once, she had taken me to choir practice and I had a rather messy accident. I did have an adult diaper on, but it was not enough to control this particular accident. Thomassina got me out of the church quickly and quietly, driving me home as fast as she could and helping clean me up once we got there. I hated that my friendships had become so humiliatingly intimate.

On one of my better days, when I was able to get out of bed, the pure misery I had been living with inside my head and heart took over and finally broke me. There was simply more agony than there was me, at that point. I was completely focused on the paranoid thoughts that my illness seemed to have prompted some of my friends, family and nurses to steal from me. I felt betrayed and so hurt. The feelings of abandonment, by family, friends, and all the balletomanes had overwhelmed me. Many of those whom I had considered to be my closest friends would not even speak to me, much less visit me. I found myself destroying everything in my house, breaking lamps, smashing everything. It was as if I was sitting outside my body watching myself do it but I was powerless to stop myself.

During my rampage, who was to arrive at my house unexpected, but Gyula Pandi. This wonderful man whom I admired so much was the one to see me at my absolute worst. I remember that he held me in the tightest grip possible, as I wailed, not allowing me any leeway to break anything else or hurt myself. He must have held me for hours. Gyula stayed until he was able to get me calmed down, medicated and back in bed. He then began the process of cleaning up my destruction, both the physical destruction of my home, and my own emotional destruction. Mr. Pandi began the process that would eventually give me back my life. This man would once again change the direction of my life, as he had done so many years before when he convinced Agnes de Mille to hire me. He went back to Winston-Salem and told Frank Smith and Mindi Lawrence, two of the teachers at the School of the Arts about what was happening to me.

I must interject something here that I learned from living this nightmare. It is about the true nature of friendship. Sometimes, those with whom you have the most intimate of friendships are only "verbal-emotional" friends. They are not always friends that you will be able to count on at the absolute worst moments of your life when you most need help. This is something that is impossible to recognize in someone until you have lived through something horribly frightening like my own situation. I have come to realize that the betrayal is not malicious, meaning that these friends would never set out to hurt you. Dealing with death is difficult for everyone. Some people seem to comfort themselves through the possession of the dying person's things. Others comfort themselves by negating the dying person's existence. Not everyone whom you love in your life, will have the strength of character to stand by through a super storm and that is all right. God and/or the universe will make sure that you are taken care of.

Probably the most important thing I learned during my time living this hell is that there are true angels living among us. These are often friends with whom you do not even realize, and neither do they, the depth of their friendship until they are needed. These angels are the people who see your need and act upon it, often knowing that it is going to mean great sacrifice to them and even to their families. I can count on my fingers who these people are in my life and still have most of my fingers left over. Kevin Self, Gyula Pandi, Karen Brown, Frank and Noel Smith and Mindi Lawrence are six such friends, as are Ronald Perry and Peter Frame. After hearing of my predicament from Mr. Pandi, Frank Smith and his wife, Noel, drove down to see me. We were more colleagues than close friends, respecting each other's work and genuinely liking each other. I remember nothing of this visit, except that I told Frank that I suspected that some of my friends, as well as the caregivers, were stealing from me. Although I do know that I was suffering from some paranoia, by this

*Mindi Lawrence, teaching a class at UNCSA, early to mid 1990's.
Photo courtesy of UNCSA.*

*Frank Smith, teaching a class at UNCSA, late 1980's / early 1990's.
Photo courtesy of UNCSA.*

time, I also knew that the pilfering was happening, as I had started consciously watching the movements and behaviors of those who came and went.

According to Frank, he and Noel were horrified at the state of both my health and my home. I was living in absolute squalor and did not even notice. I was lying in a bed made up of filthy-sweat-stained sheets. Garbage cans were full of my used diapers. The caregivers were obviously not giving me or my home any care. Bill collectors kept the phone ringing relentlessly, that is when the phone was not cut off due to lack of payment.

In Frank Smith's words:

I remember Mel was at death's door. This was the dark period, very dark. He was still living in his house. I don't remember how we, Noel and I, discovered that things were so bad for Mel. It might have been from Pandi, I'm not sure. It was over twenty years ago now. We decided to drive down to Charlotte and see Mel. We were horrified at the condition Mel was in, at the shape the house was in. No one was taking care of him, and he was not able to take care of himself. The house was a complete mess. There were dirty dishes everywhere, garbage, opened cans and stale food on the counter. No offence to Mel, but it was awful. Unopened bills were everywhere. Noel and I were stunned. We knew we had to do something. I remember talking to Mindi about it – Mindi Lawrence, another one of the teachers at the school. We talked about trying to get Mel some better help at his house. He had a couple of caregivers, one named Jackie, I remember, who Mel did not like at all. We didn't like her much either. I believe Karen Brown had found the agency providing the caregivers.

Mel told us that he felt that Karen, as well as these caregivers, were taking advantage of him financially. He believed things were being taken from the house. It was obvious that Mel was dealing with some paranoia. We saw no evidence that Karen or anyone else was doing anything wrong. Noel and I were concerned about Mel's feelings, his state of mind, but more importantly, we were concerned that Mel was not being properly cared for. I went to an attorney in Winston-Salem, and explained what was going on. Mel had asked me if I could be his power of attorney, so I asked how this could be done. The attorney said he could draw up papers for Mel to sign. This wasn't anything that I forcefully did, it was at Mel's request. The papers relinquished Karen's power of attorney and gave me the power of attorney, giving me the control needed to get some things done. Karen had done her best for Mel, but she did not live in the state, and Mel was at a point where he really needed more care than could be dealt with long distance. There were bills that needed to be paid, there was debt on some cards, things like that.

I remember saying to Mindi, that we needed to set up a fund, something for Mel. We wrote a letter to the community here at the School of the Arts and sent it out. There was no email then, at least I was not using it yet if there was. We sent it to the faculty and staff here at the school, saying that our dear friend, and former alumnus and faculty member, Mel Tomlinson is very sick and needs your help. We set up an account at the credit union, the State Employees Credit Union, and asked that checks be made out to the Mel Tomlinson Fund. I remember receiving numerous checks from people on campus. There were a couple of Deans who were quite generous. One in particular, Gerald Freedman, who was the Dean of the Drama Department at the time, was incredibly generous. One of the theaters in our Performance Place at the School of the Arts, is the Gerald Freedman Theater.

So anyway, we were collecting money for Mel, but we were realizing that it was never going to completely satisfy the needs for his care. He needed private-duty nursing around the clock, seven days a week. The current helpers were not nurses, they were basically babysitters, but they still needed to be paid by a certain time.

I don't remember who I was talking to but it was through one of the unions, AGMA or Actor's Equity, that someone said, "Why don't you contact the Actor's Fund?"

The first thing I thought to myself was, "Well, Mel's not an actor." We had nothing to lose, though, so I got in touch with the Actor's Fund, and spoke to a very nice gentleman. I was amazed at how accessible they were. I thought there was going to be tons of red tape to go through, like forms and information they would need. They basically pretty much took me on my word. They asked me how much debt there was at this point. Thousands of dollars in checks arrived.

Claudia:

Formed in 1882, the Actor's Fund's mission is clear: "The Actors Fund is a national human services organization that helps all professionals in performing arts and entertainment. We are a safety net, providing programs and services for those who are in need, crisis or transition." As of 2015, the organization had total assets of over $70,000,000. They help arts professionals in many ways: emergency care, health care, housing, career transitions, etc.

The Actor's Fund grew out of a prejudiced world in the mid-1800's, a world that had grown even more prejudiced against theater professionals after the murder of President Abraham Lincoln by an actor, John Wilkes Booth. In those days, it was not uncommon for theater professionals who were down on their luck to be refused help by both community and religious organizations. Although many people loved the theater and regularly enjoyed performances, the people doing the performing were looked down upon for choosing a lifestyle that often kept them out late at night and provided little financial reward.

Harrison Grey Fiske, a young student at New York University, began writing articles for a paper called the New York Dramatic Mirror in 1879. A few years later, his father bought a third of the stock in the paper, and young Fiske became its editor. Fiske immediately began campaigning to raise funds to help actors. On June 8, 1882, he officially founded the Actor's Fund.

Within a few years, the Actor's Fund purchased a cemetery in Brooklyn. Up until that point, actors were often denied a proper burial in church-run cemeteries because their career and lifestyle choices were viewed as less than respectable in the eyes of those of Christian faiths. The Fund, over the years, has grown exponentially, founding a retirement home for theatre professionals, a nursing facility, and, in 1988, co-founding Broadway Cares with

Actor's Equity, its own HIV/AIDS Initiative in response to the Crisis. Today the Actor's Fund has expanded to help all professionals in the arts, those working behind the scenes as well as the performers. In recent years, Career Transitions for Dancers joined forces with the Actor's Fund, offering even more opportunities for dancers to receive information and various types of help.

Frank Smith:

The Actor's Fund was certainly the highlight in a very difficult time. There was, of course, a low light. I can picture myself sitting down in the basement where we had a playroom away from the rest of the family, on the phone, dealing with all these creditors; having to talk to these mean people. They would all say the same thing when I tried to explain Mel's predicament, 'Well we don't care. We need this money now.'

Mel had all these pills to take; in those days, it was sixty-five pills a day. His whole personality had changed, due to depression, I think, but also due to the side effects of so many of the medications. He was angry and mean to everyone. The caregivers really were putting up with a lot. None of them lasted very long, what with Mel's constant abuse and cruelty. They were not trained to deal with Mel's abusive behavior so they would get fed up and quit.

When Mindi and I were talking about this, trying to remember as much as we could – it has been twenty years – she reminded me what terrible shape Mel's feet were in. One of the side effects of some of the medications was neuropathy. It was so bad in Mel's feet that even having the bed sheet touch them was horribly painful. Nothing seemed to help relieve the pain.

I remember when we visited that the air conditioning was not working in Mel's house. It was horribly hot and sticky, stifling. I was sweating just sitting there. I believe it was August, or early September. Summer in Charlotte can be brutal. It is very humid and miserable without air conditioning, but Mel was not fazed by it. He did not even seem to notice. I called this company to come and fix it. They came out and filled it with freon, but there was a leak in the line, so within a matter of hours, all the freon had leaked out and it was not working again.

We got bills under control, and home healthcare workers in place through Hospice of Charlotte, but it still was not enough. Mel just needed more than we could do. We could not be there to monitor the nurses and make sure they were doing their jobs. Someone in our church told us about the House of

Mercy. It is a hospice specifically for those in the final stages of AIDS, run by the Sisters of Mercy in Belmont, North Carolina, a small community, fifteen miles outside of Charlotte. We made an appointment to go take a look. I think Mel did come with us to see it. He was apparently qualified to be admitted. He met their bar, whatever it was. He was definitely sick enough, and had no money left due to his illness. The House of Mercy deals with terminally ill AIDS patients, most of whom have been living on the streets. They only take six residents at a time. I think Dr. Horton was involved in this process of getting Mel in there. I remember Noel and I taking Mel to the doctor a couple of times.

Mel has told me that he has no memory of agreeing to leave his home and go to the House of Mercy. He also doesn't remember making any arrangements for the care of his dog, Yogi, a very large, 150-pound Bouvier des Flandres, or his cat, Gypsy. One of the last caregivers took them both, along with Mel's car. He went to the House of Mercy with nothing but the clothes on his back.

We used to get this newsletter from the House of Mercy. I remember that there was a story in it about this dog, a collie/shepherd mix, I think (According to Shirley Stowe, Head Nurse at the House of Mercy, the dog was a female yellow lab named Hope). This dog would apparently know when someone was going to die. It would go into the person's room and be with them, sleep there. The dog did not let the people die alone. I remember thinking that they better keep that dog out of Mel's room so he won't die.

It was a great relief for everyone who loved Mel to know that he was in the House of Mercy, being cared for properly. None of us expected Mel to recover and ever leave the House of Mercy. I have no doubt that if he had not gone to live there, he would have passed within a matter of months.

Several years later, I think it was around 2001 or 2002, I was in Studio A, the Lindgren Studio, at the School of the Arts about to teach a pas de deux class. I looked up and saw Mel standing in the doorway. I remember thinking to myself, I need to introduce Mel to the students. I invited Mel in to sit and watch the class. Unsure of exactly what to say, I started talking anyway, "Students, I'd like for you all to know that the gentleman sitting here in the front of the room, his name is Mel Tomlinson. He was a student at the School of the Arts. He was in Agnes de Mille's Heritage Dance Theatre, which most of you probably don't even know about. He was a principal dancer with the Dance Theatre of Harlem, a soloist with New York City Ballet, and he was also a principal with Alvin Ailey's company, Boston Ballet and the North Carolina Dance Theatre. The students, of course, were impressed and they started to applaud.

Mel stood up, gestured to me, and said to the students, "And this man saved my life." The applause just got louder and louder. Mel and I hugged. Class began and life went on.

Frank Smith, a former Soloist with American Ballet Theatre, and the man who saved Mel's life. Frank teaches at UNCSA. Photo courtesy of UNCSA.

Chapter Sixteen

But They Don't Check Out
December 08, 1998 – Sept 10, 2000

I do remember my first moment waking up at the House of Mercy. I knew I was not in my own bed. With my eyes still closed, I used my other senses to explore this new bed. It was definitely clean; I could smell it. And it was incredibly comfortable. I did not yet know all that this bed could do. It could move to any position for comfort at the touch of a button. The mattress was heated, also at the touch of a button. As I turned over, nothing hurt in those first few moments, not even my heart.

When I opened my eyes, I was horrified. It was definitely not my house. None of my things were in this tiny cell of a room, eight by ten feet, with one small window. It was not like waking up in a hospital, where everything looked white and sterile. It was more like my life was now devoid of all color. I was living in grey-scale. The furnishings were sparse and cheap, all but the bed which was state of the art. The view from the window was of an empty alleyway. Later I would find out that this was the alley in which the hearses would pull up and park to load in the dead.

The House of Mercy is a six-bed hospice specifically for AIDS sufferers, managed by an amazing woman named Shirley Stowe. Part of the Sisters of Mercy convent, which also includes the much more well-known Holy Angels nursery, a home and hospice for severely disabled children, whose parents, for

House of Mercy, Belmont, NC.

various reasons, cannot care for their children at home. The House of Mercy was opened in 1991 to answer a community-wide need for care for those suffering from full-blown AIDS who have nowhere else to go. The house is nestled at the far back reaches of the Sisters of Mercy campus. There is even a sign pointing out all the facilities and housing there. Every arrow points the same way except the one pointing the way to the House of Mercy AIDS Residence. Every time I saw that sign when coming or going from the house, I felt the isolation of being an AIDS patient.

I found myself to be in the middle of a great confusion and struggle. I will never forget my fight and my desire to survive. However, when I woke up at the House of Mercy that first day, I was terrified. In my heart, I knew that I was placed there to die. Just being there brought home to me a fact with which I had already been struggling. For a long time, I had been fighting the thought that I had fulfilled my purpose on earth and that it was time for me to go home to my Maker. It was quite easy for me to believe this. After all, had I not had the most amazing life? Had my career dancing in several of America's top ballet companies come about despite my lack of early ballet training? Had I not been a principal dancer in all those companies, except the New York City Ballet where I was a soloist and one of the last of the dancers hand-picked by Balanchine himself? Had I not traveled all over the world, performing for royalty and presidents? Had I not already accomplished much more than most? That life, my former life, was better than any dream I could ever have, or so I thought at that moment. Certainly, it had been beyond any of my dreams.

I started trying to bargain with God. "God, if you let me live I promise……" I promised anything and everything that I could think of. I was not ready to go yet. I wanted my old life back so desperately. The thought of dying a severely ill and broken man was devastating. I wanted to be at the top of my game when I died, but obviously, that was not to be. It had not yet occurred to me that the very fact that I was still alive after so many brushes with death over the past three years just might have already been the answer to my prayers.

Funny, but at that time, I would call pain my friend, because it let me know that I was still alive. This thought made it easier for me to live day in and day out with so much discomfort. It also made it harder for me to let go. This was just another of the contradictions that had been my life from the very beginning. I believed then, and still believe, that long-suffering and pain are often part of God's plan, as found in the book of Galatians. Looking back, I can now see that all of this was part of my instruction as a very human being and believer in God's word. It was also my lesson in compassion and empathy for others, something I had not had much of throughout my life. My focus for so long had been on myself because so much good was happening in my life. Now, my focus was also on myself, but I could see none of the things happening to me as good things. With all the good in my life a seeming distant memory, I would learn to really see others and be happy for them. It took quite a while, and was a terrible emotional struggle for me, but I learned to give love to others even in the face of my dire circumstances. I realized that some of my friends who had given up on me, taking my things, thinking that I was going to be gone anyway, had always been like that. I had been complicit when they had treated others the same way and I had not cared. It was not until they treated me that way that I realized how awful it was. Ronald Perry had been right all along.

That first day at the House of Mercy, I met Shirley Stowe, the Head Nurse and Case Manager, as well as her staff. I liked Shirley right away. She was obviously the most intelligent person working there, and well-educated. She listened carefully to my questions and answered them in much detail. Shirley never made me feel rushed, or that she had anything more important to deal with than me. This is the very nature of Shirley's being. She is like that with everyone who is lucky enough to cross her path. At the time, that was just what I needed. Unfortunately for me, and for them, none of the rest of the staff made me feel that way.

Mel visits with Shirley Stowe in his old room, #6, at the House of Mercy, 2016.

Shirley told me that the only real hard and fast rule at the House of Mercy was that everyone, if physically able, gathered to have supper together each night. I joined the group for dinner that first night, but that was both the first and last time. I was horrified to find that the other five people living at the House of Mercy were uneducated, drug-addicted, street people. In my still-haughty mind, they were beneath me. These were the people that I had stayed away from my whole life. They were the people that I had worked so hard not to be like. I had great disdain for them all. The Civil Rights Act was over thirty years old, and I looked down upon any black person who did not or could not get an education and join the white middle class. The thought that I was here, with them, and would most likely die here, with them, was more than I could stand. I was most definitely Mrs. Tomlinson's son.

It was important to me to hold on to my past life. I needed to feel that the people around me all day appreciated who I was. In my mind, I had been important and I needed them to understand this and respect me for it. No one seemed to care about my feelings or respect me enough, except Shirley, whom I suspect just understood me enough to humor me. The black people on the staff as well as the black AIDS residents seemed to think I was just the same as them, poor, under-educated ghetto people. I had great disdain for them all. Maybe I was dark-skinned, but I had always felt that I was an upper-middle class white man on the inside. Never had I allowed myself to identify as one of "them." I was as racist in my thoughts and feelings towards them as any white supremacist would have been.

At that first dinner, I knew that there would never be any common ground between me and the other residents. There was absolutely nothing that we could talk about, except maybe sex and how we had each contracted AIDS, but I had no interest in talking to them about that, and I definitely did not want to hear about their drug-induced, high-risk sexual exploits. For most residents, the House of Mercy was a safe house. It was a safe place to come to die. For them, it was much better than dying alone in an alleyway, or seedy, "No-Tell

The House of Mercy AIDS Hospice in Belmont, NC.

Motel." For me, the House of Mercy was a place to recover. From that first day, I told myself that, even though in my heart, I knew that it was not the reason why I was supposed to be there. It took a slow metamorphosis over the almost two years that I was there for me to realize how healing my time there had been, not just physically, but emotionally and spiritually as well.

The staff did cater to my every need and sometimes, even my wants. I treated them all horribly, and for that I am truly sorry. I hated everything about them, but most of all I hated that they could not have cared less about my past, about who I was. They treated me the same as everyone else and I could not tolerate that.

In the words of Shirley Stowe, Director of Nursing/Case Manager, House of Mercy:

When Mel was originally referred to the House of Mercy, he was referred by Hospice of Charlotte who were, at that time, following him in his home. He could no longer live alone and he needed more care. It was a tough, tough adjustment for Mel. It is a tough adjustment for everyone, but Mel, having lived the lifestyle that he lived traveling all over, being so independent, had a particularly difficult time adjusting. Even though this is a beautiful home, and we foster a loving environment, for Mel the adjustment was excruciating. To say that he isolated himself might be too strong a term, but he spent just about all his time in his room. He did isolate himself from the other residents and some of the staff.

Because we are a group home, we do ask that the residents come together at meal time, but Mel really did not participate in that either. Keep in mind, we serve people from all walks of life, from the homeless population to the professional. Mel was at the extreme end of the "professional." For him to relate to many of the other people here was difficult. He had nothing in common with anyone else. There were caregivers here who would have rather died than go into Mel's room. He had no patience or kindness at that point. He did not want to be here.

Mel was so sensitive, and aware of the fact that people who lived here were going to die. He did not want to get close to anyone and then lose them. It is hard living somewhere with other people who all have the same disease that you have and knowing when any one of them dies. Each time, Mel agonized over the deaths, wondering why they had died and he had not. He was always worried that he would be next.

I get chills when I think back to some of the memories. I think it is safe to say that Mel and I developed a really special relationship and he trusted me. Part of that journey was traveling together, all around the state to schools. I would wheel him in, in that wheelchair – he could no longer walk at that point and he would talk to the students about living with AIDS.

At one point, Mel became so sick that he could no longer keep food down. Dr. Horton knew something was wrong with his kidneys and did a scan which showed a huge kidney stone. There was nothing that could be done, so Mel came back here and we all really expected him to die. But he didn't. He started to rally and miraculously got better. As a nurse, I have a background in kidney issues, and getting better in Mel's situation just does not happen. It was a miracle.

Mel being the spiritual person that he is had a wonderful relationship with our Chaplain, Allison, as well as the Sisters. If someone doesn't believe in divine intervention and the power of prayer, then they haven't met Mel Tomlinson.

Many of Mel's friends came to visit. Mabel Robinson came down from Winston-Salem often and was very involved here. Tommy Sinabaldi, Mel's tap teacher, would come down from New York. He bought Mel a computer.

One day, Mel summoned me into his room and asked if my passport was in order, then told me that we would be going to London together so he could see one of his friends, Kathleen LaCamera, one more time. I remember that the neuropathy in his feet was very bad on that trip. Mel could not walk at all then. I remember on the flight over, even though Mel couldn't walk, he could still stretch. He sat in his seat with his legs wrapped around the back of his neck. Everyone thought he was some kind of contortionist. Whenever Mel was well enough, he would go outside and do his stretching routine to keep in shape.

There were so many goodbyes, so many near-death moments. The pain and energy it took to live through the horrible bouts of illness was wearing Mel out. He was on Demerol and a morphine drip quite a bit then. Back in those days, most everyone who came here died. Mel was an exception. Mel had always done what Mel wanted to do, both sick and well. He never totally succumbed to what the reality of AIDS was in those days. Once he decided to live, there was no stopping him.

The meals, when I could eat, were always excellent at the House of Mercy.

When I refused to take my meals with the rest of the residents, the staff brought my meals to me. I think they were happy that I wanted to be alone, as I was so hateful to them all that none of them could stand being around me for very long. My room, #6, was at the end of a hallway, right next to an exit door leading to the alleyway. I always knew when one of the residents made their transition to the afterlife. I could feel their spirits leaving them, watching, as their bodies were carried out that exit door to be driven away. It was always eerily overwhelming to me. Each time, I wondered if I would be next.

In the one year, nine months, and two days that I lived at the House of Mercy, I had many physical and emotional highs and lows. During the times when I was relatively well and not in too much physical pain, I traveled. I went to London, New York and New Mexico. These were not pleasure trips, but were trips that I took to say goodbye to people who were important to me; loved ones whom I wanted to see one last time, but due to their own lives could not at those moments come to me.

Shirley accompanied me to London and, also on day trips to do talks about AIDS in schools in Winston-Salem and other nearby cities. I went to London to see my friend, Kathleen LaCamara, who was a minister, a graduate of Yale's Divinity School, and producer of NBC's documentary, "With a Clear Voice," a documentary film on racism that I was in back in my Boston days.

While in London, Kathleen made a reservation for me to stay at a very nice Bed and Breakfast. Shirley stayed at Kathleen's home. At first, I chose to believe that Kathleen was not comfortable with the idea of having me stay in her home. Such were the times. By then, I had grown accustomed to the ostracizing effect of my illness on so many of my friends and family, and did not take offence in the least. I knew that Kathleen loved me and I wrongly assumed she was simply protecting herself and her family. It did not take me long to realize I was wrong. It was the lack of proper access for my wheelchair that would make it impossible for me to sleep at Kathleen's home.

In the words of Kathleen LaCamera Coughlin:

I met Mel in the early 1980's when I was living in New York City. But it was only after I moved to London in the early 1990's that we had a chance to properly work together. I asked Mel to be part of a film I was making about the experience of being a "first" black man in different professions in different cultures. The film featured a British Member of Parliament called Paul Boateng (who was the UK's first black man to be elected to the House of Commons) and Mel (one of the first two black men to dance with the New

York City Ballet).

Mel was a terrific contributor. At the time of filming, he was dancing with the Boston Ballet. He very graciously let us follow him around from rehearsals to home and then out and about in Boston itself. One memorable filming disaster-turned-opportunity during those filming days with Mel came on a very snowy Saturday morning. We'd arranged to film Mel working with some of the youngest children in the Boston Ballet's Citydance school program. The snow was so heavy that the class was cancelled which left us with a big hole in our film.

We put our heads together and hatched "Plan B" which was to film Mel performing an improvised work in the empty ballet studio space. But we needed music for him to dance to that wouldn't saddle the film with expensive copyright issues. Mel's brilliant solution was to persuade a talented pianist, Maurice Gordan, to brave the snow and come over to the studio to improvise accompanying music to Mel's improvised movement. The result was stunning and provided a beautiful and dramatic major visual element – including the film's opening – for the documentary.

Mel's interview was interwoven with the improvised dance and music to wonderful effect. As a producer/director, I so appreciated how candid Mel was with us about the hard road he traveled as a young black man growing up in the rural south only to find even more obstacles to studying and then performing ballet. Mel shared his story in very moving, insightful ways, but always with a good dose of humor, gratitude and hope. Of our two main contributors, Mel definitely provided the real "heart" connection for audiences in the film.

"With a Clear Voice" was broadcast on NBC in 1993 and went on to be named a finalist in the CINE (Council on International Non-Theatrical Events) awards that same year.

In the later part of the 1990's, Mel decided it was high time to come over and see me and my family here in the UK. My husband Chris, son Mike, and I were all thrilled. We'd hoped for some time that Mel would be strong enough to make the trip and he finally pulled it off with the support of the wonderful Shirley Stowe.

Mel wasn't able to stay with us in our home given the wheelchair access issues, but he was able to visit during the day. He ended up staying close by in a wheelchair accessible hotel room just a few minutes' walk from our home.

I have a clear image of Mel in his wheelchair, all wrapped up in a scarf, hat and coat making his way – Shirley propelling the chair down the uneven sidewalks and roads between his hotel and our house. I wondered then, and still do, what people looking out their windows must have thought watching our little entourage making our way past their houses – usually in the rain.

What I remember most from that time is how much our son, Michael, then four, enjoyed Mel and how well they got on. I seem to remember them cuddled up on the couch with Mel reading a picture book to Mike, who is now twenty-one, studying art and design at university. He still remembers Mel's visit with great fondness.

We often marvel and laugh looking back at how truly miraculous and crazy that very unlikely visit was. I'm so grateful to Mel for giving Mike such a positive experience of what it looks like to live well and optimistically with a catastrophic illness. As you can imagine, we so hated saying "good-bye" at the end of our very special visit.

My last trip was to New Mexico, in the spring of 2000, to see Kevin and Michele Self. I had called them and told them I was doing well and would like to come see them for a short visit. I did not tell them that I was wheelchair-bound and was not doing as well as I let on. I knew that if I was dying, I wanted it to be there, with them. I had an overwhelming feeling that it just might be going to happen then. At one point during my visit, I asked Kevin to take me up into the nearby mountains. I just wanted to sit there, alone, and find God's peace. Not only did I find it, but I also found that I had a renewed energy. I knew it was not yet my time to go.

In the words of Kevin Self:

I tend to have a very selective memory when it comes to bad times. I think that is the only reason I survived my wife, Michele's death a few years after Mel's visit. I do remember Mel visiting us sometime in the mid to late '90's. It was during the spring, right around our spring production. He had indicated to us he was feeling well enough for the flight, so we prepared for an upbeat reunion.

His exit from the plane in a wheelchair exposed his true condition which was confirmed by his admission that he was "ready to die in New Mexico." I think Michele was more heartbroken than myself. This was the woman who had graciously shared our income to pay Mel's house payments for over two years, to give him comfortable and familiar surroundings. She was first to greet Mel and did not skip a beat welcoming him to our home.

Mel would have good days and bad during his stay. He needed an oxygen machine at night, and help getting around during the day. At one point, he deteriorated, so we brought in a hospice worker. After several more days, Mel decided to return to North Carolina. The morning of his early flight, we tried our best to get him quickly through his routine of bathing, dressing, and a breakfast of boiled egg, toast and juice.

As we got to the airport gate, all three of us watched as the plane pulled away. Mel's remark was, 'That's what happens when you're on CPT – colored people's time.'

Thankfully, the airline found him another flight. Sadly, we sent him off thinking we would never see him again.

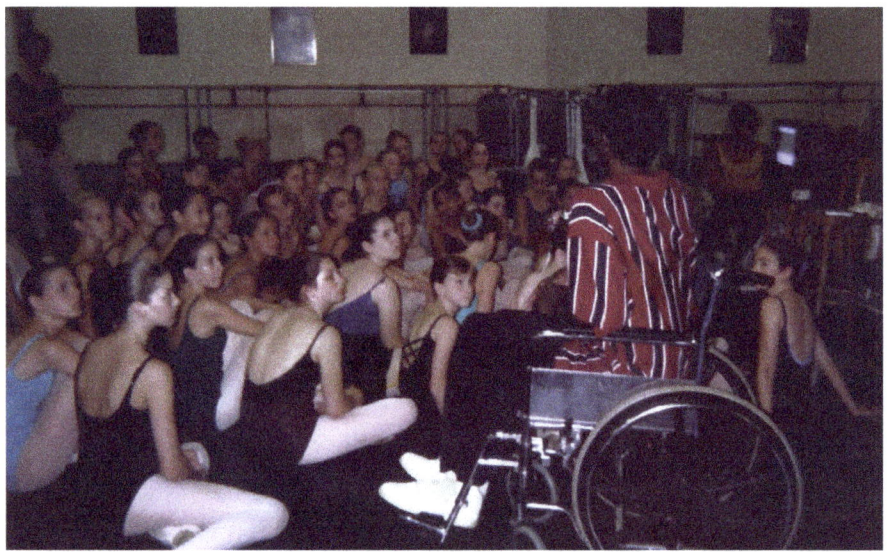

Mel, discussing Balanchine's choreography while showing a video to a ballet class at the Charlotte City Ballet School after teaching their ballet class from his wheelchair, 1999.

Besides my travel while living at the House of Mercy, I also taught ballet locally for both the Charlotte City Ballet and the University of North Carolina at Charlotte. Each time I taught during that time, it was from my wheelchair. Shirley would often take me to the studios, or Claudia or Keith Darby would pick me up. I was emaciated by this time, down to around 120 pounds. Some days, I was lucky to be able to choke down a small cup of plain rice. I would have to be fed, as I did not have the strength to lift a fork to my mouth most days. The few times I got to go teach were more sustenance for my body and soul than any food could ever have been. Until that time in my life, I had no idea how important it is to the human soul to feel relevant; to feel needed and appreciated. The love I felt from the dancers sustained me for months afterwards.

I continued to attend my church, St. Paul's Baptist Church, as often as I was able. I also sang in the choir and went to choir practice as much as I could. My church family was very kind and supportive, especially that angel of a woman named Thomassina Craig, who took it upon herself to make sure I got to church. She had not been one of my close friends, but just a woman who went to the same church as I did. She made visits practically every day, both while I was still in my home and while I was at the House of Mercy.

Thomassina saw me through some of my worst days. She was there with me when I had radiation on my big toe for the only Kaposi's Sarcoma lesion I ever had. Having AIDS and only ever having one of those hated purple lesions was, in itself, a miracle. When I was suffering from awful pains in my head, due to fluid pressing on my spine and brain, Thomassina was the one who held my hand during three terribly painful spinal taps. These procedures were very intricate. The smallest wrong move from me could have been fatal if the six-inch needle did not hit the exact-perfect spot on my spine. The fluid removed looked like thick, murky water. Each time I had a spinal tap, the pressure on my brain would be relieved and my headaches would stop for a while.

I could not have gotten through those spinal taps without Thomassina. Why she chose to take on the burden of caring for me, I probably will never know. She asked for nothing in return. In fact, when I was at my worst, and everyone was sure it was the end, I gave her many things that were important to me, posters, articles, memorabilia. When I got back on my feet, a couple years later, Thomassina gave me back all the things I had given to her, saying she was merely keeping them safe for me. Her kindness touched my heart in such a powerful way. I had never known anyone quite like her.

Three weeks into my stay at the House of Mercy, I marked my 45th birthday. Each year, since I had first found out that I was sick at age 41, I felt strongly that if I could make it to my next birthday, I would make it one more year. I was now 45 years old. I marveled at the thought that I was in my mid-forties. I was middle-aged with nothing to show for it except a disease-riddled body and soul.

I decided it was time to get my life in order. I reached out, writing to friends and family. I registered for some correspondence courses through the Carolina University of Theology in Stanley, North Carolina. I had repeatedly seen their commercials on TV and started to believe that maybe God was giving me a hint as to what I should do if I could just recover. After taking those first courses, I declared my major to be theology and Christian psychology, two things I had always had great interest in, partly because I wanted to understand my mother's behavior and how it had affected my life.

Living in the hospice, I had lots of time to read, write, and turn in my assignments. I have always loved school and having assignments and deadlines. Even while working with me on this book, Claudia would give me weekly homework and, as we got nearer to the end of the book, I missed having those assignments.

Although I now had my schoolwork to look forward to, I was still stuck in a rather fatalistic mindset. I was irritable; still resentful of everyone around me for not putting me on a pedestal and worshiping me. One day, all my desperation to be remembered and respected as a dancer was finally satisfied, thanks to a visit from a complete stranger. Her name was LaTanya Johnson.

LaTanya was a liturgical dancer. She danced for her church and worked with seniors and those in wheelchairs as her personal Christian ministry.

In LaTanya's words:

It wasn't a job. I just felt strongly compelled to share movement and empower others through movement. A friend at my church had told me about Mel several times. She was sure we would get along well. It was about six months later that we finally connected. I was at church. The service had just finished and all I can say is that the spirit moved me and I knew it was time to go to the House of Mercy and meet Mel. He was very sick at that time, probably days away from dying.

I arrived at the House of Mercy and asked if I could see Mel and if there was somewhere I could dance for him. We moved the furniture out of the way in the living room and waited for Mel. A few minutes later, he was wheeled into the room in his wheelchair. He looked confused and slightly annoyed, but I quickly told him that I had choreographed a dance to Curtis Dean's "He Cares."

I performed my dance for Mel and he asked if I could please do it again. He moved to the other side of the room and watched me from there as I repeated the dance. He gave me some pointers as to things I could do to make my dance better. I asked him about his career. He had many fascinating stories.

Mel and I became friends. I would visit often and started taking him to some of his doctor's appointments. I loved hearing all his stories, and he helped me with my dancing. When he left the hospice, we lost touch for a while.

About a year later, when Mel's health was finally stable and he was teaching a liturgical dance class at his church, St. Paul's Baptist, we re-connected and ended up working together. We even danced together a few times and, for me, it was wonderful.

The last time we worked together was a bit rough. Sometimes Mel could be insecure as to why I wanted to be his friend and dance with him. I cared about him, not because he was a ballet star, but because he was a person. I'm so happy that he is doing well and that our paths crossed right at the perfect time for us both.

After a few months, I suddenly realized that I was *living*. I was studying and I had goals. I was going to get both my Masters and Doctorate. That day I had the first glimmer of hope that I might just survive and have something else that I needed to do with my life. I was far from well, but now I had a reason to go on, even when the headaches were intolerable or I could not keep down food. I found myself wanting to make those closest to me proud of me again, especially Kevin. He is one of the smartest people I know, finishing college in only one year. I really wanted to impress him and make him proud of my efforts because he had always been such a major inspiration in my life.

My family members did not seem to be impressed. I felt the separation from them more keenly than ever. To this day, my sisters believe that I am an unforgiving soul, but forgiveness had nothing to do with my decisions. I had long ago forgiven my mother for whom and what she was. However, I was not, and still, am not able to forget or condone her cruelty and callousness. When Claudia was interviewing my brother Marlon about our lives, the subject came up and I, for the first time, told Marlon what had transpired between Mrs. Tomlinson and me when I visited her right before her death. Marlon's comment was, "I never knew that. Now it makes perfect sense why you were not at her funeral." There is a huge difference between forgiving someone for doing heinous things that they believed were the right things to do, and giving that person a pass for completely rejecting who and what one is. I understand that Mrs. Tomlinson beat us because she grew up in the "spare the rod and spoil the child" mindset. I will never understand how a mother can reject her own child because she perceives that child's very being to be an embarrassment to her. Mrs. Tomlinson's reaction to my very essence was a knife in my heart, but it was the beginning of my own awakening to true compassion for others.

Slowly, in my time at the House of Mercy, I found something that I did not even know I had missed during my years living on top of the world: compassion for, and genuine caring of others. My focus gradually shifted away from myself and to giving others hope, encouragement and a better life. Shirley was a big help in this metamorphosis. She and I went to schools and talked to the students about AIDS. Being a part of these trips was a powerful part of my recovery, both physically and spiritually, and of my journey as one of God's children.

I started befriending some of the other residents and a few of the nurses. One nurse in particular, Joyce Kloninger, became my dear friend. She, like Thomassina, showed me what love and true caring were all about. Our friendship had nothing to do with who I had been or what I had accomplished. For the first time in a long time, I was not judging people on how impressed they were with what I had done as a dancer. Joyce was funny and positive and a great cook. I genuinely liked her for who she was, without the prerequisite of her being impressed by me. At one point, Joyce left on vacation. She left me a gift, a sound machine, and a note that said it had been a pleasure knowing and working with me. Being as physically delicate and emotionally sensitive as I was at that time, I took her note to mean that she expected me to be dead when she returned. I was devastated and filled with fear once again. But I was also filled with determination to be there when she returned, and I was. I playfully sat straight up in bed and said, "I'm still here!" We both beamed with smiles of relief. Joyce had worried that I might be gone when she returned. This was at a time when my kidneys were not doing so well. Adult diapers were a way of life for me. Joyce changed my diapers, making sure to keep me dry. She bathed me and dressed me. I trusted her with every ounce of my being, the same way I trusted Thomassina. Looking back, I am humbled to have been so loved and cared for. This House of Mercy had become my home, and thanks to such wonderfully generous souls as Joyce, Shirley and my church friend, Thomassina, it would not be my final resting place.

During this time, my old friend, Peter Frame found out I was ill and contacted me. Peter and I talked more than a few times. I could talk to Peter about certain things that I could not talk to anyone else about. Most people would think I was a raving lunatic if I was to speak to them of the spiritual things Peter and I would talk about. We were both in a place in our lives where we understood that there was much more to life, health and happiness than appeared at first glance.

Peter Frame's thoughts:

Almost 45 years ago, a very bright light by the name of Mel A. Tomlinson shined radiantly upon me and illuminated my life with pure joy, laughter, fun and adventure. As our friendship began, so it continues onward with a growing meaning, value and purpose that is nurtured from consistent respect and gratitude for one another.

Due to a sustained back injury in 1990, I retired from the New York City Ballet and said farewell to this extraordinary life as a professional dancer, and my close friends and colleagues; bravely walking away from now a very familiar world and into the unknown. Just as Mel had chosen to do in 1987, it was time for me to reinvent myself.

But first, I needed to heal my back. I often found myself in crisis mode with my back frequently in painful and debilitating spasms. I did not want to undergo surgery to the affected two discs, so I reached out for other healing modalities.

I soon committed to extensive emotional therapy where I discovered how interconnected my continued back symptoms were to my emotional body. Suppressed feelings caused pain to manifest in my body. The more I was able to feel what was underlying the "dis-ease" in my back, the more my physical symptoms dissipated. Yes, the rigors of the ballet can cause physical injuries, but there was more to it than that for me.

Several years had passed after leaving New York City Ballet and once again my path crossed with Mel's, but this time it was with news that he was suffering from a physical illness. I immediately did what I could on the physical side and reached out to our dance community to create a fund to help Mel through this difficult period.

I also had heart-to-heart conversations with him to support him emotionally. He had so much to share, not so much about the fear of having a physical illness, but more about what he was experiencing spiritually, the revelations and insights. Mel was humbled on so many levels from this and in awe of how it was touching him on a whole other level. Mel and I are "birds of a feather" on this subject and I could wholeheartedly relate to his words. Maybe we are twin brothers after all.

I shared with Mel my own physical and emotional healing experiences along with the profound life lessons that accompanied them. I shared with him what I came to understand and experience about how the physical body can be at "dis-ease" within itself and the profound healing tools that helped me be at more "ease" within my body. I gave all that I could to my friend and what I shared with Mel in these intimate conversations seemed to resonate with him. There was some truth within it all that raised his demeanor and lifted his spirits. I do recall that I was quite passionate and assertive at times with Mel to remind him that the impossible is possible.

Those very sacred conversations granted us the opportunity to experience one another in a different light and context outside of the familiar setting of the ballet world, discussing the relevance and essence of life itself.

We were now grown men with our careers as professional dancers in the rearview mirror, having some of the most mature and intimate conversations of our friendship and lives. Mel's resounding spirit guided him through those rough currents and dark nights and blessed him with healing, both within and without.

And with gratitude and pure joy beyond measure our paths have continued to cross from New York City Ballet's 50th Year Celebration, his visitations to the School of American Ballet and consistently priceless yearly phone messages to wish his 'twin brother' a Happy Birthday.

It was a great help and much comfort for me to hear Peter's wise words. I was reminded that every day, I was surrounded by great people and that I did have wonderful friends. My psyche was lifted up and I was, for the first time in a long time, able to see that all was not lost. I now knew that being sent to the House of Mercy was one of the greatest gifts I had ever received.

The House of Mercy was located at the back of the Sisters of Mercy campus, a Catholic home to both nuns and priests. I often joked that we had to be hidden at the back of the campus so no good God-fearing Christians would know that the sisters were being kind to the gays and drug addicts. It really was not like that at all. Living in such a holy place, there was no shortage of faithful people with whom to pray. I had grown up in the protestant Baptist faith and had not had a great deal of exposure to Catholics, but I found that they were pretty much just like the Baptists, just quieter, which I liked. I have never been a "Bible thumper." I have always been more the quiet type when it comes to my faith. One thing I had figured out long ago was that although those of faith will fellowship together, finding salvation is much more personal, the rules being solely between oneself and one's God.

On my good days, I often got into the motorized wheelchair that Dr. Horton had helped me get and traveled across the campus to visit the nuns. They lived in small rooms, just like mine, only smaller and even more cell-like. I remember the wooden floors in their dormitory shined with such incredible gloss that I could see my reflection in them. I loved visiting with the sisters and praying with them. I felt so protected by them and at the same time had a sense of freedom and independence from the sheer fact that I could get into my wheelchair and go visit with them. The Sisters gave me such comfort and strength.

Susan Moore, a chaplain from outside would visit with us. Susan spent a lot of time visiting with me. She listened to my poetry, of which I wrote a lot in those days, as well as to my prayers. We prayed together in my room often. The House had no chapel, which I thought was ridiculous. I talked about this fact vociferously and pushed for a small chapel to be added to the House of Mercy. Susan and the nuns gave me a sense of peace and reminded me that I had once had an indomitable spirit that I could find within myself again. I listened. Though I really could not remember ever having that kind of strength in my soul, I told myself to trust these generous people. Maybe they were right. There seemed to be so much that I could not remember and such confusion in my head and my heart. I felt that I was a stranger within myself, like this very-lost, weak, sickened soul had taken up residence within me and had totally engulfed whoever had lived within before.

During one particularly bad bout of illness, I became sure that my end was coming and I asked Thomassina to take me to church. I wanted to address the congregation and let them know that I loved them and was thankful for their kindness and all their prayers. I also wanted to ask them to please continue to pray for me as I felt that I needed their prayers desperately at that point. I spoke to the congregation through a microphone set up in a small room because I was too sick to join them in fellowship. Before the service was over, I had to ask Thomassina to get me back to the hospice quickly as I had once again soiled the only remaining diaper in a serious way. We rolled the windows down and drove quickly back to the House of Mercy. I remember feeling so grateful that I was with Thomassina at that moment and not home in Raleigh where I never would have survived the "I told you so's." I realized that sometimes all you need, to have the strength to fight is love and patience. It was dawning on me that I was getting plenty of that. Slowly, I was gaining both strength and wisdom.

Chapter Seventeen

Thinking Ahead for the Dead: The End of the Beginning

I really believed that I was living in what would end up being the final chapter of my life. My health and my frame of mind had been bad for so long. I had come to accept the fact that there was no possibility that anything would get better. Almost all my friends had deserted me. They had chosen to disappear out of my life for one reason or another – my cruelty and paranoia, the need to continue to live their own lives, their discomfort with death and the dying. I felt abandoned and forgotten. Even those friends who had not given up on me did not visit as much as they had in the past. It was clear that everyone, not just I, was tired of my illness and ready to move on. Once again, I allowed myself to drift back to that place where I could no longer see anything in my life worth living for. It was time to move on to the afterlife and learn the secrets of God's mysteries. Once again, I was making the mistake of thinking I knew what God's plan was.

I had become quite apathetic, not caring anymore about what people thought of me or how they felt. I was sick of my visitors, when I had visitors. I resented what I believed was their pity and judgement. In retrospect, I do realize that they were not judging me; I was judging myself, mercilessly. I was still proud of my successes, but struggled with great shame over some of the things I did by choice and just plain recklessness. I was still fighting within myself the last vestiges of shame over who and what I was. It has taken most of my life to find peace with my choice to lead a homosexual lifestyle. I knew I could have chosen to lead a heterosexual lifestyle, but what kind of "choice" is it when what you are choosing is to live inauthentically? Which was worse – choosing to live in truth or in a Christian-accepted lie? I could have made the choice to live the way my mother and others in my Christian upbringing believed I should live, even though it would have been choosing to live a lie. But living such a serious lie concerning the very core of my being would have surely separated me from God in such a profound way that my life would have meant much less. If God created me and He did not make mistakes, then who was I to be ashamed of myself, one of God's creations? I spent much of my time in prayer, asking God for comfort and forgiveness, and asking Him for clarity so that I could fully understand the incredible nuances He had put in front of me.

I decided to plan my funeral. Most people never get to thoroughly plan their own funeral. They only share some of their wishes in passing, and buy a burial plot. I had all the time in the world, and at the same time, I had very little time. I was being practical, not pessimistic in this particular decision. I was not always the most practical of thinkers. In many ways, my illness had forced me to learn to think in more practical terms.

I decided to plan my own funeral for two reasons. First, the thought of being in control of how I was remembered appealed to the control freak in me. Second, I knew my death was going to bring out the worst in my family members, and I wanted to head off as much nastiness as possible. There was little left for them to fight over. Most of my best memorabilia was gone. Much of it I gave away, but some of my best photographs, posters and other things had been taken without my permission. The same could be said of all my possessions – furniture, appliances, my car, and clothes. It was all gone. What was left were things that mattered to only me – my poetry, letters, journals, and some family photographs, school papers and yearbooks. I wanted to be sure that these things went to someone who would take care of them. If my father had still been alive, I would have sent those things to him. He was gone, so I packed most of it up and gave some to Thomassina Craig and sent the rest to Kevin. I made a will so there would be no doubt as to my intentions as far as things I wanted to give to family members.

I had recently found out that my sister, Ellen, had, years ago, taken out life insurance policies on both me and my younger brother, Marlon. I guess she figured that our life styles, me as a gay man and Marlon as a drug user, made us the most likely to die first. I remember wondering if she had taken one out on Janie Robbins, my youngest sister who died in her twenties due to complications from diabetes. Ellen inherited her consciousness of death from Mrs. Tomlinson. Both would go immediately to the obituaries in the paper each morning to see who had not made it through another night. Daddy and Dexter would go first to the Sports section, and I, to the Arts and Entertainment section. It is interesting to me to muse on what this says about each of us.

I knew that making my will would head off most arguments between the siblings. The main trouble between them would be over money to pay for my funeral. By planning it all and paying for everything in advance, I knew that a great burden would be taken off them. I sought the assistance of my deacon from St. Paul's Baptist Church, Alfred Alexander. Alfred's family owned – still owns - the Alexander Funeral Home in Charlotte, a 103-year-old, independently-owned, funeral home. The Alexander family, one of the oldest and most respected African-American families in Charlotte, was brought to the Charlotte area as slaves by one of the oldest of the "first families" of Charlotte, the white Alexander clan. Both families were known for their community involvement, political activism and willingness to do whatever was needed to help those in need. I knew I would be in good hands. Alfred understood my need to be frugal as well as my desire that my funeral be a celebration of my life. I honestly believed that I was ready to die because I had figured out my purpose on this earth and had served it, thus completing my reason for being here.

The first order of business was to figure out who would write my eulogy. I immediately thought of Mrs. Allison, my tenth grade English teacher, who had inspired me to reach beyond the Chavis Heights projects, both figuratively and physically, and to aspire to that which was beyond my dreams. Throughout my life, I had kept in touch with Mrs. Allison. She was happy to help me and wrote a beautiful tribute to my life. I still have it, but won't print it here. I will keep it for the day for which it was written.

The Bible says, in Genesis 1:19, "…for dust thou art and unto dust thou shalt return." It seemed to me at the time that the process of cremation would be my best choice and would get me there fastest. It would also mean that the cost of a casket and burial could be avoided. I liked the simplicity and the sense of completeness and order. I purchased a vase in which my ashes could be carried.

One of my favorite songs was to be sung, *Will He Remember Me*, and I requested that it be sung by fellow church member Linzetta Gatty, who could bring life to that song and bring meaning to all who would be present. I requested that my then-current minister, Dr. Rev. Gregory K. Moss, officiate.

There was only one thing that I had not settled – Who would receive my ashes and where would they be distributed? I never did decide this, even though I knew that it would most likely cause problems with my siblings. In retrospect, I think I knew that my oldest sister, Ellen would take charge of my ashes, but something in my heart kept me from finalizing that. I was very tired now and ready to go. Things from this point on, happened very quickly, but not in the way that I had assumed they would. I continued to get weaker and sicker, but something was different. It sounds odd, but I believe that reading Mrs. Allison's eulogy subconsciously triggered something inside of me that set some amazing changes in motion.

Claudia remembers:

I remember that I was sitting at my desk, at home in my kitchen, when Shirley called from the House of Mercy. She said, "It's time to come say your goodbyes. I don't think Mel has more than a couple of days left at best."

Can I bring my children and a couple of the dancers who Mel was particularly close to," I asked.

I was not looking forward to this visit. Final goodbyes are few and far between in most people's lives. They are reserved for those at the end of life; those one will never see again in this life. Many people never even experience final goodbyes. Their loved ones pass quickly, often before anyone realizes that the end is near. If someone is not dying, then saying "goodbye" is not so final as there is always the possibility that your paths will cross again sometime.

Aside from being uncomfortable with the whole situation, it just felt "off." Mel and I had only recently, five years before, begun to build our friendship. I felt that I really did not know Mel well at all, because in the short time I had known him, I had watched as he went through massive changes, physically, mentally and emotionally. It just felt so wrong to me that he was going to be dead so soon because in many ways, he had not yet become his best person. I knew Mel well enough to know that there was much more inside of which he had not yet tapped, much less that he had time to explore. It was such a tragedy, in my mind, on so many levels, not the least of which was that, in some ways, Mel reminded me of a child, full of eager potential to learn and understand all to which he was exposed. An innocent was being taken and that was never right.

We arrived at the House of Mercy, all a bit nervous and uncomfortable. One of the nurses greeted us as we walked through the open door. Shirley came through the living room door almost immediately, as if she had been waiting there in the hallway for us and she walked us down the hall to Mel's room, quietly warning us that Mel had declined quite a bit since we had seen him last.

It was late Spring, probably mid-May, 2000, as we were preparing for a performance, and getting ready to leave shortly afterwards to spend four weeks down in Charleston, where I would be teaching ballet at the Charleston

Ballet's summer intensive and having some much-needed family beach time. I remember that when we walked into Mel's room, even with Shirley's prior warning, none of us were prepared for what we would see.

It had only been a couple weeks since any of us had last seen Mel. I had last picked him up on a Saturday morning, at the end of April, to teach a class. He had been quite weak, teaching from his wheelchair, and his train of thought had been scattered. The class combinations were confusing and un-musical, and Mel was constantly speaking gibberish in the middle of his explanations. I remember thinking that it had been a mistake to push him to come in and teach that morning. He looked closer to skeletal remains than to the vibrant and powerful dancer he had once been.

Now, only two or three weeks later, he was emaciated to the point that his lower legs, which he had on top of the covers, looked like decaying fleshless bones covered in deep, dark-chocolate brown paint. His head looked much more like a garishly lifeless skull, than that belonging to a live human, too large in proportion to his body, and again, covered in deep brown paint. Mel's long neck seemed incapable of holding up his head which lay supported by several pillows and the raised head of his hospital bed. His eyes were set so deeply into his head that you almost could not see how yellow they were.

What was most alarming to me was that he was not Mel. The only way I can describe him is that he was this crazy, manically-raving, not-quite-human stranger. I was not sure, at first, if he even knew who we were, but then he saw Molly Herboth, one of the dancers who came with me, and spoke her name with such tenderness that it was obvious how much it meant to him that she had come. "Molly, you came," he said.

A few seconds later that crazy, manic person was back, raving to someone whom only he could see. Watching Mel like that brought to my mind a quote from Ralph Waldo Emerson, "Of all the ways to lose a person, death is the kindest." With that thought came the realization that death would be kindest for Mel at that point.

One of my sons, Marcus Oxendine, remembers feeling profoundly sad because it was so obvious that Mel had given up. *'I could just see that he had given up, he was not Mel anymore. I didn't really know him well then, and I had no idea who he was as a dancer. I was fifteen or sixteen and relatively new to ballet and to the family. To me, he was this really funny friend of yours (Claudia's) who taught us ballet sometimes. I had lost my birth mother to AIDS just four years before, and had become a member of this family only a year later. Seeing Mel really reminded me of her and how my mom gave up near the end.'*

According to Shirley Stowe, what was going to finally take Mel was his failing kidneys, due, it seemed, to a very large kidney stone that was much too big to pass and could not be safely removed surgically due to Mel's completely weakened and compromised physical state. He was on heavy painkillers. That and the toxins that had built up in his blood from the failure of his kidneys to do their job, were most likely causing the hallucinations and ravings.

Throughout our visit, Mel would switch back and forth between perfect lucidity and psychotic mania. It would happen in a split second, right in the middle of a sentence. At one point, it became clear to me that he was talking to his father. Much of what he said was gibberish, but then he would yell out, "Daddy!" with such commanding force and anguish that I half expected his father to come running through the door. We left that day sure that the next time we would see Mel would be at his funeral.

While we were in Charleston, I kept in touch with Mel through Shirley. She told me that Mel was hanging in there and somehow seemed to have rallied both physically and mentally. Mel just seemed tired and ready to get off the phone when I talked to him.

It was five weeks later, when we had only been back from Charleston for a couple of days when Mel called to tell me he had an apartment and would be moving out of the House of Mercy in September. It was early August.

"Can I have a job?" Mel asked when he called. By that time, I had left the Charlotte City Ballet to found Tutu.Com, a ballet costume company.

Mel's rapid-fire banter was back. 'You might not know this but I did work-study in the costume shop at the School of the Arts and I can sew. I can also talk, I could answer the phones.' I was speechless. I was talking to Mel, the Mel I used to know, not the desperately depressed, dying Mel who I had been spending time with over the past few years. It was confusing and overwhelming and wonderful. Mel was back.

It was moving day, September 19th, 2000. Joyce, my favorite nurse at the House of Mercy, had helped find me a small apartment nearby that I would be able to afford with my monthly disability check. I had not seen the apartment yet and had no idea what to expect. Thomassina picked me up at the House of

Mercy and drove me "home."

What now, I thought, as I stood leaning on my walker with one hand, my cane dangling from the other wrist, and looked up at the two long flights of stairs to my new home. I knew it was going to be the longest walk of my life. "You can do this, Mel," Thomassina gently coaxed, taking my arm. We walked those stairs together, slowly, knowing that when I made it to the top, my new life was there, waiting for me. Twenty minutes later, I was at the top. I looked back down that long stairway and then I turned and looked at that strange new door. What now, I thought again for the hundredth time over the last hour. This door seemed even stranger than any I had ever faced before.

Only an hour before, I had waited for Thomassina to pick me up at the House of Mercy. It had felt so strange, knowing that it was to be no ordinary outing. I wasn't on my way to the hospital in crisis. I wasn't even on my way out temporarily for tests. I had said my goodbye's to the staff and other residents, and had been over to the nun's residence to say goodbye to the Sisters. I was leaving permanently, and not the way most people leave a hospice, in a body bag. I was going "home" to resume my life, a life I had unwillingly stepped out of over five years before. Really, it was more like I had fallen out of my life, and straight down the rabbit hole. Everything had been upside down for so long. It was hard to comprehend that I had found my way back up out of that rabbit hole.

As I waited for Thomassina that sunny day, I mused for the millionth time, "Why me? Why had I gotten sick when so many others I knew had not? Why had I recovered when so many others had not? There was obviously much more going on here than I would ever know.

Claudia remembers:

> *It was the fall of 2000, October, the best time of the year here in the almost-always-sweaty south. My business, Tutu.Com, was still in its' infancy, and operating out of our converted garage. We lived in the woods, full of deer and other wildlife. There was no grass, just lots of trees. The driveway was covered in leaves and black walnuts. Every few years the walnuts would have a huge harvest. 2000 was one of those years. The leaves covering the walnuts made our driveway quite treacherous on which to walk. I watched out the window as Mel, feeling his way carefully while leaning heavily on his cane, made his way down our driveway through those leaves and walnuts. He had parked his new, used Ford Taurus, which Keith Darby, one of his former School of the Arts students, had helped him find and buy, out at the*

curb. It was a slow, almost painful process to watch, which took him about fifteen minutes to complete. The stairs leading up to my front porch were yet another obstacle for Mel to overcome. The fact that Mel was here to make his way through those slippery leaves and walnuts at all made watching his slow, gingerly-placed steps, for me, an absolute joy. My first instinct was to run out there and help him, but something stopped me. Mel needed to do this himself. I remember knowing that, although he still had a long way to go with his recovery, he was going to be alright.

Mel worked at Tutu.Com, answering phones, ruffling tutu layers, making beautiful headpieces, off and on for almost two years. He moved to an apartment much closer to us, only about ten minutes away in what was then a newer area of Charlotte called Ballantyne. He continued to get stronger physically and emotionally every day. During that time, Mel graduated from divinity school, receiving both his Masters and Doctorate. When it was his turn to walk across the stage and accept his diplomas, he suddenly leaned his cane against the wall, and with that unmistakable Mel A. Tomlinson posture, set out across the stage unsupported physically, but completely supported emotionally by everyone in that room. He left his cane where he had placed it, never to lean on it again.

I was so sure that I would never teach again. Who would hire me? When I had first gotten out of the House of Mercy, I felt forgotten. Working at Tutu.Com had been the beginning of my feeling relevant and needed again. At first, I was sure no one would ever hire me to teach ballet again. The Gaston Dance Theatre director, Pat Wall, for whom I had guest-taught in the past, asked me to coach one of her very-talented young students, Brittany Summers, after hearing from Claudia that I was both alive and well and looking for work. Pat Wall was the first person outside of my immediate sphere of close friends to encourage me. It turned out to be the beginning of realizing that I could have my former teaching life back.

Brittany was a wonderful, young talent, who went on to dance at the School of the Arts and later Boston Ballet. While coaching her for a performance of Don Quixote, I also made her tutu, thanks to what I learned working at Tutu.Com. Claudia encouraged me to take the plunge.

That summer, I taught at my alma mater, the University of North Carolina School of the Arts, for the first time since I had become ill. It felt so good to be home. I also taught in New Mexico, thanks to a phone call I answered at Tutu.Com. That phone call was what gave me the courage to let the School of the Arts know that I was available to teach. At that point, I remember looking back over the seven months that had gone by since leaving the House of Mercy. It took my breath away to realize that I had climbed completely back out of the rabbit hole.

It was the early Spring of 2001, when I answered that phone call at Tutu. Com that would prove to be my new beginning.

"Hello, Tutu.Com, this is Mel Tomlinson speaking. How can I help you," I said. It was around noon on a sunny, warm day.

"Mel? Mel Tomlinson?" said a vaguely familiar voice on the other end of the line. "Not THE Mel Tomlinson? The ballet dancer? Is it really you? I thought you were dead!?" said the voice on the other end.

"Yes, I said, "This is Mel Tomlinson, the ballet dancer, and no, I am most certainly not dead. How may I help you today?" I was still as formal as ever, using the phone etiquette drummed into me by Mrs. Tomlinson so many years before.

It was my old friend, Patricia Dickinson on the line, calling from Festival Ballet-Albuquerque, in New Mexico. Her assistant had, not ten minutes before, been on the phone, ordering some tutu-making supplies. When she finished placing her order and got off the phone, she asked Patricia if her old friend, Mel Tomlinson, was the same Mel Tomlinson working for Tutu.Com.

Patricia immediately called to find out. "I'm so happy to hear that you are all right! Are you still teaching? Or is Tutu.Com your retirement job? You really must come out here and teach for our summer intensive this year." And that was the beginning of my new beginning.

Patricia Dickinson remembers:

I first saw Mel in 1972 or 1973. He was a student at the School of the Arts in North Carolina, and came down to Atlanta to guest with Southern Ballet of Atlanta, the regional ballet company that I was a member of. The company was directed by Pittman Corry and his wife, Karen Conrad, a former ballerina with Ballet Theatre, the precursor to American Ballet Theatre. We had one African-American dancer in the company at that time, Karen Wright. Mel was brought in to dance with Karen because those were still the days, in the south, when it was considered wrong for blacks and whites to dance together. I was chosen as Karen's understudy even though I was white, I guess because I had olive skin so I was the next darkest girl in the company.

The next time I saw Mel was six years later, when he was on tour, in Dallas, Texas. By then, he was a principal in the Dance Theatre of Harlem.

That was the night of my first date with the man who would become my future husband. Mel danced the part of the snake in Arthur Mitchell's "Manifestations." He had become everything I knew he would become. We waited for Mel afterwards and caught up at the stage door.

We kept in touch off and on over the years. The day I found out that Mel was still alive and surviving AIDS was a great day. I invited him to come out and teach for my summer intensive in Albuquerque at Festival Ballet. I asked Mel not to tell my students and parents that he was sick. There were still many people who did not know the facts of the disease and how it was spread. I also did not want the student's first knowledge of who Mel was to be that he was an AIDS victim. I wanted them to know him as a great dancer and teacher. Mel choreographed for our end-of-summer-school performance. It was so wonderful to know he had survived.

That fall, 2001, I was asked to coach several local students to compete in the Youth America Grand Prix (YAGP), a ballet competition that was still in its infancy, just beginning its' stupendous journey. Its mission is "To support and develop world-class dancers, ages 9-19, of all economic, ethnic, and geographic backgrounds by providing scholarship auditions, performance and education opportunities, and by serving as the global network of dance, connecting students, teachers, schools, dance companies, dancers, and audiences."

Being involved with coaching dancers for competition at the YAGP was instrumental in helping me to re-connect with old friends and colleagues. In 2002, I won the Outstanding Choreographer Award at the Winston-Salem regional YAGP for my ensemble piece, 'Il Protetto Cuore,' danced by Charlotte City Ballet student, Mollie Sansone, now with the Nashville Ballet, and Sean Hyatt, from Gaston Dance Theatre. I had first taught Mollie,

Mel poses with a very young Mollie Sansone while guest teaching in New Bern, NC in 1994.

an exceptionally talented dancer, when she was around seven or eight, in the small town of New Bern, NC, before she and her family moved to Charlotte. It was right before I got sick, and now I was teaching her again. This was especially meaningful for me since the competition was held, that year, at my beloved School of the Arts, and many of my mentors and colleagues at the school were there to see my success.

During the late summer of 2002, I realized that I was 100% back. Recently, I had finished staging *Carnival of the Animals* for the local Charlotte Youth Ballet. I had been living on my own, out of hospice for almost two years. I had been teaching again, quite a bit, both locally and nationally, had gotten both my Masters and Doctorate, and was in my second year working part-time at Tutu.Com. I had made a new life, despite AIDS, and it was time to talk publicly about it.

Back in 1995, when I first became ill, I made the decision to speak publicly about having AIDS. Honesty was still a relatively new idea as it pertained to AIDS, both in our government and in the minds of those stricken. Back then, there was still so much shame associated with the disease.

I was inspired, over the years, by several courageous celebrities who had spoken publicly about their AIDS infections – Rock Hudson, Magic Johnson, Arthur Ashe, and Bob Hattoy, the man who spoke at the 1992 Democratic National Convention, talking about living with AIDS. These men helped the general public begin to understand that this disease was a force to be reckoned with and need not be ignored.

I gave an interview back in 1995 or 1996 to the *Charlotte Observer's* arts critic, Tony Brown, which was picked up by the Associated Press and published around the country. I hoped to help de-stigmatize those who had been suffering silently alone for so long. I thought about Sal Aiello, who could not go public here in Charlotte about his illness for fear of losing funding for the North Carolina Dance Theatre (Charlotte Ballet). I thought of all the dancers I had known in New York who had died so young.

It was now seven years later, and I decided to call the Winston-Salem Journal's Janice Gaston and offered her my story. I wanted to be sure that my friends and colleagues at the school of the arts who had been so generous and supportive would know that I was alive and doing well, thanks in large part to many of them. The story was shared, on the front page of the Journal, on October 6, 2002. I may be well now, I explained, but I had and still have AIDS and that was a fact that was not going to change. I wanted the world to know that AIDS was no longer a death sentence. One could live with it, and one's life could be well-lived.

Coming out publicly about having AIDS, and living with it, for me was much like coming out as gay had been. It was terrifying to reveal my true self, but it was also liberating. I was not a larger-than-life, perfect God-like creature. In fact, I was much less than perfect. I was fallible and dealing with consequences to actions of which I would never be sure exactly when I had taken. I realized it had been a long, painful journey, but I was proud of whom I had become, a kinder, more generous person and a teacher who truly knew that all was possible.

Looking back, now, over twenty-three years since I first found out I was sick with AIDS, and probably closer to thirty years since I was first infected, I am amazed to realize that I am now part of currently the largest group of AIDS sufferers in the United States – those who have survived for over twenty years. When I was first infected, no one thought there would ever be a group of people like us. Back then, no one was expected to survive and very few did. Today, researchers are on the verge of finding a cure. There is already a pill, called Truvada, that helps to prevent one from catching the HIV virus if exposed. There is even one man, an American living in Berlin, who has been officially cured through a bone marrow transplant and the use of stem cells harvested from a donor with a very specific genetic mutation. The mutation, called CCR5-delta-32, protected the donor's stem cells from HIV, so that once given to the patient, those cells simply could not be attacked by HIV. When reading about this, I found that this cured patient, Timothy Brown, contracted HIV in the same time and city that I believe I contracted it – Berlin in the mid 1980's. I could not help but wonder if we had the same particular strain of HIV and if it is more easily survivable than others.

One of the facts that seems to be ignored by the younger generations these days is the fact that one can be infected with more than one strain of HIV if one does not practice safe sex. It is simply not enough to find other HIV-positive people with whom to have relationships. You must always be vigilant in your safe sex practices, both to protect yourself and everyone else.

I worry about the Millennials, Gen-X and current generation, the Gen-Z's, both male and female, straight and gay. Some call themselves the "Hook-Up" generation and are said to be sexually promiscuous, both males and females, much like those who attended the gay bath houses back in the 1970's and '80's. So many of these young people have no idea what it is like to watch many of your friends get sick with strange, mysterious diseases that no doctors seem to be able to cure, and die horrible, painful deaths. Many in my generation know what that feels like, and we do not want the younger generations to learn the way we did. Many have no concept that AIDS is still out there and is still a horrible disease. They seem to think that because there are some excellent medicines now that catching AIDS is not such a life-changing big deal as it once was. It is not the end of the world for most people who find they are infected. But it is still forever, and still a horribly virulent, dangerous disease. It is a terrible mistake for our younger generations to give themselves permission to be promiscuous because of advances in medication.

Over the years, I have wondered why I contracted HIV/AIDS when many other people I knew to be much more sexually active than I was, did not. I cannot be absolutely sure when or where I contracted HIV, but I do believe it was in Berlin from Rolfe Garski. Yes, I must admit that I spent my share of time at the gay bath houses in New York in the 1970's and early '80's. With an eight or ten-year incubation period considered to be the average these days, and the fact that I was not even diagnosed until I was diagnosed with full blown AIDS, it is just not possible for me to know for sure when I contracted it. I cannot help but wonder if my journey would have been easier had I not sunk into nine years of complete denial when I received that call about the false positive test result from my doctor the day I was leaving New York. I must give credit for my ability to so easily live my life while denying facts to Mrs. Tomlinson, who taught us all that factual truths are never as important as gilded lies.

Looking back now, it is well-known and documented that AIDS was spreading rampantly through the sexual practices at the gay bath houses. It is also well-known and documented that in New York, then-Mayor Koch's government was doing nothing to warn the gay community, even though there was ample evidence of the facts. I never so much as saw a sign in a bath house warning of the AIDS virus, much less a bowl of condoms. The painful truth is that no one cared. New York was ground zero for the AIDS epidemic back in those days. So many lives could have been saved, but were not mostly due to greed and petulant selfishness. Our Mayor and other government officials did not want to be involved. Mayor Koch was unmarried and sensitive to the whispers that he might be gay. He denied it and I believe that, politically, he felt the need to keep himself distanced from the gay community. He was a prominent politician and back then being Gay would have ended his political career anywhere in America except possibly San Francisco.

The gay bath house owners did not want to let anyone in on the fact that anal sex was the way in which AIDS was being spread in the beginning. They were making a lot of money from the gay community and the sexual revolution. The gay community did not want to know the truth either. We all cherished the fact that we had this hard-fought-for sexual freedom. No one wanted to give it up or make changes.

I have also often wondered why I survived when so many others did not. I know that I will probably never have answers to these questions. I tell myself that I must accept God's will and be happy and grateful that I have had the life I have had. The only earthly reality that I can think of that I am sure does have something to do with my recovery and survival is the fact that I do not drink alcohol, smoke cigarettes or do drugs. I also have always, from the first day of my diagnosis, done exactly as my doctor has recommended.

I very much appreciate the fact that I am, and have always been blessed. I know that the angels have definitely stood watch over me my entire life. There is simply much to be said about one's relationship with higher powers. Though prayer, meditation and any means one learns to communicate with the higher powers in one's life are important, in the long run, I found that I simply had to let go. There was no amount of begging, praying, bargaining or cajoling that was ever going to change my circumstances. Once I figured that out, everything changed, and I was able to trust God and let Him take care of me.

Mel Tomlinson, visiting the House of Mercy in 2016.

It really all happened in one very-long night at the House of Mercy. I felt the passing of someone else's soul as their earthly body was wheeled out to the waiting hearse. I was so tired and despondent. My kidneys were failing; I was heavily drugged for the pain, and I remember thinking, when the hearse outside my window pulled away, that it should have been me inside. "Why won't you take me? Daddy, I want to come home," I cried out loud, talking to both my father and my heavenly father at the same time. My daddy answered me, telling me that it was not my time yet. I continued to talk to him out loud for hours. He and I had spoken once before, again in the early morning hours, the Thanksgiving before. In the wee hours, I got up and spent some time practicing walking to my door and back to the bed with my walker, something I had not done in months. Both my fathers were there with me, encouraging me, supporting me. Around five a.m., I opened my door, and very slowly, without my walker, leaning on the wall, walked myself down to the bathroom and took a long bath in the new step-in bathtub that the House of Mercy had recently acquired. It was my first bath on my own in several years. I dressed myself and made my way back down to my room where I sat up straight and tall on my bed and waited for the first visit of the new day from my nurse. I had made it to the end of the beginning of my new life. The rest awaited me.

The End

Afterword

Sometimes God will take you to a storm only to bring you through it. I believe that this statement best describes the outcome of my journey thus far. While full of ups and downs, this journey has always been blessed with elements of hope, faith and love. When one finds oneself in the abyss, one tends to not only lose those things, but to question their very essence. Perhaps there is much truth to this cliché: That which doesn't kill you makes you stronger. I must say that I did come through my storms of loneliness, shame, doubt, guilt, fear and sorrow with a newness of innocence and a healthier outlook on life.

Up until I became sick, I believed that I was in control of most everything in my life. My illness caused me to feel such shame and remorse, and so much confusion. If I was in control, then why was this happening? Was I in control? Or had I spent my life thus far living under a delusion of self-control? Much of my emotional agony came from the fact that I felt like an abject failure for not being able to control my illness or my feelings about myself. Looking back now, I can see that it was at the very moment that I allowed myself to give up control; the moment that I was simply too tired to care about being in control any longer that things started to change. The funny thing is this: I did not consciously realize that I had not already turned it all over to God. Consciously, I assumed that God was in control. I had been taught that my whole life so I assumed that was the reality. It was what was happening deep inside of me emotionally that was preventing me from letting go. My confusion over what love was, along with my need to be appreciated for my career and accomplishments before I would show respect to others kept me from letting go. For it was not just the disease for which I needed God's help. I needed to find my way back to my innocence, something I had misplaced at some point along the way.

In the loneliness created by my selfishness, I was forced to reflect on the consequences of the wrong choices I had made and wrong actions I had taken. Looking back now, I am so grateful for this heaven-sent time-out. I do not believe it was ever the intention of God for me to leave this earthly realm due to my illness. I feel sure that I am still here for a reason, whether it is for the ministry or to continue to teach ballet or possibly both reasons, I may never know. It doesn't matter. I am here, and I am a better person than I was before I became ill, a living testimony to the power of love. Where will my journey take me next? Only God knows, and I am happy to go along for the ride, wherever He takes me.

Index

A Piece of the Action 160
A Rose for Miss Emily 49
Abarca, Lydia vi, 34, 90, 112, 114, 123, 152
Actor's Fund, The 229, 230
Adams, Diana 65, 116, 138
Afternoon of a Faun (Aiello) 182, 185
Afternoon of a Faun (Robbins) 123
AGMA (*see* American Guild of Musical Artists)
Agon i, ii, iii, 63, 65, 90, 107
Aiello, Sal (*see* Aiello, Salvatore)
Aiello, Salvatore v, 38, 141, 156, 163, 167, 173, 175-176, 178-179, 181-182, 185
Aikens, Vanoye 56
Ailey, Alvin v, vi, 20, 37, 57, 63, 66, 181
Alexander, Alfred vi, 253
Allegro Brilliante 97, 98, 156, 163, 194
Allen, Sarita 86, 154
Allen, Woody 124
Allison, Mrs. (*see* Allison, Muriel)
Allison, Muriel 27, 253, 254
Alvin Ailey American Dance Theater 82-83, 86
American Ballet Theatre 37, 41, 49, 63-64, 72, 77, 80-81, 86, 100, 122, 161-162, 187, 193, 197, 200, 232
American Guild of Musical Artists 75, 80, 83, 109, 175, 229, 259
Angelou, Maya 92, 167-169
Apollo i
Aponte, Christopher 179
Ardolino, Emile 96
Ashe, Arthur 261
Ashford and Simpson 169
Ashford, Nick (*see* Ashford and Simpson)
Ashley, Merrill 126-127, 156
Astaire, Fred 104
Atlanta Ballet 41-42, 190, 201, 206
Atlantic Coast Conference Tournament 1
Augusta Ballet 41
Austin, Debra 65
Bacon, Julie 197
Badua, Patrick 186
Bailey, Michelle 135

Baker, Josephine 76
Balanchine, George i, ii, v, 22-23, 36-37, 43-44, 63-67, 89, 96-98, 100-108, 112, 114-119, 122, 127, 129, 130-134, 136-141, 145, 149, 153, 155, 157-159, 161, 163, 179-181, 183, 190, 194, 222, 234, 242
Ballet Austin 184
Ballet Folklorico de Mexico 85
Ballet of the XX Century 100
Ballet Russe de Monte Carlo 37, 44, 66
Ballet Society 37
Ballet Theatre 37, 44-45, 123, 259
Banks, Marilyn 20, 86, 155
Banks, Marilyn "Bunky Lee" (*see* Banks, Marilyn)
Barnett, Mary 87
Barwick, Beverly 30
Baryshnikov, Mikhail 77, 86, 134
Bass, John 101, 135
Bates, Ronald 135
Bauer, Elaine 55
Bejart Company 77, 81
Bejart, Maurice 77, 81-82, 100, 189
Bejart, Mr. (*see* Bejart, Maurice)
Bennett, Tracy 135
Bernstein, Leonard 36, 91, 123
Bessmertnova, Natalia 58
Beyonce' 197
Black Ritual 45
Black, Maggie 77
Blue Goose, The 173-175
Blues Suite 84
Blum, Tony 135
Bobby Lindgren (*see* Lindgren, Robert)
Bolender, Todd 65
Bonnefoux, Jean Pierre 132
Boston Ballet vi, 63, 127, 150, 193, 197, 212, 224, 232, 240, 258
Boston Ballet School 195
Boston Conservatory of Music 197
Bourman, Frank vi, 193, 195-197
Brown v. Topeka Board of Education Decision 2, 3, 65
Brown, Isabel Mirrow 37
Brown, Karen vi, 41-42, 63, 80, 89, 91, 152, 156, 163, 203, 206-208, 216, 220, 222, 228
Brown, Kelly 37
Brown, Timothy 262
Brown, Tony 261

269

Browne, Leslie 37
Bryant, Homer Hans 70
Bugaku 89, 158
Bujones, Fernando 193-194
Bush, Barbara 99
Bush, George W. 99
Bushman, David 186
By Lamplight 183
Cagney, James 91
Calegari, Maria 125, 136, 157, 166
Campbell, Edward vi, 180
Cantwell, Don v, 188, 190-192
Cantwell, Patty v, 188, 224
Caras, Steven vii, 114-117, 124-126, 138, 157-158
Carasco, Diego 186
Career Transitions for Dancers 230
Carnival of the Animals 261
Carolina University of Theology 11
Carolinas Medical Center 208-209
Carter, M. Elena 89, 153
Carter, Susan 54
Castelli, Victor 119
Cats 141
Cavanaugh, Jennifer vi, 185, 215-216, 222
Charleston Ballet Theatre 188-189, 191
Charlotte Ballet (*see* North Carolina Dance Theater)
Charlotte City Ballet Company vi, 176-177, 211, 214, 220, 242, 256, 260
Charlotte Symphony 178
Charlotte Youth Ballet vi, 261
Chavis Heights Housing Development 2, 6-7, 16, 253
Cherry Tree Carol, The 49
Citydance 193, 195- 197, 240
Civil Rights Movement 3, 65
Civil War 2, 189-190
Cliburn, Van 58
Clifford, John 65, 131
Clinton, Bill 170
Clowns and Others 189
Cocteau, Jean 57
Coles, Charles "Honey" 55
Collins, Patsy 151
Colton, Ron 41
Concert, The 127
Concertno 107, 126-127, 128
Concerto Barocco 153
Conrad, Karen 259

Coppelia 194
Cordell, Fanchon v, 161, 200, 206
Corry, Pittman 259
Cosby, Bill 160
Costa, Mary 58
Costello, Robert vi, 208
Cragun, Richard 58
Craig, Thomassina vii, 224, 243, 252
Creation du Monde 136, 157
Cunningham, Mia 186
Curtis Institute 35
D'Amboise, Chris 125
D'Amboise, Jacques i, 131, 137
Dabney, Stephanie 153
Dali, Salvadore 60
Dance in America 92, 96, 99, 101
Dance Place 177, 186
Dance Theatre of Albuquerque vi
Dance Theatre of Harlem i, vi, 20, 30, 43, 61, 63, 66-83, 85, 88-92, 95-101, 103-105, 108-112, 114, 117, 120, 122-123, 135, 150, 152-153, 158, 161, 169, 194, 207, 221-222, 231, 259
Dancing with Demons 126
Dandridge, Dorothy 76
Danilova, Alexandra i
Darby, Keith vi, 214, 242, 257
De Lapp, Gemze 55
De Lavallade, Carmen 66
De Mille, Agnes v, Dedication, 37, 44-45, 47-61, 64, 68-69, 79, 83, 86, 90-91, 100, 104, 143-144, 151-152, 161, 174, 179, 226, 231
Denvers, Robert 77, 184
Diaghilev, Serge 130, 189
Diaghilev's Ballet Russes 130
Dickinson, Patricia vi, 213, 259
Dietrich, Marlene 76
Dingman, Nolen v
Disciples of Christ Church 9
Divertimento #15 89, 157
Don Quixote 258
Don't Bother Me, I Can't Cope 172
Dougla 69, 76, 96
Dove, Ulysses 124
Dracula 188-189
Drouin, Jacques and Mary 145
Drouin, Matthew 145
DTH (*see* Dance Theatre of Harlem)
Duell, Joe vi, 136, 157
Duell, Dan vi

Duell, Joseph (*see* Duell, Joe)
Dunham, Katherine vi, 56-57, 69
Dunleavy, Rosemary vi, 70, 96, 114, 139
Eathorne-Bahr, Jill v, 188-189, 191
Ebert, Roger 160
Ecstatic Orange 107
Egerton, Walter 5
Ehle, John 35
Ellington, Duke 36, 86
Elliot Norton Award 196
Ely, Stephanie 152
Emerson, Ralph Waldo 255
Evans, Albert 145
Evans, David 55
Fancy Free 122-123
Farrell, Suzanne 103, 106, 137, 156
Faulkner, William 49
Feld Ballet, The 181
Festival Ballet - Albuquerque 259-260
Firebird, The 153-154, 188-189, 191-192
Fiske, Harrison Grey 229
Fitzgerald, Ella 76
Floyd's Guitar Blues 56-57
Fokine 109, 189
Folts, Claudia v, vii, 112, 176, 201-202, 211-212, 229, 242, 244-245, 254-255, 257-258
Fontanne, Lynn 91
Fonteyn, Margot 44, 58-59
Ford Foundation 36, 49
Fountain III, Primous 70
Four Temperaments, The 89, 107
Fox, Dayna vi, 161
Frame, Paul vi
Frame, Peter vi, 31-32, 101, 105, 107, 119, 208, 227, 246-247
Frankie and Johnny 89
Franklin, Robin 181, 186
Freedman, Gerald 228
Freedman, Susan vi, 96, 100-101, 119, 155
Freedman, Susie (*see* Freedman, Susan)
Frohlich, Jean-Pierre 119
Fugate, Judith 158
Gades, Antonio 58
Garland, Judy 52
Garske, Rolf 209, 263
Gaston Dance Theatre vi, 258, 260
Gaston, Janice 261
Gatty, Linzetta 253
Gelfand, Jennifer 197

Gershwin Concert – Concerto in F 125
Gershwin Concerto 120, 127
Giannini, Christina 54, 75
Giannini, Vittorio 35
Glass Pieces 107
Gosnell, Robert vi, 201-202, 205, 207
Grady-Smith, Noel v, 227-228, 231
Graham, Martha 152
Grant, Alexander 58
Grant, Micki 172
Gray Goose of Silence, The 187
Grundvig, Marjorie (Margie) 184
Hall, Yvonne 91
Hamilton, Margaret 52
Hanes, Joan 36
Hanes, Philip vi, 36, 143
Hanes, Phil (*see* Hanes, Philip)
Hanlon, Kati 186
Harkness Ballet 86, 165, 174-175, 179, 189
Harkness House for Ballet Arts (*see* Harkness Ballet)
Harkness, Rebekah 174
Harvey, Cynthia 187
Hattoy, Bob 261
Hawkins, Erik 28
Haydee, Marcia 58
Hayden, Melissa v, 65, 161-162
Hayes, Helen 36
Hazard (*see* Tomlinson, Marlon Dale)
Helpmann, Sir Robert 58
Hemingway, Ernest 112
Henry, Hazelline 10
Henry, Mama Jessie vii
Henry, Reverend John D. vii, 9-10
Henson, Jim 96
Herboth, Molly 255
Heritage Dance Theatre vi, Dedication, 44, 48, 50-51, 53-56, 58, 60, 62, 68, 79, 83-84, 92, 152, 174, 231
High Point Ballet 199, 201, 204, 207
Hines, Jerome 58
Holder, Geoffrey 66, 69, 76
Homage to Verailles 183
Homek, Linda 142
Hooper, Geraldine 171
Hope, Bob and Dolores 99
Horgan, Barbara 104, 112
Horton, Dr. James 208-209, 215, 220-221, 224, 231, 238, 249
Hoskinson, Rick 135

House of Mercy vii, 231, 233-238, 242-244, 246, 248-249, 254, 256-259, 264-265
Hoving, Lucas 84
Howard, David 77, 212
Hubbard Street Dance Chicago 201
Hudson, Rock 261
Hungarian National Ballet 53
Hunt, Governor James B. 160
Hurok, Sol 44, 58, 60, 69
Hyatt, Sean 260
Icarus 84
Il Protetto Cuore 260
Intrieri, Anita 184
Irving, Robert 58, 118
Jamison, Jamie 55
Jamison, Judith 82-84, 86, 153-154, 158
Jamison, Judy (*see* Jamison, Judith)
Janie Jolly Griffith Jewelers 13
Jenner, Bruce 21
Jenner, Kaitlyn (*see* Jenner, Bruce)
Joffrey Ballet School 63, 99, 175, 189
Joffrey, The (*see* Joffrey Ballet School)
John W. Ligon High School 5, 25-26
Johnson, Jerome 162
Johnson, LaTanya vi, 244
Johnson, Magic 261
Johnson, Marguerite Ann (*see* Angelou, Maya)
Johnson, Virginia 97, 98, 153
Jones, James Donnie 7
Jones, Mable A. (*see* Tomlinson, Ma Mable)
Jones, Melvin vi, 86
Jordan, Julie 152
Joyce, Nurse vii, 246, 256
Julliard 35
Kammermusik #2 107, 131
Karinska, Barbara 76, 105
Keene, Christopher 190
Kelly, Desmond 58
Kennedy Center Honors 90, 92, 100
Kent, Allegra i
Ketley, Alex 194
Killian, Jiri 182
King and I, The 123
King, Alonzo vi
Kirkland, Gelsey 126
Kirstein, Lincoln i, ii, v, 38, 129-130, 140, 142-143, 173, 177, 212
Kisselgoff, Anna 120, 124
Kistler, Darci 125, 156
Koch, Mayor Ed 263
Koner, Pauline v, 28-29, 38, 49-50
Koslov, Valerie 102
Koslova, Valentina 102, 157
Kovach, Betty v, 25-29, 151
Krispy Kreme Donuts 13
Kroll, Kathy 152
Kumery, Jerri vi, 180, 212, 216
L'Enfant et les Sortileges 95-102, 119, 155
La Malinche 50
La Valse 141, 156
LaCamera, Kathleen vii, 238-239
Lamb, Rael 155
Lambrou, Lambros 183-184
Lamont, Deni 135
Lavery, Sean 126-127
Lavrovsky, Mikhail 58
Lawrence, Greg 126
Lawrence, Melinda v, 161, 227-228
Lawrence, Mindi (*see* Lawrence, Melinda)
LeClerq, Tanaquil 65, 71, 116, 122
Lecon de la Dance 199
Lee, Harper 36
Leon, Barry 186
Leonard, Part 6 160
Ligon High School (*see* John W. Ligon High School)
Limon Company 50
Lindgren, Robert v, 28, 37-39, 41, 44, 48-49, 55, 63, 68-69, 141-143, 159, 162, 164, 173, 177, 181, 185, 187, 211-212, 231
Logger's Clog, The 53
Lopez, Lourdes 107, 125, 131, 156
Louisville Ballet Company 176
Lovelle, Susan 70, 91
Lubovitch, Lar 85
Luders, Adam i
Maloy, Heather vi, 185, 216, 222
Manhattan School of Music 35
Manifestations 70-71, 74-75, 92, 260
Marceau, Marcel 37
Marks, Bruce v, 127, 193, 197
Martin, John 45
Martins, Peter i, vi, 22 102-103, 106-107, 112, 119-120, 129, 132, 134, 137-138, 140, 142, 155, 163
Mason, Breanetta v
Mayfield, Mary Helen vi

McBride, Patricia vi, 65, 104, 158
McCullough, Rick 182-183
McCullough, Susan McGee 165
McDaniels, Keith 86
McKayle, Donald 85
McKinley, Gayle 91
Menotti, Gian Carlo 190
Miami City Ballet 131, 158
Midler, Bette 104
Midsummer Night's Dream (Vesak) 187
Midsummer Night's Dream, A (Balanchine) 63, 107
Miller, Evelyn v, 30-31, 75, 118
Miner, Scott vi, 192
Mitchell, Arthur i, v, 19-20, 43, 63-68, 70-72, 74-78, 80-81, 85, 88-93, 95-97, 99, 100, 103-105, 107-114, 116, 118-119, 122-123, 138, 149-153, 157, 179, 186, 221, 260-261
Mitchell, Miss 2
Mofid, Afshin ii
Moncion, Frank i
Mones, Steve 86
Moore, Carolyn 5
Moore, Deborah 5
Moss, Dr. Rev. Gregory K. vi, 253
Mr. B (*see* Balanchine, George)
Muldrow, Henry 5
Muller, Jennifer 188
Muppets, The 96
Murphy, Gillian 162
Myers, Milton 86
Nashville Ballet 201, 260
National Council for the Arts 36
National Endowment of the Arts 175, 188, 192-193
NCDT (*see* North Carolina Dance Theater)
NCSA (*see* UNCSA)
NEA (*see* National Endowment for the Arts)
Netherlands Dance Theatre 165, 182
New York City Ballet i, ii, iii, vi, 22-23, 30, 32, 37-38, 43-44, 64-67, 71, 74, 76, 95-96, 99, 101, 103, 105-111, 114, 121-123, 127, 129-130, 135-137, 139, 140-145, 148-150, 155, 158, 161-163, 173-174, 177-180, 182-183, 193-194, 205, 209, 212, 221-222, 231, 234, 247-248
Nichols, Kyra 157

Night in the Tropics 183
Nijinsky 185
Noble, Duncan v, 19, 28, 43, 49, 72, 119
North Carolina Black Repertory Company 172
North Carolina Dance Theater vi, 38-39, 49-50, 63, 141, 150, 161, 163, 167, 172-177, 179-184, 187, 189, 191-192, 194, 215-217, 261
North Carolina Dance Theatre (*see* North Carolina Dance Theater)
North Carolina Governor's School 5, 25-26, 28, 35, 61
North Carolina Prize 140, 160
North Carolina School of Science and Mathematics 35
North Carolina State University 1
Notturno 188-189
Nowlin, Shanequa 91
Nureyev, Rudolf 44, 150
Nutcracker, The 39, 44, 65, 155, 194
NYCB (*see* New York City Ballet)
Oklahoma! 50
Opera Carolina 178
Orpheus 141
Owens, Traci vi, 181, 186
Oxendine, Marcus 255
Padgett, Bruce 101
Page, Ruth 89
Pandi, Guyla Dedication, v, 39, 45, 50-51, 53, 55, 72, 79, 200, 225-227
Paquita 89
Paris, Carl 88
Pas de Duke 86
Paul, Billy 42
Peerce, Jan 58
Penn, Cynthia 152
Perry, Edith 74
Perry, Mr. (*see* Perry, Ronald)
Perry, Ronald vi, 73-74, 77, 80-81, 87, 90, 100, 123, 135, 218, 221, 227, 235
Perry, Viola vii, 74
Persephone 106-107, 141
Persons, Melanie 222
Peters, Roberta 58
Phiffer, Cassandra 91
Plessy v. Ferguson Decision 2-3
Plevins, Marcia v
Poitier, Sydney 160
Potts, Pearl 180
Preobrajenska, Olga 44

273

President Johnson, Lyndon B. 36
Price, Leontyne vi, 91
Price, Sheron 200
Prodigal Son i, 88, 147
Rainbow 'Round My Shoulder 85
Reagan, President and Mrs. 99, 148, 154
Reagan, Ron, Jr. 99
Regional Ballet Association (*see* Regional Dance America)
Regional Dance America 41-42, 152, 190, 201, 204, 212
Revelations 84-85
Reynolds, Regina vi, 152
Rhodes, Lawrence 179
Richmond Ballet 181
Robbins, Jerome v, 107, 120-126, 132, 134, 136-137, 185
Robbins, Jerry (*see* Robbins, Jerome)
Robinson, Joe (*see* Robinson, Kierron)
Robinson, Kierron vii, 171-172
Robinson, Mabel v, 170-172, 238
Rodeo 49-50
Ross, Diana 169
Rowland, Greg vi, 186
Royal Ballet of Flanders 184
Royal Danish Ballet 102, 137
Royal Winnepeg Ballet 175
SAB (*see* School of American Ballet)
Saland, Stephanie 157
Salem College 5
Sales, Roscoe 200, 205
San Francisco Ballet 42
Sanford, Terry 35
Sansone, Mollie 260
Satto 163, 180
Scheherazade 109
Schetter, Peter 101
School of American Ballet 102, 104-105, 112, 130, 137, 142, 149, 173, 177, 190, 194, 248
School of the Arts (*see* UNCSA)
Self, Kevin vi, 19, 24, 40-41, 48, 55, 57-59, 63-64, 68, 72-74, 87, 174, 221-222, 227, 241, 245, 252
Self, Michele vi, 221, 241
SERBA (*see* Southeastern Regional Ballet Association)
Serenade i
Seymour, Lynn 58
Shellman, Eddie vi, 80-81, 93, 109, 154, 221

Sherman, Maxine 86
Shook, Karel v, 43, 64, 66
Sinabaldi, Tommy vii, 238
Sisters of Mercy, The vii, 231, 233-234, 248
Sleeping Beauty, The ii
Smith Jones, Selena 7
Smith Temple Baptist Church vii
Smith, Floyd 56, 57
Smith, Frank v, 161, 216, 225-227, 230-232
Socrates 20
Sothern, Ted 186
Soto, Jock ii
Southeastern Regional Ballet Association 41-42, 152, 190-191, 201, 204
Spellbound Child, The (*see* L'Enfant et les Sortileges)
Spirit Square Center for the Arts 177-178
Spoleto Festival 190
St. Paul Baptist Church vii, 243-245, 253
Stahl, David 191-192
Stallings Lippert, Carla 197
Steele, Jim 167
Steinbeck, John 36
Stern, Isaac 58
Stia (*see* Giannini, Christina)
Stowe, Shirley vii, 231, 233, 235, 237, 240, 256
Strasberg, Kyra 197
Stravinsky, Igor ii, 189
Suarez, Adriana 197
Summers, Brittany 258
Swoboda, Maria 44
Swan Lake ii, 45
Swan Lake, Act II (*see* Swan Lake)
Swan, Ashley Lazenby 188
Swan, Peter 188
Symphony in C 140, 141
Taanila, Gertrude 44
Taanila, Sonja (*see* Tyven, Sonja)
Tabbert, Jonathan 188
Tallchief, Maria 132
Talley, Duane 87
Tanny (*see* LeClerq, Tanaquil)
Taras, John 107, 132, 134, 158
Taylor, Erica Moe vi, 192
Taylor, Gary vi, 199-200, 203, 206
Taylor, Rita vi, 199-200, 203-204, 206
Tennenblatt, Don 212

Texas Fourth 45, 51, 53-54, 56, 91
Thatcher, Margaret 99
Theatre Charlotte 178
Thompson, Katherine 182
Thompson, Mel 1
Tomasson, Helgi 179
Tomlinson, Bessie 8
Tomlinson, Coray Alexander 1
Tomlinson, Dexter Gale vii, 1, 4, 7, 13-14, 16-17, 27, 43, 57, 152, 161, 218, 252
Tomlinson, Ellen Henry vii, 1, 7, 11-12, 14, 27, 29, 43, 57, 159, 161, 208, 223, 252-253
Tomlinson, George Adolph 8
Tomlinson, Janie Robbins 1, 14, 252
Tomlinson, Ma Mable vii, 5-8
Tomlinson, Marjorieline (*see* Mrs. Tomlinson)
Tomlinson, Marlon Dale vii, 1, 4, 7-8, 14, 161, 245, 252
Tomlinson, Mrs. vi, 1, 4, 6-7, 10, 11-17, 21, 26-27, 29-30, 33, 42-43, 48, 58, 62, 68, 74, 79, 82, 100, 110, 121-122, 125, 143, 159, 160-161, 208, 223, 236, 244-246, 251-252, 259, 263
Tomlinson, Tommina Jo vii, 1, 4, 10, 14, 161, 223
Tomlinson, Tommy vi
Tomlinson, Tommy Willie Amos 1, 7, 11-15, 17, 21, 62, 74, 86, 120, 122, 160-161, 202, 218-219, 221, 252, 256, 264-265
Turning Point, The 37
Tyven, Sonja v, 36, 39-40, 44, 49
Uncle Duck (*see* Tomlinson, George Adolph)
UNCSA v-vi, 29, 31, 35-37, 40, 49, 61, 106, 119, 141, 143-144, 159, 162, 164, 170, 173, 225-226, 232
Van Hamel, Martine 70
Van Hoven, Jane v
Van Scott, Glory 55-57
Verdy, Violette 105, 183
Vereen, Ben 89
Verrett, Shirley 58
Vesak, Norbert 187
Vidal, Gina v
Villella, Edward 96, 98, 131, 137
Von Aroldingen, Karen 107, 157
Wall, Pat vi, 258

Watts, Heather i-iii, vi, 112, 114-118, 138, 141, 156, 159
Weber, Andrew Lloyd 141
West Side Story 124
West, Mae 76
Who Cares 180
Wilkinson, Raven 63
Williams, Derek 152
Williams, Ebony 197
Williams, Stanley 149
Williamson, Liz v, 37
Wilson, Clerow (*see* Wilson, Flip)
Wilson, Flip 171
With A Clear Voice – Documentary 239-240
Wiz, The 57, 69, 100, 171
Wizard of Oz, The 52, 69
Wonder, Stevie 169
Wood, Donna 154
Wright, Karen 42, 259
Wright, Terri Lynn 186
Wyatt, Joseph 89
Wynn Valdez, Zelda (*see* Wynn, Zelda)
Wynn, Zelda 75-77
YAGP (*see* Youth America Grand Prix)
Yarborough, Sarah 85, 154, 189
Yeager, Timothy 185
Youth America Grand Prix 260
Zorina, Vera 106-107, 157

CPSIA information can be obtained
at www.ICGtesting.com
Printed in the USA
LVHW07*1505250918
591321LV00020B/275/P